FROM ANXIETY TO ZOOLANDER

FROM ANXIETY
TO ZOOLANDER
Notes on Psychoanalysis

Anouchka Grose

KARNAC

First published in 2018 by
Karnac Books Ltd
118 Finchley Road
London NW3 5HT

British Library Cataloguing in Publication Data

A C.I.P. for this book is available from the British Library

ISBN-13: 978-1-78220-393-3

Typeset by Medlar Publishing Solutions Pvt Ltd, India

www.karnacbooks.com

For everyone at CFAR

CONTENTS

ACKNOWLEDGEMENTS

Thank you so much to Constance Govindin, Oliver Rathbone, and Rod Tweedy at Karnac for asking me to write something, and to Cecily Blench, Martin Pettitt, and Kate Pearce for their help along the way. Thanks to Nathan Burton for his help with the cover. Also thanks to Darian Leader for making me do all these talks. If it weren't for you I would have spent my Saturdays doing something a bit easier. And thanks especially for all the book loans and brilliant advice and ideas. Thank you to Camille Germanos, Ivan Ward, Julian Bell, Phillip Allen, Geneviève Morel, Michelle Willett and Susan Forster for inviting me to do talks in interesting places. Very big appreciation to Vincent Dachy, Noga Wine, Astrid Gessert, and Darian again, for their inspiring Saturday lectures throughout my training, and since and to Bernard Burgoyne and Lindsay Watson for being such exquisite listeners. And to everyone at CFAR who's been generous enough to listen to my stuff, and ask difficult questions about it, over the years. Mega-thanks to my analysands for being so interesting, and for illuminating and contradicting psychoanalytic theory in such endlessly striking ways. Huge gratitude to Antonia Manoochehri and Jackie Lenoir for improving my life with their loveliness. As ever, thanks to my parents, Roslyn and

Peter, for being the way they are, and also to my brilliant sister, Tamara. And at the core of everything, thanks to Dot Grose Forrester and Martin Creed for being the loveliest, most challenging, and funniest life companions imaginable. I love you guys.

ABOUT THE AUTHOR

Anouchka Grose is a practising psychoanalyst and member of the Centre for Freudian Analysis and Research, where she regularly gives lectures. She is the author of two novels, as well as several non-fiction books including, *No More Silly Love Songs: A Realist's Guide to Romance* (2010), and *Are You Considering Therapy?* (2011). She is the editor of *Hysteria Today* (2015), a collection of essays on hysteria in the contemporary psychoanalytic clinic. Her journalism is published in *The Guardian*, and she also writes for numerous art and fashion publications. She has taught at Camberwell School of Art and gives talks on art and psychoanalysis in museums and galleries, as well as sometimes speaking on the radio.

INTRODUCTION

This book definitely begins with anxiety. Each chapter started out as a bundle of notes for a talk. Like so many other neurotics, I'm terrified of public speaking. I worry about saying something stupid, not making sense, being boring, inadvertently revealing unsavoury aspects of my character, and generally being a jerk. This means I have to make quite thorough notes—if I left things up to chance my mouth would dry up, I'd start to shake, and that would be the end of it. The problem is that watching someone read aloud is extremely tedious. In order to avoid sounding like a Dalek I've developed the brilliant technique of writing notes in pidgin English to make it impossible for me to read them aloud word for word. This way I have a hope of putting ideas across in a followable sequence while still appearing human. The word "pidgin" apparently originates in nineteenth century Chinese traders' mispronunciation of the word "business". Somehow my awful notes manage to broker a deal between my ego and my superego, making it possible to speak.

Most of the talks were given at The Centre for Freudian Analysis and Research, where I trained as an analyst. In a sense, the teaching there is quite old-fashioned; people give long, uninterrupted lectures followed by questions from the room. There are no "learning games", no going off in groups to draw spider maps before feeding back to the class. Once, while I was training, a man became very angry about the archaic teaching methods, asking how on earth people were supposed to learn under such austere conditions. The person giving the lecture gamely replied that she wasn't there to teach anyone anything. If people got something out of the things she said, great, but it was entirely up to them. This is very much in keeping with the analytic approach of forgoing advice and education in favour of allowing analysands to deal with things in their own idiosyncratic ways.

All of which is to say that teaching at CFAR can be quite a burden. Speaking at length to a room full of quiet, analytically minded people, who might or might not give a damn, risks being an anxious speaker's worst nightmare. You really have very little idea of where your speech is landing, although you are probably aware that some people have come with the hope of finding out something about psychoanalysis, while others have PhDs on the exact subjects you're trying to tackle. It's a perfect scenario in which to face Lacan's question regarding anxiety: "Who am I for the Other?" There's no way you can even begin to kid yourself you're addressing a consistent, knowable entity.

On the bright side, it does mean you have to do tons of preparatory work in order to protect yourself from the baleful gaze of your imaginary listeners. As a result, you end up with loads of notes, albeit, in my case, written in the style of Tarzan. The good thing about these notes is that they aren't trying to be clever. They're just stating ideas as clearly and efficiently as possible. If you sit down and try to write properly about psychoanalysis you risk losing yourself in a labyrinth of contradictions. Anyone who's ever attempted to paraphrase Freud will know how difficult it is to come out the other side making any kind of sense. But if all you have to do is get a few prompts down on paper so you can speak for an hour and a half, the consequences of over-simplifying seem less dire. Your words will fly past people. Half of the audience will be asleep anyway. Even the ones who stay awake will lose concentration here and there. There can be fractures in your arguments, false starts, dead ends, but no one will be able to call you on all of it because listening isn't reading. People will be distracted by their phones, your hand movements, the person in the next seat's cough. Unless the things you say are brazenly idiotic you'll probably escape unscathed.

The problems come when you get it into your head that this huge pile of notes could somehow be put in order. The questionable things you've been saying for the last decade suddenly start to look different. It's OK to prattle fleetingly, in real time, but what would it be like if those words stuck around? Plus, there's the hard labour of translating them into readable language. Still, it might be worth it if the brevity and directness of the notes made up for their obvious flaws. The trick would be to tidy up, maybe even redecorate a little, but not be tempted to build from scratch. The sketchiness would be the point.

While writing can look like the cowards' option in relation to live speaking—you can say what you like to your laptop—it's actually infinitely scarier. As Hilary Mantel warns writers, "Try to mean what you say. [… N]othing ever really goes away" (2016). If the spoken word is a fleeting vibration, the written word is more like an indestructible Christmas puppy that may turn out to bite. It's the polar opposite of sentences spilled in a psychoanalytic session, which can be as scurrilous/foolish/petulant/unreasonable as you like. Writing entails responsibility, and that's not always nice. As Walter Ong pointed out in *Orality and Literacy: The Technologizing of the Word* (1982) the shift from speech to writing is traumatic. When you move from the spoken to the written word you lose as much as you gain. Your printed words look sinister and stony, like they've been stared down by a Gorgon. They seem hideously transformed. Inside every nervous public speaker is undoubtedly a rampant megalomaniac trying to break out. Writing can help to set the monster free. Where before there was breathy hesitation, in its place comes uncompromising inertia. The printed word has something almost intrinsically hectoring and self-important about it. If you disagree with it, it doesn't care.

Another bad thing about publishing lectures is the possibility that you will look like a person who loves Lacan so much you want to be just like him. I don't want to protest too much, but I actually worry that I don't like him nearly as much as a Lacanian analyst is supposed to. I do feel sorry for him, though, because he *was* mostly just speaking, and the fact that his speech is now preserved in a form that we can pore over maybe isn't fair. He says terrible things all over the place, sometimes even berating himself for it. To attack him for his spoken blunders can seem a bit rough, but then again he has enough proper acolytes to make up for the odd backslider. And his written words can be pretty cruel and rash in places too.

It's strange, looking back through the notes, to see how much time is devoted to trying to sort out who's the best, the object relations people or the Lacanians. This is perhaps because there are so many of the former and so few of the latter in the UK; any Lacanian training organisation risks feeling a bit embattled. A great deal of time gets spent on marking out the differences between the sets of theories and modes of practice. While one hopes it isn't always a foregone conclusion which side one will come down on, it's probably harder to disidentify with one's clan than one would like. All in all, my struggle to represent theoretical differences probably says as much about my own oedipal make-up as it does about psychoanalytic theory. What comes through most strongly, perhaps, is a schism between bossy/boring mother Klein and ludicrous/bombastic father Lacan, with lovely grandpa Freud holding everything together. This kind of family structure also happens to be echoed in many of the case studies that appear here—including the historic ones—suggesting it may form a pretty functional framework for large numbers of people. It allows parents to be flawed without triggering a total loss of belief in "grown-ups".

The last thing I ought to apologise for is any idea that an A to Z suggests something complete. This book is anything but. I hope it's not too wheedling to say that I meant it more on the side of the arbitrariness of the letter than anything encyclopaedic. A great deal is left out. As Dorothy Parker apparently said of Katherine Hepburn, "She ran the whole gamut of emotions, from A to B." So here comes the psychoanalytic equivalent …

Acting out

Centre for Freudian Analysis and Research, 2007

It's unfortunate that the term "acting out" begins with a letter "a" because it's hardly a natural starting point for a general book on psychoanalysis. It's a notoriously imprecise idea and, unlike "anxiety" or "wish fulfilment", isn't much in circulation in the outside world. On the bright side, it invokes the broader problems of speech, action, listening, and understanding, which are central to analytic work. While it might require a fair bit of untangling to get anywhere near the bottom of the concept, there's a chance it might be worth it if, *en route*, we stumble across a series of ideas or questions about what one person might be attempting to do with another, both in the consulting room and beyond. While there might be doubts about the validity of the term, its very imprecision could be the thing that ultimately proves enlightening; an attempt at an explanation should take us straight to the heart of some of the knottiest problems of clinical practice.

Here are a few very basic definitions, just to give some idea of the problems of trying to say exactly what "acting out" is. From randomly selected psychoanalytic websites we have; "discharge by a means of action rather than a verbalisation", "something repeated as opposed to remembered", or acting out as a form of defence; for instance, a man has an affair because he can't recognise or name the feelings of helplessness he experiences in his marriage. From Wikipedia, we get: "Acting out is usually anti-social", an example being a tantrum, or the so-called "cry for help" activities like shoplifting or self-harm.

Maybe at first glance these sorts of definition seem OK. At least we can say that they don't *not* describe acting out, the trouble is that they also describe other psychoanalytic phenomena—bungled actions, symptoms, sublimation, the compulsion to repeat, or, on some level, any action at all. It might be worth bearing in mind Otto Fenichel's warning at the beginning of his essay on the subject (1987); you can't start with a definition of acting out, you can only end up with one having done a bit of work. Still, it's far from certain that he ends up with anything very clear-cut so perhaps we should be wary of following his advice.

Show and tell

Phyllis Greenacre tells us to look for the first appearances of the concept in chapters eight and nine of Freud's *Psychopathology of Everyday Life* (1901b). These are the chapters on bungled actions, and symptomatic and chance acts. She seems to be referring to a couple of vignettes where the "mistake" is very clearly addressed to someone else. Unlike other examples—for instance when Freud flips off his slipper with exquisite precision and breaks an ornament—these aren't private acts but ones that seem to require a viewer. There's the young boy who sits making figures out of dough as he talks to Freud. Each time he finishes one he scrunches it up and starts again. He makes a figure with an enormous penis and crushes it immediately, then proceeds to make other figures where the giant appendage appears out of the shoulder or the head, as if to cover up for the first one. Freud recounts a story where a king sends a message to his son via a dumbshow. The boy gets the idea, accepts that the bread figures may carry a meaning, and allows Freud to get on with curing him. Or there's the case where a young man meets Freud for the first time with a huge stain on the crotch of his trousers. He clocks Freud noticing it and explains that he had a sore throat so swallowed a raw egg, and that some of the white had spilled onto his clothes. As soon as Freud gets him alone he thanks him for making his diagnosis so much easier and they go on to discuss his compulsive masturbation. In each case the person has done something apparently quite inadvertently, perfectly designed both to conceal and reveal unconscious material. Greenacre seems to be suggesting, then, that acting out may be a special kind of bungled action or symptomatic act intended to be witnessed by someone else.

A decade or so later the concept of acting out comes up again in the technical papers, where Freud falls just short of representing the whole of analytic treatment as a battle against the patients' tendencies to act out. He says:

> The unconscious wishes do not want to be remembered in the way the treatment desires them to be, but endeavour to reproduce themselves in accordance with the timelessness of the unconscious [… The patient] seeks to put his passions into action without taking any account of the real situation. The doctor tries to compel him to fit these emotional impulses into the nexus of the treatment and of his life history, to submit them to intellectual consideration and to understand them in the light of their psychical value. (1912b, p. 108)

In other words, in psychoanalysis, the point is to try to make people remember things and verbalise them rather than to rush around actually *doing* stuff. Freud represents the patient's capacity to act out as something of a menace that has to be brought into line. But there's an interesting paradox here in that the main weapon at the analyst's disposal is the transference, which is itself, according to some, a form of mindless repetition, or even a type of acting out. If the analyst is lucky and the patient has a positive transference then that will make them want to please their shrink by coming up with all the right information, and producing all sorts of fantastic memories and associations. This "good patient" performance is largely built on a person's wish to make herself lovable to her analyst, using the means constructed in her own history in relation to her early caregivers. Freud tells us, "It cannot be disputed that controlling the phenomena of transference presents the psychoanalyst with the greatest difficulties. But it should not be forgotten that it is precisely they that do us the inestimable service of making the patient's hidden and forgotten erotic impulses immediate and manifest" (Freud, 1912b, p. 108). It's a form of mindless repetition that can be put at the service of analysis by making something present and visible, as well as by making the patient more biddable and engaged in the work.

This brings to mind a distinction that's often talked about in the world of fiction writing; new writers are always told that they must show, not tell. They have to construct scenes and demonstrate ideas through action rather than using reportage. This way they will apparently draw the reader in and captivate them on a gut level rather than presenting them with a detached account which will fail to engage them emotionally (assuming the reader likes action-packed, realist fiction). In psychoanalysis, Freud seems to be saying, we have to work towards the opposite. We have to tell and not show. Perhaps by "showing" something to our analyst we are hoping to draw them in rather than simply to present them with the information. Their job will be to resist the allure of the scenes we present.

In another of the technical papers, "Remembering, Repeating and Working Through" (1914g), Freud brings up the old analytic rule (which we no longer use because of the extended length of so many contemporary analyses) concerning a ban on the patient making important decisions during treatment. This will supposedly save her from taking certain catastrophic actions. But, Freud says, there's nothing you can do to stop your patients putting smaller decisions and choices into action, "even if they are foolish; one does not forget that it is in fact through his own experience and mishaps that a person learns sense" (Freud, 1914g, p. 153). This is a good one coming from Freud as it goes against all psychoanalytic thought and experience, which tells us that we don't learn from our mistakes but carry on repeating them our whole lives. In terms of disingenuousness, it's up there with, "Sometimes a cigar is just a cigar."

The idea of acting out as a problem that has to be guarded against in analysis is brought out again by Otto Fenichel in his 1945 paper, "Neurotic Acting Out". He describes the phenomenon as an "acting which unconsciously relieves inner tension and brings a partial discharge to warded-off impulses", but concedes that this won't do as a definition as it would also do for too many other things besides; it's something one might just as easily say about the psychological symptom. Elaborating on Freud's ideas about transference, Fenichel says that analysis itself, as well as encouraging transference, also inadvertently encourages acting out. It does this in two ways: on the one hand the analyst, by being quiet and unresponsive, doesn't react to the patient in the manner that he may have come to expect, and this may push him to greater extremes in order to force a response. On the other, analysis mobilises repressed impulses and encourages people towards less convoluted forms of satisfaction, which is why acting out tends to be so frequent during treatment.

Fenichel introduces the idea of an "acting out type"; someone who is inclined to deal with psychic tension with action, whether they are in analysis or not. He defines these types as narcissistic, orally fixated people who don't deal well with frustration, comparing them to addicts. He argues that their impulsive acts are often desperate bids at warding off depression. Inside analysis their actions have to be treated as resistances because they are attempts at avoiding repressed thoughts or wishes—exactly as Freud had said too—although they don't *necessarily* do damage to the treatment. In fact, they may even be advantageous, providing a good source of material and serving to persuade the patient that childhood influences aren't so distant from his present state. But this will only be so if the actions are interpreted immediately, before they can be written off as simple mishaps. Another fortuitous aspect of acting out would be in the case of the patient who is very introverted and cut off from his feelings. A spell of acting out may be a sign of progress, although it may also present a danger if it isn't kept in check by the analyst. Fenichel recommends careful, well-timed interpretation of the transference and states rather melodramatically: "Some types of acting out are reminiscent of inoperable malignant tumours whose operation was omitted." Alarmingly, in this account, acting out is seen as a potentially fatal menace which it is the analyst's responsibility to defuse. If it can't be done subtly the practitioner may even have to resort to a prohibition, creating the further risk of his being identified with a castrating parental figure. This in turn will then have to be interpreted back to the patient as soon as possible and with any luck it'll all work out in the end. By the conclusion of Fenichel's essay, not only do you still have a very imprecise idea of what acting out is, you have the added worry that it's extremely difficult to deal with clinically and that your failure to handle it adequately might have dire consequences for your analysands.

Five years later Phyllis Greenacre steps in with her article "General Problems of Acting Out" (1950), where she elaborates on Fenichel's ideas. She takes up his notion of acting act out as a particular form of remembering, describing "memory expressed in active behaviour, without the usual sort of recall in verbal and visual imagery". She adds to Fenichel's idea of orally underpinned acting out the possibility that certain behaviours may be informed by "a special emphasis on visual sensitisation producing a bent for dramatisation (derivatives of exhibitionism and scoptophilia), and a largely unconscious belief in the magic of action". Ostensibly, certain people act out because they are fascinated by the ideas of seeing and being seen, or because they think they can make something true by acting as though it is. Greenacre also talks about chronic acting out in patients whose early speech was delayed or disrupted, and who now show a preference for action over discussion. She associates neurotic acting out with the tendency to somatise in hysteria, pointing out its structural similarity. As in Fenichel's paper, Greenacre's text has the advantage of not taking the term for granted, and of showing it to be more problematic than it may at first appear. Still, Greenacre suffers the same uncertainty around the question of what qualifies as a symptom and what can properly be called acting out. Would the compulsive hand-washing of one of Freud's female patients, which both drew attention to and away from the "dirty" thing she'd been caught doing with her hands as a child, be called an acting out? (Her mother had caught her masturbating and now, whenever the doorbell rang, she had to greet the caller with the spectacle of her freshly cleaned hands.)

To give a contemporary clinical example, a male patient used to turn up every week with a little request. In his first ever session he asked for a glass of water. After that he would come up with something every single week; another glass of water, an umbrella, could he borrow my A to Z? Then one week, could he take off his trousers and put them in my drier? (I didn't hesitate to say no.) He had problems with paying for his sessions—an uncle was going to cover the first few and after that he would have to do it himself, but he could only manage if I gave him a reduced fee. When the time came for him to handle his own payments he asked whether he could do it in the form of gardening (again, a no). The favours and demands for special care really were incessant. He described growing up with two rather bohemian parents, who separated when he was ten years old. Even before the separation his life was chaotic. They were incapable of getting him to school on time and sometimes he'd be so embarrassed about his lateness that he'd hide in a bus shelter all day rather than go in and face comments from his friends and teachers. Home times were just as bad—no one would collect him and finally the porters would have to lock up the school, leaving him out on the pavement. During these moments, he would long for his mother to appear and take him home, allowing him to feel that he was loved after all.

After his parents' separation, he lived for a while with his mother but found her too erratic so asked to move in with his father. His dad gave him a key and made sure there was food in the fridge, but little more than that. The boy stopped going to school and sat around eating junk food and watching TV. After a couple of years his parents agreed to send him to a military school where the teachers organised him, got him up in the morning and told him what to do. He loved it.

One of the first things he said about himself was that if he had money he didn't have love, and if he was in love he never had money. If he fell for a woman all he wanted to do was stay in bed all day; it seemed somehow wrong or inappropriate to mix this with going out and trying to make a living. But because of this, his girlfriends would ultimately leave him because he seemed like a bad financial bet. Money had been a big issue between his parents—his father only took on jobs he liked, and was therefore a little unreliable when it came to the bills. Their marriage, while it lasted, seemed to be very much a matter of passion rather than of practicality.

The little favours the patient demanded in sessions seemed to demonstrate that he needed to be looked after, as well posing questions about love. In the accounts of his day-to-day life he often used the example of his partner bringing him a glass of water as a kind of index of how much she cared about him—if she brought one without him having to ask it was a top-scorer in terms of proof of devotion. If I said, "Really? A glass of water?" and maybe looked at the one sitting next to him, he'd brush it off as an irrelevance. It really seemed that the thing being acted out was a way of getting satisfaction without allowing the underlying material to become conscious.

According to some writers, this would be an example of "acting in" as opposed to acting out. The patient doesn't go off and do something, but instead does it with you. In this case, it was hardly a dangerous form of acting out, although the tendencies he displayed through it were dangerous both for his love life and his rent.

Next, we have Helen Deutsch's paper "Acting Out in the Transference" (1963) in which she comments extensively on Greenacre's earlier text. Deutsch reiterates the problem of finding a definition and tries to hone it by saying that something can only qualify as acting out if it is done in relation to the transference. It doesn't have to happen in the room, with the analyst—she cites a bit of acting out that happened in the Far East—but it must be linked with what's going on in the analysis at the time. She mentions a patient, troubled by a break in her analysis, who goes on holiday and takes on her analyst's identity, giving herself a version of her analyst's name—"French" instead of "Deutsch"—and claiming to be a shrink from Vienna with a doctor husband and a small son (exactly Deutsch's own situation).

Deutsch depicts an ideal analytic set-up whereby the "healthy part of the patient's ego" works in collaboration with the analyst to analyse the transference, but says that this may be hard to sustain, as the transference is experienced on an emotional level, and that it can lead to a sort of dry analysis where everything is intellectualised and the relationship ultimately collapses. If analysis ideally requires a more sentimental type of transference, this can easily lead to various forms of acting out when the feelings that have been mobilised can't be put into action in the normal ways. If you fall in love with your analyst, for instance, you can't sleep with them, so, according to Deutsch, you may have to look for another outlet for your pent-up feelings.

So, those are the key theories. If for Fenichel and Greenacre acting out is a particular mode of remembering, for Deutsch it is a way of working off excess feeling in relation to the transference.

Food for thought

Lacan came back to the theme of acting out again and again, often using the same cases as examples: Freud's young homosexual girl, Ernst Kris's fresh brains man and Ruth Lebovici's case of transitory perversion. I'll focus here on what he has to say about the fresh brains case and the Lebovici case, which both introduce the idea of acting out as a correction of the analyst. But before I talk about these cases it's perhaps worth mentioning Lacan's dodgy methods.

There is a book called *U and I* (1991) by Nicholson Baker where the author talks about his admiration for John Updike's work. Instead of going through Updike's work carefully, re-reading it and finding out precisely what it was that made such an impression on him, he develops a technique he calls "closed book interpretation". This means *not* reading the texts again but simply talking about one's own distorted memories of them with the idea that the disfigurements may be the thing that's really interesting or useful. To say that Lacan may have been employing a similar approach in his readings of his colleagues' work may be far too generous; his tone in the discussion of the Ernst Kris case, at least, is quite vindictive. He constantly misrepresents Kris's text to suit his own ends and then criticises his own fictionalised version of it.

When Lacan first mentions Kris's paper in the "Rome Discourse" (2006) in 1953 he mocks its poor use of language, comparing the analyst's interventions to a "nonsensical stuttering". This is with particular reference to a moment at the end of the paper where Kris reports inadvertently using the phrase "need for love" in the place of "demand for love", thereby producing a surprising reaction in his patient. Kris emphasises the switch from the active verb "demand" to the more passive "need", which exposes a previously unexplored trend in the patient's unconscious. Lacan completely misrepresents this, saying that Kris stupidly failed to differentiate between the two verbs. Kris puts his point across rather self-effacingly, which makes it more galling that Lacan chooses to rip him apart for it, and on completely false grounds. Shortly after this there's a brief discussion of the same case in Lacan's *Seminar I: Freud's Papers on Technique (1953–1954)* (1988) in which some of the details are, again, skewed. Here it isn't being used to talk about acting out so much as the ideal ego and negation in relation to the Other. This mention is fairly civil in tone. Then, in 1955–1956, there is a discussion of the case in the psychosis seminar (1993a). This is one of the most vicious, and also least accurate. Later, in "The Direction and Power of the Treatment" (2006), Lacan becomes far more complimentary about Kris again, and it's interesting that he seems at this point to give a reasonably factual account. Then in 1963, he's back on the attack, having forgotten everything, presenting case as though the patient is a kind of Hannibal Lecter, whereas in fact all he is reported to have done was to go and read a few menus.

To recap a little on the story, Kris tells us about a man who comes to him for a second analysis. He's already worked with Melitta Schmideberg, Melanie Klein's daughter, but now wants to speak to a man. He is a scientist in his early thirties who is unable to advance in the academic world because of his inability to publish his work. This, he explains, is due to a constant impulse to steal other people's ideas, especially the ideas of one of his colleagues. While he's seeing Kris he gets to the point of being about to publish something when he finds a book in the library, which he vaguely remembers having read, and which apparently contains the same ideas. He tells Kris about the book with a tone of satisfaction that makes his analyst curious, and which, Kris tells us, prompted him "to inquire in very great detail about the text he was afraid to plagiarize". Then Kris says—and these are his exact words—"In a process of extended scrutiny it turned out that the old publication contained useful support of his thesis but no hint of the thesis itself" (1951). In other words, Kris asked lots of questions and established that, by the patient's own account, the book didn't actually say the same thing as the patient was saying in his work. What's more, as the discussion continued, it transpired that the patient's colleague was actually more likely to be stealing *his* ideas than the other way around. Kris relates all of this to the man's identification with his father. The patient's grandfather had been a distinguished scientist, but his father had failed to make any kind of mark in his own field. The patient's attribution of worthwhile ideas to paternal figures was interpreted by Kris as a wish on his part for a more successful father. Only other people's ideas were interesting to him. If he found himself with an idea of his own he had to quickly palm it off on someone else in order to win back the impression that he was stealing it. Kris says, "Only the ideas of others were truly interesting, only ideas one could take; hence the taking had to be engineered" (ibid). When he interprets this back to the patient there is a pause.

> At this point of the interpretation I was waiting for the patient's reaction. The patient was silent and the very length of the silence had a special significance. Then, as if reporting a sudden insight, he said: "Every noon when I leave here, before luncheon, and before returning to my office, I walk through X Street [a street well known for its small but attractive restaurants] and I look at the menus in the windows. In one of the restaurants I usually find my preferred dish—fresh brains". (ibid)

In other words, when Kris makes his interpretation, the patient comes back with a new piece of information which not only confirms Kris's interpretation, but shows that the patient has understood it. He basically says, "Oh yes, you're exactly right, I *want* to eat other people's brains." In other words, the intervention produced new material and marked some kind of turning point in the patient's understanding of what was going on. As Kris said, the work of the analysis had been to discover how the feeling that the patient was in danger of plagiarising had come about. This was done through slow and detailed tracing of the patient's ideas and history, gradually making conscious the mechanism of attributing one's own ideas to other people so that one could increase their value, at the same time as barring one's own access to them.

Kris represents the case as something of a success—the patient was apparently helped—without making extravagant claims for it. The work seems to have been conducted extremely carefully and it's hard to see why anyone would take such exception to it. Unless, of course, one had a double agenda. Kris was a colleague of Heinz Hartmann's, and an adherent to the school of ego psychology. The fresh brains case takes up about two pages of a fifteen-page essay in which Kris also discusses the problem of analytic interpretation in the light of resistance, and the fact that one is inevitably going to have to introduce the patient to ideas he doesn't like. As Freud had already warned, the analyst can't simply apply interpretations dictatorially and expect people to accept them. Kris's essay is rather tentative, promoting caution and careful timing with respect to one's interventions—ideas which Lacan also takes up, coming to very similar conclusions. It may be a claim early in the paper that Lacan takes exception to; the moment when Kris says that ego psychology has brought about a number of changes in the technique of psychoanalytic interpretation. The changes he is explicitly referring to are a move away from a bossy, authoritarian approach, whereby the patients' resistances are seen as a form of naughtiness, towards an understanding of resistance as "part of the 'psychic surface' which has to be explored" (ibid).

So, let's see how Lacan (mis)represents the case in the psychosis seminar. First of all, he introduces it by saying that Kris considered his intervention to be a stroke of genius. This isn't at all true—he simply represents it as the culmination of some very laborious work. Then Lacan goes on to state:

> When the subject alludes to the work of one of his colleagues whom he claims he has plagiarized yet again, one takes the liberty of reading the work and, observing that there is nothing there that merits being considered an original idea for the subject to plagiarize, makes this known to him. One considers such an intervention to be part of the analysis. We are fortunately both honest and blind enough to give as proof that our interpretation is well-founded the fact that the subject brings this nice little story along to the next session—on leaving the session he had gone into a restaurant and treated himself to his favourite dish—fresh brains.
>
> One is delighted; there is a response. But what does it mean? It means that the subject has himself understood absolutely nothing

of the matter, that he understands nothing of what he brings us either, so that one fails to see very well where the progress that has been brought about is situated. (1993a, pp. 79–80)

You can see that Lacan skews the case in a number of ways. He gets the source of the plagiarism wrong; he conflates the library book and the colleague. He suggests that Kris went away and read the work that had supposedly been plagiarised and then came back and stated that there was no plagiarism involved. Kris, of course, did no such thing. And then Lacan completely twists the patient's reaction, claiming that he left the session without having consciously understood anything and went and ate some brains—also entirely untrue.

If we're going to take the most generous approach and say that Lacan is practising a kind of closed-book interpretation, what might his version of events show us? He accuses Kris of practising "the most elementary psychotherapy" and intervening at the level of reality. The fictional Kris had listened to the patient's complaints and set out to prove, empirically, that they were unfounded; he went away, read the book, then came back and informed the patient that his work was original and that he had nothing to worry about. Because of this crassness, the fictional patient is then pushed to demonstrate that, actually, it's not quite like that. He's not simply afraid of plagiarism; in fact, he gets a good deal of unconscious satisfaction from it. If his fictional analyst is too stupid to recognise this he'll have to go out and eat some brains. So, we are given the idea that acting out is a correction addressed to the analyst. Lacan refers to it as a renewal of the symptom. The patient is showing the analyst that he's barking up the wrong tree.

As a theory of acting out it isn't necessarily bad in itself, it's just that Lacan's means of illustrating it are extremely dishonest. This is often attributed to the fact that he was at war with the ego psychologists and, according to stalwart Lacanians, rightly so, because they were an awful bunch, developing a terrible brand of psychoanalysis that had little to do with proper Freudian thinking. Still, if you read Kris's paper you see that Lacan isn't correcting or arguing against him at all, but is appropriating ideas from him and then attempting to re-write history by giving a false account of his text. It's curious that Lacan should be doing this using a case that revolves around plagiarism. We see Lacan's assault on Kris for failing to distinguish between need and demand, whereas in fact Kris was quite clearly *making* that distinction. We have Lacan's false representation of Kris's interventions, which actually put into practice the "Lacanian" recommendation of not imposing one's interpretations on the patient but, instead, thoroughly investigating material he brings. And you get a complete obliteration of one of the paper's main points, which is to re-iterate Freud's idea—also taken up by Lacan elsewhere— that you can only judge the validity of an intervention by the patient's subsequent response.

It's quite amazing that Lacan came back to this case so many times, like a criminal compulsively returning to the scene of a crime. One can only wonder what made him treat it in such a bizarre way, sometimes being quite complimentary and giving a fairly reasonable account, at other times attacking it and transforming it to suit his own ends. If Kris's patient wants to attribute ideas to other people, Lacan seems to want to do the opposite—to represent others as having no decent ideas at all. Perhaps this goes some way towards explaining why he found the case so fascinating.

One might find it forgivable if the theory that grew out of it was particularly precise or clinically relevant, but is it? The other example used by Lacan, Ruth Lebovici's "Case of Transitory Sexual Perversion in the Course of an Analytic Treatment" (1956), is also apparently chosen for its capacity to illustrate the thesis that acting out is a correction of the analyst. It has in common with the Kris case the fact that Lacan had an axe to grind. In fact, two. He didn't like Ruth's husband, Serge Lebovici, and he may also have been set against the case because it was supervised by Maurice Bouvet, whom he apparently saw as one of his arch rivals. (If you have the inclination and patience it might be possible, using Elizabeth Roudinesco's detailed history, *Lacan and Co, A History of Psychoanalysis in France, 1925–1985* (1990) to track Lacan's misrepresentations of other people's writing alongside manoeuvrings and fallings out in the French psychoanalytic scene.)

Lebovici's case concerns a young man in the navy who had developed a fear of being found ridiculous because of his great height. The effect of this on him was that he had to leave the navy and go and stay at his parents' house, where he spent all day lying down in his bedroom masturbating. The mother's response to this was to organise a much older lover for him, ostensibly to cheer him up. The father disapproved of this, and of the mother's relationship with the son, but was unable to do anything about it. Early in the analysis the patient described a terrifying dream in which he was being chased by a man in a suit of armour, carrying a can of fly spray. Lebovici identifies this character as the phallic mother, and states that he is afraid of being attacked by his mum. She continues with this line of interpretation, and in response the patient begins to talk at length about his fantasies of peeing in front of a woman. Lebovici interprets this as having to do with his fear of actual genital contact; a woman watching him peeing is a more bearable idea than that of actually having sex which, according to Lebovici, is what he *really* wants. She further suggests that he's prevented from fantasising about, or actually having, straightforward sex by the idea of his castrating father. In other words, she tries to impose a classical Oedipus complex on her patient.

Lacan reads this case very differently. Rather than the father being portrayed as a frightening figure who might come and chop off your penis, it is the mother—and more particularly the desire of the mother—that's terrifying. The image of the powerful, castrating father has to be erected in order to defend oneself against her. There are moments in the case when the patient claims to be afraid that Serge Lebovici might walk into the room. Ruth Lebovici understands this in terms of the oedipal triangle and the patient's fear of being "caught" by the husband while he is lying down in the wife's room. Lacan instead sees it as his way of erecting a helpful barrier against his analyst, to whom he has a strong maternal transference.

Lebovici continues to insist on her particular set of ideas concerning her patient's unconscious. Under this regime his fantasies change from a wish to be watched by a woman while he pees to a wish to watch a woman peeing, perhaps as a response to the barrage of interpretations concerning activity and passivity. Lebovici is constantly insisting on his passivity and, even when he makes a demand—for instance to miss a session—she relates it back to this. She constantly plays the role of the great prohibitor, and his reaction is ostensibly to begin to fetishize certain aspects of her body—the feet and legs—and to tell her he wants to see her peeing. One day he says the analysis can't end until he's slept with her. She tells him he's playing a game of making himself afraid of an event which he knows will never happen. Rather than trying to find out more about what he's trying to articulate, she takes it at face value and slaps it down. This is where the actual case and Lacanian commentaries diverge. According to Lacan, the patient's next move is to find a public toilet where he can spy on women peeing, the theory being that this is his attempt to send a message back to Lebovici, telling her she is missing the point. While she insists on his being a little Oedipus, too scared to put his sexual wishes into practice, he apparently responds by showing her that he's interested in the gaze and the image, and perhaps the fact that there is something that emerges from the woman's vagina—the stream of urine—rather than its being a part of the body that lacks.

In the original case study, you see that it's not at all at this moment that the patient goes to the cinema to watch women pee. There are actually *months* in between the two events. Lebovici tells us it happens at the moment when he follows his mother's advice and starts using his grandfather's gun to go hunting—an activity which takes the place of having sexual relations with his mistress. Again, the grandfather was someone whom the patient saw as very authoritative and virile, far more so than his father, and Lebovici tells us that it was the appropriation of the grandfather's shooting equipment and the giving up of his sex life that forced him into the Paris toilets.

Again, the case has been altered by Lacan to fit his theory, which needn't of course mean that the theory is wrong. To put it in Lacanian terms again, the nightmare figure with the insect spray is an appeal to the symbolic dimension of paternity as a defence against the desire of the mother. When Lebovici fails to see what the patient is trying to do, but instead carries on insisting he wants to fuck a woman but is too afraid of incurring paternal wrath, he is forced to show her that she doesn't know what she's talking about. The reader can perhaps decide for themselves whether Lacan's closed-book technique is enlightening or obfuscatory is this case.

Later on, as Lacan develops the concept of the real, symbolic, and imaginary, his theory of acting out is modified to say that it happens when the analyst stresses one register too forcefully, causing the patient to respond by stressing another. In the Lebovici case one might say that the analyst seems determined to work too much in the imaginary, so the patient tries to reinstate something of the symbolic. However, one might argue that Helene Deutsch's definition would be equally plausible here. The patient has all sorts of feelings that have been mobilised in the transference and he needs to find something to do with them. If he can't watch his analyst pee then he'll go and find some substitute women instead.

Another dimension of Lacan's thinking around the idea of acting out is the distinction he makes between acting out and what he calls a *passage a l'acte*. Lacan talks about it in *Seminar X, Anxiety (1962–1963)* (1993c), using the examples of Dora and Freud's "young homosexual woman" (1920a), and the moments when their performances break down. In the first case, there is the moment when Dora slaps Herr K (her married suitor) in the face. Up till that point everything has been proceeding quite smoothly, if a little unsatisfactorily for Dora. She has been putting up with Mr K's letching so that her father can continue his affair with Mrs K. While Dora's not particularly interested in Mr K himself, she's very interested in his wife, and in what her father sees in her. She's also interested in the idea that she is to Mr K what Mrs K is to her father, which is what enables her to believe, unconsciously, that she is capable of taking on the role of the woman who is interesting to her father. Two triangles are formed, one with Mr K being in love with Dora while his wife hovers in the background, and another with Dora's father being in love with Mrs K while his daughter hovers in the background. Dora tolerates Mr K's attentions because it positions her in one of the triangles, in the space occupied Mrs K, her father's lover, in the corresponding triangle. So, when Mr K says, "My wife means nothing to me", according to Dora's geometric logic it's as if her father has said, "Dora means nothing to me". She loses her place in the drama. No longer is she the woman who is capable of exciting her father's love, but suddenly she's repositioned as unloveable and uninteresting. Her response to this is to whack the person who delivered the unfortunate message in the face. Lacan likens the *passage a l'acte* to an exit from the stage or, more particularly, a toppling off it. It's a moment when the show can't go on.

In the case of the young homosexual girl this would be the moment when, after seeing her father's angry look in the street, the Lady—the object of the girl's affection and the figure she is using in order to show her father how a woman should be loved—tells her to stop following her around. The world that the girl has constructed according to her specifications has been snatched away and, in response, she throws herself over a railway siding. Lacan mentions intense embarrassment preceding the *passage a l'acte* as if, without the role or the mask provided by the drama, the subject is suddenly left exposed, acting spontaneously in the face of absolute discomfort and mortification.

The *passage a l'acte* is not without meaning. The fall from the stage doesn't imply a pure break from language or social relations—perhaps you'll remember that Freud interprets the girl's fall in terms of giving birth and falling pregnant. It's just a moment when something radically changes. The previous state of affairs is no longer viable, but nothing has yet been built in its place. Lacan calls it a "switching point". Of course, it's an extreme and unpredictable moment, and one where all sorts of things might go wrong—the girl's jump was a serious enough attempt at suicide—but it's something about which one might, if one survives, have something to say.

People in Lacanian trainings often ask whether acting out is more popular with neurotics, and the *passage à l'acte* with psychotics. This is perhaps thanks to the greater extremity and "un-ciphered-ness" of the *passage à l'acte*. It isn't encrypted by the unconscious in the same way as a piece of acting out, so may be more appropriate to psychotics who, to follow Lacanian thinking, have trouble with metaphors. Still, rather than separating the camps in this way, it might be more helpful to think about the possibility of psychotic acting out, where the point isn't to cipher one's impulses through eloquent acts, but to organise something for the subject.

To give another clinical example, a patient turns up with a number of symptoms, the most bothersome of which are his compulsive mastur-bating to a really limited and precise set of fantasy scenarios and what he describes as constant "rampaging thoughts". He also feels as though strangers can see into him and observe something of his shameful fan-tasy life. He begins his analysis when the woman he has lived with for the past ten years leaves him. He's worried there will be nothing now to stop him masturbating, and no one to talk to to give form to the rather frightening chaos in his head. He is worried that I will find him disgust-ing and that the sorts of things he needs to speak about will be too much for a woman to hear. After a few sessions, he starts to say that he thinks he's falling in love with me and is worried he will become too depen-dent on the analysis, and also find it exciting for all the wrong reasons. He is someone who knows a fair bit about psychoanalysis and has all sorts of ideas about the types of things a shrink might want to hear. He has an overbearing, invasive mother who engaged him in all sorts of "acceptable" erotic activities as a child. At first, he was constantly afraid that the big revelation we were working towards was the idea that he wanted to fuck his mother—a thought he found extremely disturbing. He was always trying to second-guess my reactions to things and to view his own material in the way he imagined I would see it. Sometimes he might come and talk about something going well at work and would then say, "But of course I'm only saying this to impress you" or "I'm probably only telling this story in order to make myself look good". He hadn't had sex with a woman since his girlfriend had left, and had begun to think that sex was impossible for him; if he ever found himself in the unlikely position of being in bed with a woman, he wouldn't be able to do it.

After a break, he came in quite flustered and said that he couldn't bear it any more. He'd talked to a friend about what was going on in his analysis, and how upsetting and frustrating he was finding it. His friend had said that either he had to find a way to make something happen or he had to get a new analyst. I asked him a few questions about his other experiences of love, to move the subject away from me and to try to understand a little more what he might mean by the word "love". A few days later he came back and said that he had spent the whole weekend fucking a woman he'd just met. He was keen to talk about how well it had gone and how he'd managed to give her lots of orgasms. After this he said, "But of course I'm only telling you that to show off." Maybe someone going by Helene Deutsch's definition might conclude that his encounter with the woman was a bit of acting out, both to impress the analyst and to work off feelings of frustration in relation to her. But to follow Lacan one might say instead that perhaps the man's ideas about doing things in order to impress me were his way of forming a link to the Other. The real, live encounter with this woman was extremely disconcerting to him; his idea that he was just putting on a show for me may have been his way of introducing a kind of form and logic into the experience. Rather than being baffled and overpowered by the woman's presence, he could turn it into a spectacle and a story, giving himself the distance necessary to get the job done.

To conclude, if one is to proceed with the idea that there is such a thing as acting out, then one finds oneself confronted by a series of choices or conundrums. Is it this or that? A correction? A relief? A catastrophe? Can it be all three? This, of course, is no comfort at all to either new or experienced analysts but, as we might say amongst ourselves, if it's comfort you're after you're in the wrong field.

Anxiety

Centre for Freudian Analysis and Research, 2008

One man in a clinic where I worked had become so terrified of cats that he couldn't leave his house unaccompanied. Another woman was so afraid of shops, trains, boats, and planes that she could never go with her husband to the supermarket or on holiday. In both cases, it was impressive to see how perfectly the situation seemed to suit them, not to mention their partners. The first case demanded a high degree of interdependence, while the second necessitated plenty of separation. Although they both claimed to want to "get better" it wasn't hard to see some of the benefits of their symptoms—company for the former, freedom for the latter. You'll often hear it said in psychoanalytic circles that the treatment of phobias is a very delicate matter; trying to remove them may be a very bad idea. While they might be making a person's life impossible on one level, they might also be making it possible on another.

I'd like to look at some of the Freudian and Lacanian ideas about anxiety and phobia before discussing a case of phobia in a woman. Very loosely speaking, it's easy to get the idea that Freud thinks it's all about the scary, castrating father while Lacan thinks it's all about the scary, overwhelming mother. Obviously, it's not so simple. I'll focus on Freud's "Little Hans" case (1909b), although I know, for some, it will be all too familiar. Still, perhaps it's worth picking through the details in order to see that Freud is already saying some of what Lacan goes on to say in *Seminar IV, The Object Relation (1956–1967)* (1993b), namely that the phobic object stands in for a number of key figures in the subject's life, not just one.

There's also the idea of "educating" children, which Freud introduces at the end of his case study. What is it appropriate or helpful to tell them? What are you supposedly aiming at in the upbringing of a child? Do you want them to be happy? Or socially useful? Or both? And are the two aims compatible, or is it all about reaching a workable, not too painfully neurotic, compromise? While Freud's case may have a quaint hint of Victoriana about it, it's also shot through with post-Internet levels of frankness, not to mention very contemporary-seeming parental angst. Hans's mum and dad are precursors of the *Mumsnet* generation, desperately hoping to dodge the failings of their own upbringings and to produce a well-balanced, unproblematic child.

There has been a great deal of criticism of Freud and Lacan's respective theories of the Oedipus complex and the Name-of-the-Father (their two different but interconnected ways of thinking about childhood "education"). Much of the criticism focuses on the idea that these theories are offensively normative and promote the idea of the old-fashioned, authoritarian father; and so, by extension, a patriarchal society. Lacan is seen by some commentators to be putting forward the retrograde notion that fathers have to be strong, forbidding law-enforcers if they don't want their children to be psychotic. Freud could be said to be more liberal—he believes that children need to be given the facts of life by kind, tolerant parents.

The contemporary case I'd like to discuss is one of phobia in a woman. Or, to be more precise, it's an attempt at a phobia in the face of an overload of anxiety. If you've seen the Roman Polanski film, *Repulsion* (1965) the woman shares certain features with the film's main character. She has a strong sense of the uncanny and is basically afraid of her own house, imagining all sorts of terrible things happening to her inside it. She was brought up by liberal parents who never smacked her or told her off, and gave her a great deal of information about sex. Freud talks about the Hans case as an experiment in child rearing, slightly lamenting the fact that the experiment wasn't taken far enough. In Freud's view, Hans wasn't given the facts of life, but was instead told all sorts of nonsense about God and storks. In this contemporary case you could say that Freud's "experiment" was fully realised, and it was hardly a breeze for the subject. But is the only solution to have stuffy, strict parents who bullshit you? Another particular feature of the case is that the woman has undergone two analyses—a short period of work with an object relations person before speaking to a Lacanian for nearly ten years. The first analysis managed to subdue the phobia, although the woman herself had only a vague idea of why the work was so effective. The second carried on the process, giving her more of an articulable idea of what might have been at stake.

Freud's famous phobic

"Little Hans", aka Herbert Graf, was the five-year-old son of Max Graf, an author and musicologist who attended Freud's Wednesday night meetings and had a serious interest in psychoanalysis. Hans's mother, Olga, was an ex-patient of Freud's. They were both keen to bring up their son in an open-minded, non-coercive, "Freudian" way. Freud knew the boy and liked him, but during the course of his phobia saw him only once. Max Graf spoke with his son himself, making notes and reporting back to Freud as they tried between them to untangle what was going on. The first thing Hans's parents noticed was his state of general anxiety—he was having trouble sleeping at night and would want to come into his parents' bedroom. Quite quickly this morphed into a fear of going out and, more particularly, the idea that a horse might bite him. Evidently his parents were quite surprised. They seemed to have some vague idea that the way they were bringing him up was somehow symptom-proofing him. They appear perplexed by the possibility that this marvellously modern upbringing hadn't quite panned out as expected.

Freud himself is perhaps a little less idealistic about psychoanalysis than Hans's parents. His interest in the case has more to do with trying to back up some of his ideas from the *Three Essays on Sexuality* (1905d), published four years before "Little Hans". The problem with Freud's hypotheses on infantile sexuality was that they could only be inferred by looking at effects, or symptoms, in adults and trying to trace the cause back logically or imaginatively. With Hans, here was a five-year-old boy—most likely in the thick of his oedipal wranglings—who could maybe throw some light onto some of Freud's impossible-to-prove ideas. You have to feel a bit sorry for poor Hans when you think of his father assailing him with all sorts of bizarre questions. And, in the background, Freud, "the professor", trying to extract peculiar information from him. The conversations between father and son are sometimes quite extraordinary:

> "Why did you want Berta to make you widdle?"
> "I don't know. Because she looked on at me."
> "Did you think to yourself she should put her hand to your widdler?" (1905d, p. 61)

Still, it's great for the advancement of psychoanalytic theory. Hans appears to be every bit as perverse and sexually curious as Freud might have hoped; all his suspicions about infantile sexuality are confirmed. Plus, Hans's phobia goes away relatively quickly; the "treatment" is a great success.

The story begins with Hans's outburst of anxiety and continues with his fear that a white horse will bite him. We hear right at the beginning that his father believes the ground for his nervous disorder "was prepared by sexual over-excitation due to his mother's tenderness". Freud thinks the Dad is maybe in a bit of a rush to jump to conclusions and suggests we don't follow him too readily. Still, Hans is represented from the very start as a "little Oedipus" who wants to get his Dad out of the way so he can possess his mother. He has had a fair bit of luck with this already on a family holiday where his father's presence was quite intermittent. While the Dad was away he was allowed into his mother's bed, so he has worked out what he needs in order to be with her; his dad has to be gone. This keenness to be with his Mum also provides a motive for his illness (the "gain"). Being ill is a way of keeping her with him.

Like all of Freud's cases, Little Hans is incredibly detailed and complex. If you attempt any kind of summary you risk simply having to repeat the entire case. All the parts are elaborately interwoven and don't really make sense on their own. Suffice to say, I'm over-simplifying wildly …

To enter into Hans's world, or Freud's account of it, there are a number of things you need to know. Primarily, that he is very interested in his "widdler". His initial idea about widdlers is that they are the things that mark the difference between animate and inanimate objects. People and horses have them, tables and chairs don't. The idea is gradually introduced, though Hans has some resistance to hearing it, that the presence or absence of the widdler in fact marks the difference between males and females. At the beginning of the study, he imagines his mother must have a widdler the size of a horse, but by the end he is forced to realise that neither his mother nor his sister has one at all.

There is also the question of where babies come from, and how they get there. He knows that his mother had a big belly, that his baby sister suddenly appeared, after which the bump vanished. But he has been told that his sister, Hanna, was brought by the stork. He seems quite sure that he is being lied to, but can't work out the truth. He has long chats with his Dad where he tells his Dad outrageous lies concerning his sister, as if to say, "If you lie to me, I'll lie back." Some of these untruths involve horses. Then there's the question of how babies get out of tummies. Do they come out like lumf? (Hans's family's word for shit.) And how do they get there in the first place? Hans asks his father to explain how come he is a father. If only women can get pregnant, then what is the man's role in the proceedings? He has the vague idea that widdlers are somehow involved, and that it's all very exciting. Hans imagines that the baby is inserted into the woman's body via some act of violence and imagines a plumber boring into his own chest. He also fantasises about committing small acts of violence, such as breaking a window, accompanied by his father.

By what process does all this baroque trivia get turned into a phobia? Like any symptom, according to Freud, the phobia is as much a solution as it is a problem. There's something in the logic of the symptom that attempts to quell a difficulty for the subject. Hans finds himself confronted with a series of unanswerable questions and impulses he can't act on. He's in a very over-excited state. He's been masturbating and getting excited about all sorts of activities involving the people around him—not just his mother, but also the children he plays with. He wants to watch them go to the loo. He wants them to watch while he does. He wants them to touch him, to be his babies. But if he tries to act on these wishes he's likely to be told off. Sometime before he gets ill he suggests he'd like his mother to touch his penis, and she slaps him down immediately saying it would be "improper" and "piggish". Immediately before the illness, he commends his penis to her again and is rejected.

Hans has been flooded with overwhelming feelings—he's in a great state of excitement and he doesn't know what to do with it. It's got something to do with his widdler and with his mother, but as soon as he tries to put them together and get some satisfaction it all goes wrong. The previously pleasurable feelings suddenly become problematic. Now, instead of enjoyment, Hans is awash with anxiety. Everything suddenly feels awful. He exists in this state for what appears to have been a very short time—his parents notice that all is not well with him, but it's nothing they can pinpoint. Then suddenly, hey presto, he's afraid of horses and can't go out into the street. So how did he do that? What kind of psychic operation is it? He saw a horse falling down in the street, which seems to have set things in motion, but a number of things already had to be in place in order for that trigger to be effective.

As Freud puts it, "It was this increased affection for his mother which turned suddenly into anxiety—which, as we should say, succumbed to repression" (1905d, p. 25). Freud initially suggests that this repression may have been necessary because the intensity of Hans's feelings had become unbearable to him. At the same time, he explains that this can't be the whole story. He makes a very clear point about repression and pathology. In the initial period of Hans's anxiety, he doesn't want to go out into the streets with his nanny because it means being separated from his mother; all he wants is to stay at home and "coax" with her. (Another word particular to the case, coaxing means to hang out and cuddle, possibly in bed.) So, Freud here makes a distinction between simple longing and repressed longing. On the one hand, if you consciously long for something and then you get it, you are likely to experience satisfaction (although it might not last very long). But if your longing is repressed, then it becomes unsatisfiable. After the first miserable outing with the nanny Hans kicks up a fuss and his mother takes him out instead. But, thanks to the repressed component of his longing, he can no longer be satisfied by her presence and continues to be anxious in the street. Even though his mother is physically there, he still suffers from his unsatisfied yearning for her because it has been broken off from consciousness and therefore can't be sated. Satisfaction of a repressed wish is a special type of hell, as the repression prevents you from acknowledging your enjoyment. He's a little bit better—when she's there he can actually go out, unlike with the nursemaid—but far from completely OK. In this state, Freud says, it becomes necessary for Hans to attach his anxiety to an object. On this walk with his mother, Hans mentions for the first time his fear that a horse will bite him. Why is it this possibility, rather than any other, that presents itself to him? Freud's idea is that the phobia is built out of the same complexes that caused the repression. The forces or ideas that are keeping Hans from fully accessing his feelings about his mother are the very same things that give the phobia its particular form. The trick is to find out what caused the repression and then you will have the key to the phobia. Freud sets out like Sherlock Holmes (with Hans's Dad playing Watson) to sniff out clues. The only thing Freud is absolutely sure about at the beginning is that there *will be clues*. Although there are lots of things about the phobia that don't initially make sense—why is Hans afraid a horse will come into his room at night, for instance?—Freud insists that nothing must be attributed to the silliness of children, everything must be taken seriously and looked into. He tells us, "A neurosis never says foolish things, any more than a dream" (1905d, p. 27). The other mistake, according to Freud, would be to assume that Hans has been mistreated. Last of all, we certainly mustn't imagine that Hans's mas-turbation was making him ill. In fact, it seems that it's Hans's attempts to *stop* masturbating that are leading him into difficulties.

Hans's Dad follows him around with a notepad and occasionally says things that Freud has told him to say, much like in the popular TV programme, *Supernanny*. Freud reads through the father's notes and tries to understand Hans's logic. Hans's phobia appears to Freud to be made out of a very large number of things. In some senses a horse is like Hans's father. It has a black band around its mouth, just like the Dad's moustache. The biting, especially the biting of a finger, signifies castration. Hans is afraid of being punished by his father because of his feelings for his mother. But Hans had also already identified his mother with horses too, believing his mother must have a large wid-dler just like a horse. She was also horse-like in that horses pull large carts, which are somehow like the boxes the stork brings babies in, in other words they are a bit like pregnant women's bellies. There are also moments when Hans identifies with horses himself. He described the fallen horse as "making a row with its legs"—something he also did during a tantrum when he was called away from playing in order do "do lumf". Doing lumf was incredibly important in Hans's scheme of things because it seemed to have something to do with having babies. It was also exciting and interesting in itself, although possibly a bit less fun than playing with his friends. The question of "enjoyable" or "not enjoyable" was understandably very important to him, and this may well have carried over to the question of whether it was nice or not nice for his mother to have babies—both the act of giving birth and the mys-terious act that put the baby there in the first place. But this is possibly already to extend a little bit beyond Freud. Once you've looked at some of the Lacanian literature on the subject it can become hard to separate the Lacanian re-reading from the original text. Still, it's very clear from reading Freud that what he says about the make-up of Hans's phobia can't be reduced to a simple fear of a castrating father; there are all sorts of other things going on besides.

Freud seems to believe that Hans's Dad is doing a good job. His only criticism has to do with Graf's blaming his wife for their son's neurosis. Max Graf and Lacan actually seem to be in more agreement about the genesis of the illness than Graf and Freud (although Lacan clearly thinks that Max Graf is totally pathetic). While Hans's Dad says it's all his wife's fault for being too snuggly with Hans, Freud says it's hardly her fault that she is Hans's mother and is therefore bound to find herself the object of his excessive love. It's funny because she is an ex-patient of Freud's, and he too seems to be quite taken with her, mentioning her beauty more than once. You could say he's hardly an impartial observer—he's excited about the mum in a not dissimilar way to Hans. He thinks she's doing a great job and it's simply the fact of her being a mother that lands her in trouble (which is different to Lacanian readings, which are more inclined to pick up on her exhibitionism and all-consuming, perverse, maternal womanliness).

To sum up and compress even further, the Freudian reading goes something like this: Hans's libido is directed towards his mother and he hopes to get some kind of satisfaction from her. His masturbatory phantasies are linked to her, but if he makes any kind of attempt to get satisfaction he is soon slapped down, either by her or his father. He comes to realise that his desires are socially unacceptable and, as a result of this, repression sets in. The mother and father appear to be equally important in this process of "civilisation" or "education". Both of them tell their son what he is and isn't allowed to do. When Hans makes seductive moves towards his mother and she rejects him, he has to make some sense of this rejection. His widdler is extremely precious to him, but when he offers it to his mother she ticks him off. Is it because it is inadequate—not big like a horse's, but tiny like a little boy's? In which case, what *would* satisfy his mother? A bigger, grown-up one? Or something else altogether—another baby, for instance? And what do babies have to do with his father? And with his father's widdler? It's all extremely confusing. The incredible thing is that Hans manages to work it all out in the end. He certainly gets his parents' attention with the phobia, and then he manages to get himself out of that too, with the help of Freud and his father.

Hans seems to have been quite a success story. He went on to have a brilliant career as an opera director and wrote several books. I have no idea whether he was a miserable wretch in private or not, but he was certainly very productive unlike, say, the Wolf Man. Whatever kind of "cure" it was it doesn't seem to have done any harm, and maybe even did some good. While Lacan, as we'll see in a minute, is critical of both parents, as well as having quite different ideas from Freud about the dynamics of the case, the fact is that it all *appears* to have gone extremely well. Not only does Hans cleverly use his phobia to place some kind of limit on his free-floating anxiety, he also uses his conversations with his father to reorganise his phobia—and therefore his entire psychic economy. While one could argue that Freud is missing the theoretical point, it would be hard to say how things might have gone better, at least clinically. While Lacan's theorisation of the case is quite different, his ideas about the treatment of phobia fit very well with what Max Graf and Freud actually did.

Lacan and phobia

Lacan's re-reading of the case is found in *Seminar IV (1956–1957)*. He goes along with Freud in saying that a phobia is a means of organising anxiety, making life more bearable for the subject. He sifts through the case showing all the different things a horse can be for Hans, agreeing that the horse phobia is doing all sorts of stuff, representing different things at different moments. The horse isn't a signified, but a signifier that can be linked to a number of signifieds: the father, the mother, Hans, Hanna, some of Hans's friends, shit, babies.

The place where Lacan really begins to diverge from Freud is in his theorisation of the father's role in the family, and therefore in the phobia. Lacan thinks that Hans's Dad, by being a bit of a softie, has failed to make himself the agent of castration and to take up his proper place in Hans's Oedipus complex. When Hans starts getting over-excited, masturbating and fantasising about his mother, this inevitably becomes a source of anxiety for him. What does his mother want from him? Would he be able to give it? What would happen to him if he did? Would it damage him? Or her? What would his father make of it? By stepping in and putting Hans in his place, Hans's father would supposedly be helping him out. Far from becoming a terrifying castrator, by playing the role of the forbidding father Max Graf might actually *reduce* his son's anxiety. He would make clear the limits of Hans's relation to his mother. Under a properly enforced prohibition Hans could, in theory, submit to law and language, and understand something about kinship and social relations. In other words, he could become a nice, normal, disappointed neurotic person. He could think it would be great to be able to access his lovely mother a bit more if only his nasty old father would let him. Thus, he would have a far more bearable relation to enjoyment than a person who feels at risk of accessing an enjoyment without limits. Because Hans's father fails to perform this role, Hans constructs a phobia with the hope of getting the job done some other way. While Hans's parents see the phobia as something of a disaster— "How could this son, to whom we've been so nice, get sick?"—Lacan sees it as a very good scheme for introducing a symbolic dimension into a messy and anxiety-provoking situation. It might not be a lasting solution to the problem, but it is at least a way of cobbling something together in a moment of crisis. If the horse is like a castrating father, it's because the actual father *isn't* like one. And perhaps there needs to be one around *somewhere* or everything threatens to go wrong.

It's not just the Dad that gets it in the neck in *Seminar IV*. The Mum is portrayed as a bit of a pervert, treating her son as an object of satisfaction rather than as a subject in his own right. Because she gives him too much access to her body and lets him see too much, she potentially problematises his relation to desire. According to Lacan, desire needs a veil in order to function. There must be something between subject and object in order for the object to function as an object of desire, not as something terrifying that threatens to consume or destroy us. So, Hans's mum gets it all wrong, and it's not just Lacan who says so. While Freud was busy being completely charmed by the lovely Olga, lots of later writers, including John Bowlby and Eric Fromm, have criticised her mothering style, and her husband's failure to do much about it. Apparently, she was "socially avoidant" and there's a suggestion that her children may have been one of her few sources of satisfaction. Even then, people have suggested that she wasn't able to engage with them very interestingly at home. Why was Hans left to sit on the balcony and stare at an eight-year-old girl for hours? Was he in fact a bit neglected? Kurt Eissler, who was in charge of the Freud archives (before dear Jeffrey Masson) interviewed Max Graf and was told how difficult things had been with Olga, that she was a very troubled woman, and that he had felt completely unable to act as a buffer between her and the children. Hans's parents split up when he was a teenager, but perhaps the cracks were already showing at the time of Freud's intervention in their story. Mr. Graf was often away from the family, and it's possible that he let his difficult wife use their children to plug up the gaps in her own life because it kept her off his case. This seems to have been the general drift of his interview with Eissler.

Lacan aligns phobia with fetishism, in that it's something that happens when the subject's passage through the Oedipus complex becomes problematic. The phobic object and the fetish object are each a means for the subject to try to formulate something around a lack, and also to organise their world. The phobia or fetish promises to help make sense of things and to hold them in place. A phobic object is often something that the subject has previously liked a great deal. Hans was fond of horses, and even had quasi-sexual fantasies about beating them for fun, just as he wanted to beat his mother for fun.

Quite often, when a person recovers from a phobia, the previously feared object becomes an object of fascination again, and sometimes even becomes necessary for sexual enjoyment. Darian Leader has spoken about button phobias—which are surprisingly common (known as koumpounophobia)—and the way in which they are liable to morph into button fetishes. Buttons have an intimate relation to the body. They are part of a mechanism for concealing and revealing it and, as such, are a perfect phobic/fetish object. Sometimes, after recovering from this phobia, the subject needs buttons around in order to get aroused. People with button phobias often talk about the "dirtiness" of buttons, and have to wash their hands immediately if they ever touch one. The guilt and horror provoked by their excitement about these objects is precisely what feeds into the phobia. As soon as the phobia gets a bit untangled, buttons often revert to being more straightforwardly exciting.

You can perhaps also see how a phobia and a delusion have something in common in that they are an attempt at limiting anxiety. You could say that, according Lacanian theories of psychosis, madness might have been a very distinct possibility for Hans; his mother is all over him and his father doesn't know what to do about it. But Hans himself finds something that saves him. I should say here that both Freud and Lacan are very clear in pointing out that phobia isn't a psychic structure in itself, but something that happens on the way to something else.

Lacan sees it as a phenomenon that generally leads towards hysteria or obsession. In Little Hans's case it may be the thing that saves him from psychosis.

So how can you work with phobias? It's hard to criticise what Freud does when it was evidently such a success. But maybe you can separate what Freud *does* from his reasons for doing it. If Freud's idea is to soften the father's role even further by making it clear to Hans that his Dad isn't angry with him, then why does Hans get better? Isn't this precisely the thing that might make things even worse? Does the fact that Hans gets better problematise Lacan's reading, or is it possible that Max Graf's treatment of the case, under Freud's guidance, isn't actually so far removed from the sort of treatment that a Lacanian analyst might attempt?

Firstly, there's the fact that Max Graf doesn't actually do all of what Freud tells him to. Then there's also the fact, which was very lucky for Hans, that Freud and his colleagues really wanted to know what went on with children of precisely Hans's age. So, there are two strands to the father's work. On the one hand, there are the ideas that might "cure" Hans: he needs more information about sex so he doesn't spin around making nutty things up, and he needs to be told that his father isn't out to get him. Alongside this, there is Freud's wish to extract as much information as possible from him, to find out what the phobia is made out of and to really submit it to interrogation. This means asking all sorts of probing questions without any particular aim in mind other than to find something out about how children's minds work. This is not at odds with what one might also do in a Lacanian analysis. The idea might be to get the person to articulate something about every aspect of the phobia. By following every possible signification of the phobic object you might be able to unstick a few repressions and help the person to instate a new signifying system, or personal mythology. It's not that you would somehow whip the phobia away but, together, you would translate it into slightly different terms that would, perhaps, be easier for the subject to live with. You would be out to discover that the carriages are like stork-boxes, that babies are like turds, that the subject is afraid of losing bits of their body, and that it's interesting to think about whacking your mother. Instead of the phobia, the subject is left with a new story that follows the shape of the old story, but without such unnerving affect.

Still, perhaps most importantly for Hans, all of this work was being overseen by "the professor", a man who had the respect of both of his parents and who had stepped in to keep an eye on the workings of the family. In other words, Hans found himself with just the sort of "big daddy" who made his phobia unnecessary. Not only that, but this super-dad appeared to believe in the potent authoritarianism of his real dad, in whom Hans had previously had little faith. When Freud had his little chat with Hans, far from calming Hans's fear of his father, you could say that he "installed" him where Hans needed him to be—as a barrier between himself and his mother. It's a moment in which psychoanalysis offers a solution to the subject, rather than revealing to him the truth of the situation. The dad is raised from wimp to wizard in one easy step, making Hans feel instantly safer.

Catherine De-nervous

I'll try with the case that follows to show how a contemporary treatment of an anxiety disorder might go. Catherine was afraid of the dark. Or, more precisely, of being alone at night in the flat where she lived. She wasn't afraid when she was at a friend's house, nor when she had visitors. She just couldn't stand to be home alone at night. She lived in a large flat in the mansion block where she'd grown up and was mostly functional, although a bit edgy, during the daytimes. At night she would be plagued by horrific fantasies about being attacked in bed. As soon as daylight started to fade she would be overcome with anxiety, barely able to move. She had the unshakeable idea that someone had broken in during the daytime and hidden himself away in a cupboard, waiting until she was asleep before coming to attack her. She would stay in her bedroom, or in a small room with a television, hoping eventually to become so exhausted that she would sleep.

For those who've seen Roman Polanski's *Repulsion* you'll remember the terrifying scenes where huge cracks suddenly appear in the walls, or where disembodied hands reach out and grab the main character. While the movie character actually hallucinates, Catherine would experience the flat as though this sort of horror might be possible, without going so far as to actually *see* it. No amount of rationalisation helped. She didn't consciously believe in ghosts, but nonetheless had the sense she might be confronted with a terrifying apparition at any moment. As she lay in bed, her mind would fill with images of fragmented body parts and gore. One solution, she imagined, would be to rush out into the street and stay there till it got light, but she knew that, realistically, this was far more dangerous than staying inside. Over time she developed a habit of crashing at various people's houses, or inviting people to stay, so she knew she'd get a few decent nights' sleep here and there. You could say that this was one of the gains from illness; company. Going to sleep and waking up together added a level of intimacy to her friendships. On the downside, it took a great deal of organising, and she didn't want to be a burden.

One of the odd characteristics of her state of fear was a series of reversals. Initially she would wallow in the idea of someone attacking her. Then she would begin to fantasise about talking him round. She would imagine trying to make some kind of deal whereby she would promise friendship in return for his sparing her. When this fantasy stopped working and the fear returned she would think about how she might be able to fight back. Next, she would decide that it might be a good idea to arm herself with a weapon, perhaps a kitchen knife. But the idea of being in bed with a knife was frightening because of the risk that she might use it on herself; she might cut her own wrists or throat in her state of pure panic. So, there were three moments in the phantasy: being attacked, attacking someone else, and attacking herself.

The thing that had initially triggered Catherine's full-blown symptom was her parents and brother moving abroad. Her parents planned to keep their base in the London flat and return from time to time. But Catherine's extreme fear of the family home was nothing new. Whenever they had gone away on trips she'd always hated coming back. She didn't feel it was safe until everyone was inside and her father had been right to the far end and back, switching on all the lights. There were also childhood symptoms along the lines of Hans's, and at precisely the same age. She'd been terrified of going to the loo on her own. She would run away from the sound of the flush in a state of total panic. At the time, the family were spending most weekends in an old farmhouse with noisy pipes. The water system would make strange growling and banging noises. Catherine had the idea that there was an evil creature living inside it. This was the house where she remembered first masturbating, finding it so exciting that she told her brother about it. He was about three at the time, and seemed to her to disapprove. She also told her parents about the new bits of her body that she was discovering and they seemed to be highly amused by it all, while giving her the idea that this was something she should probably keep to herself. So, there had been a cluster of childhood terrors at the age of five; a frightening house with scary corners and some kind of beast living inside it, and also an earlier precursor at the age of two, shortly after her brother's birth, when she became very afraid at night.

Catherine's parents worked in television. They were liberal types, but still conventional enough. They had a monogamous marriage (as far as she knew) but there was always loads of sexually explicit material around the house. There were arty books of naked women covered in mustard, and etchings in the hallway showing scenes of orgies. The parents themselves didn't hide their sexual activities from the children, and would walk around the house and garden naked. When Catherine was six or seven, she and her brother were given a cartoon book explaining bodily functions—everything from the digestive system, to the workings of the heart, and the technicalities of penetration. If they asked a question about sex, it was answered. But they didn't have to ask much because everything was pretty much laid out for them to see. For Catherine, the problem came from not wanting to see it.

Two analyses

Catherine began her first analysis in quite a desperate state. She had no idea why she was so afraid at night. She was anxious that the therapy might reveal some sort of abuse, although she was certain she had no memory of anything. Her worst hypothesis was that her beloved grandfather had done something to her when she was a baby, but she knew it didn't feel right. She remembered telling her analyst that her relationship with her mother was fine, her brother was a pain, and her father barely existed for her. That was that, no need to mention it again. Everything she said, the analyst somehow related back to himself. He would ask her if she'd ever taken drugs, for instance. When she reeled off the list he'd say, "I think you're just saying that to impress me." If she was late he would say, "Half of you wants to be here, half of you doesn't", or "You're trying to make me miss you." She found his approach mystifying. He seemed to believe she was far more interested in him than she was, so she jumped to the conclusion that *he* must therefore be a bit too interested in *her*. On the way to sessions each week she'd stop off at a designer dress exchange and buy an outfit she couldn't afford, then fret about her compulsive shopping. In therapy, she came up with the idea that she was trying to manage the horror of her body somehow, by continually packaging and repackaging it. The main theme of the analysis was the quest to work out who the imaginary intruder was, as if he was the avatar of a single, real person who had wronged her. Was he her grandfather? Her father? Some mysterious abuser whose memory she'd repressed? One day her analyst said, very decisively, "Maybe the intruder is you." This idea was fantastic to Catherine. It was immediately alleviating to think that the interloper was a character of her own making. She also liked the idea of this *man* being a part of her. Her symptoms didn't exactly vanish, but something was tangibly better.

Quite soon after, the therapist told Catherine he thought it would suit her to attend a therapy group, instead of seeing him one-to-one. She strongly objected. She went along to the group a few times and found it a mixture of fascinating and disappointing. It was as if she'd been carelessly landed with a new bunch of siblings. Her solution was to claim immediately to be better. She announced that the group had been so fantastic she could now sleep alone in her flat, so thanks very much and goodbye. The analyst put up a fight but she left anyway, in a perfectly double-edged act that told him to sod off, but also demonstrated how superior she was to all his other patients. Look how good she was at therapy—she got better straight away!

This wasn't altogether a lie. The phobia really seemed to have vanished. The only problem was that it was replaced by the occasional panic attack and constant free-floating anxiety—exactly as anyone analytically minded might have predicted. A few years later she went back into analysis, working with the new person for nearly ten years. As opposed to the previous therapist, who had consistently interpreted the transference and been rather bossy and directive, this second one mainly just sat there and shut up. Catherine was rather afraid of him, partly due to his physical likeness to Freud plus the fact that he seemed too serious to be bothered with her silly problems. He would just grunt and say the odd fairly innocuous thing, but because of his aura of extreme wisdom she kept talking. Then one day, after about six years, he said, "You thought your mother wanted to kill you because you were in love with your father." It was so orthodox as to be laughable, but it rang perfectly, perfectly true. It's a very good example of the thing you always hear about analytic interventions; it's not what you say but when you say it. You have to strike at precisely the right moment otherwise the intervention will carry no weight.

The effect of this intervention was that Catherine suddenly began to take psychoanalysis seriously. She realised that Freud wasn't joking when he wrote that daughters wanted to have babies with their fathers; that children wanted to seduce their parents, and then became afraid of the terrible punishments that might befall them. And also that they developed bizarre sexual theories, even when they were ostensibly told everything. She happily came to the conclusion that her phobia was a repressed sexual phantasy that had been forced to take another form; guilt about her early sexual interests had provided the seeds for later fears. In short, she was a grown-up Little Hans trying to process something about sex, birth, death, and desire, and that, as with Little Hans, talking about it somehow seemed to help.

Cure

Freud Museum, 2012

Around the time of Louise Bourgeois's death in 2010, four boxes of notes were discovered; hundreds of pages of writings and drawings, some documenting her three decades in psychoanalysis. The notes, a number of which are on display in the museum, prompt questions about the aims of clinical psychoanalysis, and whether "cure" is a relevant topic for analysts and their patients—perhaps especially for those patients who are artists.

"Cure" has been an extremely labile idea in the history of analysis. In Freud's writings from the late 1890s people keep getting better. He reviews this position as he goes along until, reading "Analysis Terminable and Interminable" (1937c), you might come away with the idea that psychoanalysis doesn't make people any better at all. Indeed, many analysts see "cure" as an entirely misguided aim. This isn't because, as the popular suspicion goes, if you cure your patients they'll stop coming, but because it presupposes a medical model of sickness and health that many consider incommensurate with the subtleties of psychic life.

It appears that Louise Bourgeois felt ambivalent about analysis—both her own treatment and the set of theories in general. She seems to have thought it was brilliant, but also terrible. We know she spoke a great deal about the biographical precedents for her work; she had plenty

the analysis is a job
    is a trap
    is a job
    is a privilege
    is a luxury
    is a duty
    is a duty towards myself
    my husband   my parents
    my children   my
    is a shame
    is a fare
    is a love affair
    is a rendez-vous
    is a cat + mouse game
    is a boat to drive
    is an internement
    is a joke
    makes me powerless
    makes me into a cop
    is a bad dream
    is my interest
    is my field of study
    is more than I can manage
    makes me furious
    is a bore
    is a nuisance
    is a pain in the neck

Louise Bourgeois, c. 1958. Loose sheet: 11 × 8 ½ in. (27.9 × 21.6 cm). Credit line: © The Easton Foundation/Licensed by VAGA, New York, NY.

to say about making objects as a way of processing and responding to difficult feelings: unhappiness, rage, confusion. And we now know that she was also in analysis for a huge chunk of her life. One might deduce that she valued psychoanalysis as a practice, at the same time as objecting to any reductive psychoanalytic readings of her artworks. The idea of analysis as a key that can tell you the secret meanings of things, or as an authoritative discourse that reveals the truth about art or literature was something she understandably found extremely annoying. She would endlessly correct curators, critics, and journalists who mistook the fleshy protrusions in her work for breasts or phalluses.

In Bourgeois's notes, instead of psychoanalysis trying to explain something about art, we find out what an artist has to say about psychoanalysis. On one page, we get a list of twenty-nine observations about Bourgeois's personal analysis, including: "The analysis [...] is a trap [...] is a job [...] is a privilege [...] is a duty [...] is a shame [...] is a joke [...] makes me powerless [...] is my interest [...] makes me furious [...] is a bore [...] is a nuisance [...] is a pain in the neck."

It's a pretty thorough list, and one that invites thoughts about what psychoanalysis might be for. Is it to make people feel better? To access difficult truths? To interpret worldly phenomena? To preserve a space for people to articulate something quite particular about their own subjectivity? And will that help them in any way? Or not?

Artists and writers have historically been very receptive to Freudian thinking. Not just the surrealists; people at art school today read Freud and Lacan far more than people on psychology degree courses, who might barely come into contact with psychoanalytic thinking at all. But artists have also typically been quite suspicious of all kinds of therapy. There are two very potent myths in circulation: that female artists shouldn't have children—or even all artists, if you believe Cyril Connolly—and that artists shouldn't see shrinks. To quote Rachel Whiteread, "There have been times when people have said, 'Why don't you go and see a therapist?' and I kind of go, 'Well, you know what, I like to hang on to this stuff because it goes into the work'" (Simon Hattenstone, *The Guardian, 10th May 2008*). It seems there's a threat of losing your drive if you stop feeling screwed up. Louise Bourgeois also makes an inverse link between art production and mental anguish in her famous quote, "Art is a guarantee of sanity." Evidently art-making seemed to her to help more than an endless, sometimes boring, cat and mouse game ...

Art-making and suffering are bound together, not just according to Freud but also in the popular imagination. Everybody knows that artists struggle. In Freudian theory, art production and the psychological symptom come from the same place. The "pathogenic material" might be expressed as aches, pains, mood problems or phobias, or alternatively sublimated and expressed through novels, paintings, music or sculptures. So, if you undo repression, perhaps you'll stop creating.

In *Fashion and the Unconscious* (1953) by that most excruciating of psychoanalysts, Edmund Bergler, the author tells us about the gay fashion designers he worked with, and how their homosexuality and their urge to dress women were intimately linked. Deviating from Freud's unprejudiced stance on homosexuality, Bergler boasts that he can "cure" men of their gayness without curing them of being fashion designers. In doing so he demonstrates that, not only is he labouring under a pitifully normative understanding of the Oedipus complex, but that he has a totally unrealistic notion of cure. Instead of the human psyche being conceived as an extraordinarily labyrinthine construction of interrelated parts, with each element potentially affecting the others, he sees it more as a garden to be weeded, removing the nettles in order to allow the bluebells to grow. With people like that on our team it's hardly surprising that certain artists, and others, have steered clear.

The relationship between psychoanalysis and art can appear deadly, perhaps also due to the idea that psychoanalytic theory can explain the meanings of images, not just the overall phenomenon of art production. You sometimes come across psychoanalysts who like to say, "We're so boring and artists are so interesting. We just have our theories, but they have their drives and their imaginations ..." But what do they mean? Are they hoping to make it appear that they have a stable form of knowledge, or are "experts", while the artists are crazy, overgrown children? Many of the ideas you come across in psychoanalytic theory are as paradoxical, unstable and shocking as anything you'll ever come across in any piece of literature, film or art exhibition. It's a cunning sleight of hand to pretend things are otherwise. Freud and his circle were famously guilty of practising this ruse, although arguably for good reason—if they weren't pantomimically "proper" their whole project would be put at risk.

Many analysts find the levels of uncertainty we work with extremely disconcerting—you can't know what effects your interventions will have. You can try to be kind and find it makes your analysand extremely angry, or you can fear you've overstepped the mark with a brutally frank interjection and then hear it's the most helpful thing the person has ever heard. So, the idea that, when practising analysis, you're engaged in anything like a sensible discourse is an illusion.

In this sense, psychoanalysis can, in itself, be seen as a form of art practice. At the most pronounced end of that you'd have the clinical performances of Lacan, very much in the line of Dada or Situationism. He talked gibberish to his patients, threw plant pots out of the widow at them as they left, or apparently once dropped his trousers in a session. All this, of course, is extremely threatening to people who want to see a psychoanalyst as an authority figure, or as an embodiment of perfect psychic normality. Dropping your trousers in contemporary practice is more likely to lead to a Fitness to Practice hearing than a place in the psychoanalytic pantheon. Still, one can hope there continues to be a place for interventions that aim to take people by surprise and throw them off track, helping them to think differently rather than simply aiming to make them more controlled and sensible.

For Louise Bourgeois, psychoanalysis evidently wasn't an authoritative discourse, more a volatile human experiment. She wrote an article, "Freud's Toys", in *Artforum* in 1990, in which she's dismissive of both Freud's art collection, and his work as a whole. She portrays him as a literal-minded idiot with the visual equivalent of a tin ear. Still, her private list suggests she was very engaged in whatever it was she was doing in her own treatment, which she clearly found annoying, boring, exciting, frustrating, and important enough to be worth sticking with for three decades. It's the list of a person who's deeply engaged in analytic work and is trying to do something with it—while being very open-minded about what that something could be. This kind of work can't possibly be reduced to producing rote meanings and reducing one's existence to a sensibly narrativised biography that fully explains why you do the things you do. Nor to developing more "realistic" expectations of life. Bourgeois is speaking about the kind of delicate, difficult, fascinating process that will be familiar to anyone working in the psychodynamic tradition, and which is increasingly at odds with a culture that insists on fast, measurable results.

Family

Alton Counselling Service, 2014

In the twenty-first century, a family can take many different forms: biological or non-biological, two mothers, two fathers, two mothers *and* two fathers, no father, or any other combination you like. Still, as ever, some families seem easier and pleasanter to grow up in than others. So, what makes a good one, if not a cisgendered mum and dad who stick together to bring up the kids? Is it kind, playful parents, or strict, organised parents, or parents—in any quantity or of any sexual orientation—who understand how to be both playful *and* strict in an impeccably balanced way, who know when to tell children the truth and when to protect them from it, and all the other subtleties of child-rearing? This last description might roughly sum up a contemporary ideal, but maybe doesn't withstand too much scrutiny. Can individual members of this perfect family be replaced, as long as the new ones are just as strict and friendly? Or do the members have to stay the same? Do you need a stable, monogamous couple? (Or at least a couple who only stray in secret?) Or can you add and subtract other members? Is it best if everyone lives together? In other words, if the biological, nuclear family is no longer the aim, are you left with "anything goes", or are we still talking about variations on—or simulations of—the stable, heterosexual couple who each have a genetic stake in the kids?

No great apes, except humans, live in nuclear families; only lesser apes do. Great apes have myriad ways of going about family life. Chimpanzees and bonobos form large, polygynandrous groups. Orang-utans, who are thought to be particularly intelligent, are also among the most solitary apes. Males live alone and mate with whichever willing females cross their paths, while females form bonds with each other and with their young offspring. (This arrangement might sound familiar—it's basically a version of John Gray's *Men are from Mars, Women are from Venus* taken to extremes.) Gorillas live mainly in troops of one adult male and multiple females, plus offspring. The male is very much in charge. You also occasionally find all male groups. These tend to be friendly and sociable, and may involve homosexual couplings. Then you have lesser apes, like gibbons, who form male/female pairs and raise children together, although both males and females are compul-sive love-cheats. In short, there are plenty of different, "natural", ways of setting up situations whereby it's possible to live and breed, or simply to live.

The different shapes of "family" are brought about by changing cli-mates and vegetations, and the management of threats and resources. Bigger bodies are good for fending off predators, but mean you need to eat more. Different gains bring about different problems, demand-ing alternative solutions. All solutions are temporary because they feed back into the system and change it. So, one type of body size and mating behaviour works for a while, until there are too many of you, and some of you are forced to move out of the jungle and onto the plain, where new conditions make new demands and so on. Species branch off in dif-ferent directions, although any existing group might have behavioural variations within it, pending further evolutionary developments.

To get back to the subject of humans, in Catal Huyuk, a neolithic settlement from 7000 BC, we find biological families buried together, suggesting people may have been making the conceptual link between sex and parenthood for many millennia. One theory is that the nuclear family made it possible for different groups of pre-humans and early humans to exchange both males and females with one another—to arrange "marriages"—avoiding problems of aggression and loss of life in the competition for mates. Exchanging children was a way of build-ing relationships between groups, of collaborating with neighbours rather than killing them. This would have been good for distributing genes, and also for survival in the immediate present. When survival is already extremely difficult, you don't want to be killing each other for no good reason. In this context marriage may have made good economic/social sense.

But do speculative theories like this throw any light onto the structures and functions of contemporary human families? Rather than saying that early humans found it extremely helpful to form strong pairs bonds, so that's why we still do it, you could also say that nature is simply a series of attempted solutions to problems of resources. There might be one that works for a while, but further down the line it may not. Luckily there tend to be members of all species who do odd things, who have unusual sexual or dietary preferences, and if things don't work out for the conventional types then it may sometimes turn out that the weird ones are actually onto something quite viable. As Darwin was careful to explain, evolution is non-teleological—the world isn't on course to perfection, it's just a big mess with the odd happy accident along the way.

It's quite a big jump, perhaps, from the primeval forests of Africa, via stone age Turkey, to Europe in the eighteenth century, bypassing countless cultures with various organised mating ideas, but we haven't got all day. The economics of the patriarchal family unit came up for questioning in the eighteenth and nineteenth centuries by Mary Wollstonecraft, John Stuart Mill, Harriet Taylor Mill, and Friedrich Engels, amongst others. Western so-called civilised societies had long taken the patrilineal route, and men were, at least nominally, the rulers of the family. This was perhaps a solution that had once seemed well-designed to keep things ticking over (although there were, of course, divergences from it).

In this type of society there was (and is) a huge focus on what happened to your possessions after you died. It wasn't just about keeping yourself alive long enough to breed, but about accumulating stuff and somehow hanging onto it post-mortem. This can be put down to the relatively recent (in evolutionary terms) development of language, writing, money—things that can help you to continue to exist, or appear to exist, without your live body actually having to be around. In this system, sons got the gear on the understanding that they would produce more sons. In other words, men had invented an ingenious system whereby they apparently softened the castrating blow of death, but it only worked if your son was actually your son, not someone else's. Fathers provided the money and laid down the rules. According to Mary Wollstonecraft this scheme was only sustainable thanks to the fact that women had been hoodwinked into thinking they were weak, stupid and purely decorative, thereby making it "natural" that they should sit around at home doing what men wanted. But it wasn't "natural"—it was artificial. (Of course this is an unsustainable dichotomy. You can't always say where nature ends and artificiality begins.) Or at least it could be another way if only people were prepared to try it. Indeed, the idea of "nature" was women's enemy in this scenario because it kept a bad situation going. It bolstered the idea that women are created soft and gentle so they can be good carers. It was important to the system that women felt "naturally" pathetic. Wollstonecraft thought it would be much better for all concerned if people would stop kidding themselves and each other, and allow women to be educated in order to reach their full potential. That way they would be happier, as would men who would no longer have miserable wives and daughters, constantly succumbing to hysterical complaints in order to register their dissatisfaction.

The Mills further developed this idea of the nineteenth-century patriarchal family being detrimental to women, relegating them to the position of slaves. They argued for a change in marriage laws, giving women more agency, and allowing them to get away from violent or otherwise difficult partners.

At the end of the nineteenth century (coinciding with Charcot's hysteria clinic at the Salpetrière), Friedrich Engels published *The Origins of the Family, Private Property and the State* (1884). Here he refers to "that compound of sentimentality and domestic strife which forms the ideal of the present-day philistine". He evidently thought that nuclear, patriarchal families were horrible for men *and* women, alienating people from one another. The passing on of private property to biological male heirs was, he believed, at the heart of the problem, as it set up a terrible imbalance between men and women. Fidelity was only really demanded of the woman; the man could be as unfaithful as he liked. In fact, he'd be liable to have affairs and visit prostitutes because he'd be unlikely to get satisfaction from his miserable wife/prisoner who was forced to stay at home, barred from interesting work because this would make it much harder to police her. For Engels, a lifetime bond between two people where one holds all the power and has all the freedom, while the other is trapped and subordinated is bound to produce unhappiness. He referred back to earlier periods in human history—although it all seems a little nonspecific—where group marriage or later, "walking

marriage" (serial monogamy) was the norm. Instead of a lifetime con-
tract you had a bond that lasted while both partners wanted it to, after
which it was easily dissolved. In other words, pretty much what we
have now. (Engels seems to have held out more hope for serial monogamy than for group marriage. He was in a long-term, monogamous,
unmarried relationship himself.)

Engels argued for a fairer deal between the sexes, both at work and in
the family, with the idea that this would greatly improve male/female
relations. This would, in turn, improve the whole of life. It's hard not
to agree with him, even when we can see from experience that life is
still extremely difficult even under these greatly improved conditions.
What if one of you wants to "dissolve the bond" and the other doesn't?
Aren't separations often complicated when you have children together?
And so on.

Psychoanalysts have plenty to say about why families make people
unhappy. In "'Civilized' Sexual Morality and Modern Nervous Illness"
(1908d) Freud tells us: "A girl has to be very healthy if she is to be
able to tolerate [marriage]" (p. 195). Following on from Engels, Freud
agreed that society ought to be more understanding about the sorts of
things that can go wrong in relationships, although he doesn't appear to
agree that things can be so easily fixed by changes to the law. Regarding
child-rearing, he seems to be in largely favour of kindness and understanding rather than strictness and order, as we see in his Little Hans
case. The father is portrayed as a necessary killjoy—one just has to hope
that he doesn't do his job so assiduously that all joy gets killed for good.
It's a perfect example of a functional-but-fudged neurotic solution.
You understand the rules, although they annoy you. Nevertheless, you
accept them, at least up to a point, because not doing so would be too
much of a nuisance. It's a ramshackle psychic equation that's actually
quite practicable; while far from perfect, it can help you to stop fussing
and get on with your life.

Freud and Lacan give a different slant to place of the father, as we
saw in the chapter on Anxiety. But maybe it's interesting to go back to
a very early essay of Lacan's, before he became "Lacanian". In *Family
Complexes in the Formation of the Individual* (1989 [1938]) Lacan tells us:
"We are not among those distressed by an alleged slackening in the
familial bond. [...] But a great number of psychological effects seem
to us to come from a social decline in the paternal imago." He's not
quite up in arms about the downgrading of the paternal position, but

does appear to think that the reduced status of the father will inevitably make a difference to the development of the child, and hence have knock-on effects for society.

As time goes on, Lacan further develops his ideas about the respective roles of mother and father. According to Lacan:

> The mother is a big crocodile and you find yourself in her mouth. You never know what may set her off, suddenly making those jaws clamp down. That is the mother's desire. [...] There is a roller, made of stone of course, which is potentially there at the level of the trap and which holds and jams it open. That is what we call the phallus. It is a roller which protects you should the jaws suddenly close. (1993d, p. 129)

The idea is that the father needs to step in and triangulate relations so that it's not just a sticky mother/child dyad. A child needs a third term in order to make the necessary psychic equations enabling it to use language (rather than be invaded by it) and to navigate the law (without feeling persecuted by it). Lacan gives this third term the title "The Name-of-the-Father" and is careful to say that it needn't be the biological father who incarnates this role, just that someone or something needs to occupy this place for the child.

Still, going back to Lacan's 1938 essay, he seems to find the nuclear family particularly well-suited to encourage certain kinds of sophisticated psychic operation. He doesn't argue for its being "natural", he just finds it to be an arrangement that happens to make all sorts of things possible. "[T]he complex of the conjugal family succeeds in creating superior forms of character, happiness and creativity" (1989 [1938]). This is not simply thanks to the presence of mother and father, but siblings too. Reduced to something extremely schematic, the conjugal family gives you an exciting object at which you can direct your infantile libido, a law-giving object that stops you constantly trying, and failing, to get full satisfaction from your mother, plus you also have brothers or sisters—who might be older or younger—offering you opportunities to compete, copy, love, hate, envy, pity, and so on. You are offered the points around which to draw up a relatively reliable, yet also rich and complex, psychic map.

After many decades of polemic against the conjugal family, you get an argument in favour of it—and not just a simplistic argument that says it's "nature's way", but one that tries to show what it offers people, apart from frustration. Instead of saying that conventional families are horrible so we should give people other options, he's saying something more along the lines of, "Conventional families are horrible in a very formative, instructive way and if we mess around with the shape of them we should be aware that there may be effects further down the line." The main effect he's referring to is psychosis, which he sees as resulting from an absence of structuring paternal intervention.

Is he really saying that the breakdown of the patriarchal family is going to result in mass madness? In a way he is, but you have to remember that there are all sorts of qualifiers—apart from the one that says psychosis isn't *necessarily* a catastrophe for the subject. The "mother" could be a man or a woman, as could the "father". It's just that biological men and women often lend themselves conveniently to these linguistically constructed roles. There has to be a primary caregiver to whom you're extremely attached, and if you grow up believing you came squelching out of their body, that can also be a good thing. Then there has to be another person in whom the primary caregiver is very interested, and who helps to keep you in your place. Believing that this person packs a truncheon *can* lend imaginary support to this idea, but actually, it's all just an equation, with each of the terms being a position in the overall sum, rather than anything more particular, not to mention "natural".

However, you're still left with the model of a two-parent family, preferably with more than one child, as an ideal set-up for the formation of happy, intelligent, creative human beings. Lacan, in this essay, is dubious about one-parent families, seeing them as potential breeding grounds for psychosis. It's not a moral problem for him—he just has the quasi-architectural idea that you need a number of well-positioned points to make a stable structure.

To recap, you have the idea of a primeval scrabble for survival, with any form of family being valid so long as it buys enough time to breed. Then, following centuries of fluctuation and experimentation, you have a gradual rigidification of the idea of family in Western culture, underpinned by an awareness of death, which is harnessed to anxieties about private property. While the conjugal patriarchal family seems to work very well as an economic unit—people survive and sophisticated things get built and invented—it also very often seems to make people unhappy, particularly women. It works in one sense, but not in another.

So, people begin to put this idea of the family in question. Psychoanalysis appears on the scene with plenty to say about why families might be a source of source of suffering for all concerned. However, it also argues for the ways in which conventional families might structure the psyche and prepare us for complex relations further down the line. If you give up on the idea of the nuclear family, at least according to Lacan, you do so at your peril.

Where does this leave the contemporary family? Is the fluidity and variety of its forms a problem? Or might it be a huge relief not to have to conform to a one-size-fits-all domestic arrangement? One can probably think of all sorts of examples and counter-examples from family, friends, fiction and therapeutic practice. Two recent-ish books caught my attention, showing two very different ways of thinking about families, and especially about paternity. There's *My Struggle, Book 2: A Man in Love* (2009) by Karl Ove Knausgaard, and *About a Boy* (1998) by Nick Hornby. Knausgaard's book, the second instalment in a series of six, focuses on fatherhood and the author's relationship with his partner. It depicts a dramatic love story followed by years of domestic frustration. At the exact point at which the couple stop insanely idealising each other, she gets pregnant and they start fighting all the time. They have three children together. Both are self-employed writers and share childcare equally. Although he loves the children, the narrator—the author—suffers feeling "feminised". And this is in spite of the fact that he lives in Stockholm, which he describes rather disparagingly as a world centre for caring, super-involved dads. He struggles with his new identity, describing walking around the city with a pram feeling like a Victorian patriarch on the inside, a pitiful post-modern wimp on the outside. He spends pages ranting about the general insanity of Swedish men, who can discuss the faults and merits of various nursery food providers for hours. He doesn't believe that women should stay at home while men go out and be manly. He just suffers his situation without believing the old way was better. Still, he's totally committed to being a dad after feeling let down by his own selfish, uncaring father. The narrator even uses his commitment as a weapon against his partner, spitefully demonstrating that he can do every domestic duty efficiently, and without complaint—something of which she seems incapable. His initial solution to the problem of family is to do everything "right"—to stay with his partner although things aren't perfect, to have as good a relationship with his kids as he's able—but also to be frank with himself about the horror of it, and to write about all this at very great length.

Knausgaard is often dismissive of psychologists in his writing, but you could say that his approach is quite in keeping with some of the ideas you might find in psychoanalysis: Take families seriously. Don't expect magic solutions. Understand that, by changing something over here, you'll inevitably be changing something over there. Maybe there's something precious about the conjugal family that's worth fighting and suffering for. It's all desperately gloomy, but also dense and fascinating, serious and subtle, not to mention beautiful and uplifting in places. In that sense, it's extremely old-fashioned.

Nick Hornby's book, *About a Boy*, was written over a decade earlier, and proposes a more modern solution. (Almost anything is more modern than seeing what strength and knowledge you might be able to extract from suffering; hardly a top twenty-first century ideal.) The story follows an extremely selfish, rich, idle bachelor who accidentally befriends a twelve-year old boy. The boy's mother is depressed and unstable, insisting her son remain childlike because she's so afraid of losing him. She cuts his hair herself and dresses him up in weird clothes, making it very difficult for him to fit in at school. The bachelor can see that this is bad news for the boy, so he starts trying to teach him to be a bit more cool. The boy is desperate to get the bachelor and his mum together. It's easy to see why he might want a dad-type guy around, to stop his mother making life impossible. The problem is that the bachelor has absolutely no sexual or romantic interest in the mum.

Basically, the whole thing is the story of an unorthodox psychodynamic treatment. You get to hear a great deal about the countertransference as well as the transference. The boy comes round to the man's house every day after school. It turns out that he's doing this for two very important reasons. One is that he doesn't want bullies to follow him back to his real address. The other is that he once came home from school to find his mother crashed out from an overdose; now he's terrified of what he might find when he lets himself in the front door. The daily visits delay the horrible moment. When the bachelor hears that this is what the drop-ins are all about, all he's able to say is, "Fucking hell." He chastises himself but, as it happens, this is the most helpful thing anyone could have said to the boy. It shows that someone else understands the problem and takes it seriously, so much so that all they can do is swear.

(Rather than go through the laborious and embarrassing do-gooding motions of pressing him to speak about it, in the manner of a school counsellor.) Anyhow, to cut to the ending, the boy gradually learns to resist his mum a bit better, without rejecting her, and the bachelor falls in love for the first time (with another single mum), attributing this change to the greater vulnerability and sensitivity brought about in him by his relationship with the boy. They "cure" each other. The bachelor's girlfriend and the boy's mum become friends, and he inherits a kind of step family in the form of the bachelor's girlfriend's children. He also begins to spend time with his biological dad, who has a new partner. So, it goes from being just the boy and his mum, to a collective of inter-related people.

At the very end the boy and the bachelor have a conversation about family. The boy says: "You know when they do those human pyramids? That's the sort of model for living I'm looking at now [...] I just don't think couples are the future." For him, couples are too unstable. People are too obscure and difficult to sustain closed, exclusive relationships. If you're a child, and therefore dependent, it's better to spread the risk across a whole network of people. The book isn't dismissive of couples—it ends with two happy couples forming parts of the human pyramid. It just throws doubt on their being the most stable configuration. There's still scope for monogamy and intimacy in this new scheme—if that's what people like—but it offers more fall-back positions than a tight conjugal unit. In terms of keeping the crocodile's mouth open, perhaps a collective holds more promise than a solitary, fallible man.

Fashion

Colloque de l'A.l.e.p.h, Lille, 2006*

In *The Devil Wears Prada* (2003), Lauren Weisberger gives a fictionalised account of her time spent working as assistant to Anna Wintour, editor of American Vogue. The book has been described as "revenge lit"—a genre that began with *The Nanny Diaries* (2002), a novel detailing the unfortunate foibles of wealthy Manhattan families. In these books a wealthy, autocratic female boss is treated to a vicious character assassination by a younger female employee. *The Devil Wears Prada* is largely made up of a series of vignettes showing what a cruel, heartless monster the magazine editor is as she ritually humiliates everyone fatter, uglier, poorer or worse dressed than herself. The boss's incessant attempts at making everyone around her look foolish end up making her look like the biggest idiot of all, closely followed by everyone else in the fashion industry for buying into such a mindless system. The counterpoint to all of this is, of course, our heroine, a sensible young lady who eats burgers and chips, goes out with a schoolteacher and buys her clothes on the high street.

---

*First published in French in *Savoirs et Clinique: le corps à la mode ou les images du corps dans la psychanalyse* (Editions Érès, 2009).

But if the book is intended as an attack on the inhabitants of the world of fashion, it's curious that it begins with a series of "accidents" befalling an array of luxury garments. Within the first few pages our heroine manages to snap the heel of a Manolo Blahnik stiletto, sweat all over a pair of suede Gucci trousers and burn a hole in a pair of Jimmy Choo boots. So why is she so angry with clothes? Are they simply the objects of exchange in an economy she despises? Or is there more to it than that?

What does psychoanalytic literature have to tell us about fashion? Freud made a brief reference to women's clothing at a meeting of the Vienna Psychoanalytic Society. Like all of Freud's pronouncements on women, it needs to be approached with a certain degree of skepticism. He claimed that: "All women are clothes fetishists ..." and supported this by saying that women were characterised by a kind of passive exhibitionism; they enjoy allowing themselves to be seen. This tendency was "repressed" by the wearing of clothes, which in turn were "raised to a fetish". He says:

> Only now can we understand why even the most intelligent women behave defencelessly against the demands of fashion. For them, clothes take the place of parts of the body, and to wear the same clothes means only to show what the others can show, [...] that one can find in her everything that one can expect from women.

So, for Freud, clothes were important because they simultaneously hid and drew attention to the bodies that women wanted to show off. And, more particularly, that fashion, i.e., wearing the same clothes as other women, was important as a way of accentuating one's femininity and identifying oneself with the feminine ideal.

While it might be offensively generalising and paternalistic, certain aspects of Freud's definition might nonetheless be worth bearing in mind. Here, fashion doesn't simply mean an array of more or less appealing, more or less expensive clothes. The element of "sameness" is vital. Nothing can become fashionable without a certain degree of consensus around the idea that this style of garment is a good thing to wear right now. The wish to have what the other people have is clearly one of the driving forces behind fashion. And while this is often understood in terms of wealth or social status, it's important not to lose sight of fashion's intimate relation to the body, and therefore to the question of what bodies do or do not have.

A more sustained psychoanalytic account of fashion is provided by J. C. Flügel in his book, *The Psychology of Clothes*, published in 1930. The first part of the book deals mainly with our attitudes towards clothes in general and he agrees with Freud in saying that clothes mediate the contradictory demands of showing off and covering up. He uses the example of the sombre suit guarding against phallic exhibitionism while the top hat provides an outlet for the repressed urge.

Further into the book Flügel talks more specifically about fashion, and its emergence during the Renaissance out of the collapse of the European feudal system. He tells us that as slaves bought their freedom from impoverished aristocrats and moved to cities to set up their own businesses, the aristocracy became very worried about losing its power. As the newly formed bourgeoisie grew richer, the nobility had to invent the means by which to establish a distinction between themselves and the rest of society. One of their more desperate strategies was to introduce laws forbidding the middle classes from wearing the same clothes as them. Apart from being hard to enforce—how different was different enough?—legislation failed because the cunning masses opted instead for a perpetually transforming style of dress, which they apparently supposed would be a good visible sign of their newfound social mobility.

Flügel's idea that, "in a rigid hierarchy fashion is impossible" is obviously deeply appealing to fashion's apologists. This myth of the birth of fashion has been repeated endlessly by clothing historians keen to represent fashion as a benign force. But Flügel himself wasn't interested in arguing a case in favour of fashion. In fact, by the end of the book we see he has quite a different agenda. Flügel was an advocate of clothing reform. He believed that much could and should be done to make clothing more comfortable, attractive and affordable. He came up with the idea that "the aim of clothes should be to secure the maximum of satisfaction in accordance with the reality principle". Having said this he was forced to admit that there's no real way of measuring precisely how much showing off, covering up and protection from the external world would be permitted by the reality principle. The fact that clothing itself is a compromise formation and, as such, is always likely to arouse anxiety, ultimately leads him to argue that in the more enlightened societies of the future clothing will no longer be necessary at all. Once we have begun to understand the complex mechanisms at work in the obligatory wearing of clothes—the inhibitory impulses, the desperate management of desire and disgust, the displaced exhibitionism, the masochistic subjection of the body to various forms of discomfort—we will walk around stark naked and be much happier.

Flügel's conclusion prefigures the ending of Robert Altman's film, *Pret-a-Porter*, with its catwalk show of nude models proclaiming the death of fashion. Altman also appears to be in agreement with Flügel in that the only characters in his film who achieve any kind of happiness are a man and a woman whose clothes have been lost in transit and who therefore have nothing to wear. It seems that while clothes may promise to make our own and other people's bodies more bearable, they also bring a special misery of their own. And perhaps nowhere is this idea better illustrated than in the story of Adam and Eve. Here, clothes are associated with punishment.

Flügel may have been sad to see that seventy-six years later we are showing no signs of being cured—in fact fashion is one of the most profitable consumer industries, with every high street in every city crammed full of clothing shops. However, at least part of Flügel's vision of the future has been fully realised in the form of Gap, a shop whose entire *raison d'etre* consists of granting sartorial satisfaction in accordance with the reality principle.

At least in Edmund Bergler's 1953 book, *Fashion and the Unconscious*, everyone gets to keep their clothes on—although he would agree that fashion is the source of much misery. Bergler begins by saying that the material he has gathered during years of analytic work with numerous gay fashion designers will form the basis of his theories. It perhaps ought to be mentioned that his theories are liable to be extremely offensive to the contemporary reader due to his thoughtless heteronormativity. His key idea is that clothes are a means of taming the castration complex, the castration complex being the culmination of a series of pre-genital anxieties, the "septet of baby fears", i.e., being starved, devoured, poisoned, choked, chopped to pieces, drained and, finally, castrated. Men need women to be clothed because, naked, women's bodies are just too frightening. On the one hand they're too powerful, and on the other they have bits missing and they bleed. Because in gay men—according to Bergler—this fear amounts to something more like panic, homosexuals are particularly inclined to want to "dress" women, especially if the clothes they provide make the women look stupid, feel uncomfortable and cause them to give up all their money. Bergler refers to this situation as the "fantastic fashion hoax": in his eyes fashion is a cruel trick played by gay men on unsuspecting women. But while he is confident that he can cure his patients' homosexuality, he insists that he can't, and won't, cure them of being fashion designers. No wonder his books are so rarely read these days.

Although Bergler has a great deal to say about the men's investment in all of this, he has remarkably little to say about why women would so willingly go along with it. Indeed, instead of focusing on the female masochism necessary to keep the scheme ticking over, he seems to see stylish women as some sort of healthy ideal, portraying "sartorial anti-talents", or dowdy dressers, as unfortunate neurotics in desperate need of help. For instance, women may dress badly in order to punish their mothers, or themselves. So, analytic cure, for Bergler, may involve becoming better dressed.

Today it seems that we are confronted with two options if we want to understand something about fashion. We can either look at the various ways in which different individuals use fashion, or we can look at fashion as a system, in the manner of Roland Barthes in his book, *The Fashion System*, published in 1967.

One can always come up with plenty of cases where the first approach would seem appropriate. The young woman who spends twenty thousand pounds on designer clothes in the few days before she slashes her wrists. The successful woman who still borrows money from her parents to buy extravagant clothes. The new mother who incessantly buys clothes only to return them to the shop the next day. Or the girl who suffers from obsessive thoughts about self-harming and who regularly stays up all night cutting, reshaping and dyeing second-hand garments. All four are doing something quite different with fashion and it would surely be worthwhile to try to understand exactly what. (Having said this, while there might be as many modes of relating to fashion as there are people, an idea that one often hears is that fashion somehow promises to give consistency to the body—or at least to its reflection.)

In contrast to this approach Roland Barthes' study of fashion all but ignores the wearer, focusing exclusively on the grammar and syntax of fashion. Fashion is a chain of interchangeable signifiers that temporarily take on the meaning "fashion". He is particularly interested in the various ways in which fashion journalism links "the written garment" with the world. It is always important in the reporting of fashion to give the new look a tangible space or reason for existing. The three main ways fashion magazines provide rationalisation, via the means of text and photography, are:

Appropriate settings. The world forms a theatrical backdrop for the dress. A stark, alien landscape exists in order to give the woman a reason to dress like a Martian.

Recognisable types or personae. The femme fatale, the puritan, the businesswoman or heiress. They exist and you too could dress like them.

A response or reaction to the fashion immediately before.

Using any or all of these strategies one can make sense of any new fashion. But perhaps their multiform nature attempts to exclude or gloss over the aberrant or irrational. It seems that this network of logical explanations, constructed in such a way as to come prepared for any eventuality, conceals something arbitrary intrinsic to the workings of fashion. As Barthes says: "Clothing and the world can enter into any sort of relation [...] relation being constant, its content varied." Looking particularly at the third strategy, it's easy to see how any change can be validated when the relation to the previous style can take any form. An improvement, a continuation, an inversion or a rejection would all be seen as equally valid links between consecutive modes of dress. So not only do clothes smooth over the horror of the body, but the fashion system itself smoothes over the horror of its own semantic inconsistency.

This view of fashion differs dramatically from most historical accounts, whose aim is generally to show that each fashion is a natural and inevitable product of its own era. But these sorts of connections can only ever be made retroactively. Short skirts have been associated with women's liberation both in the 1920s and the 1960s, but at other times the wearing of miniskirts has been linked with the objectification of women by men. Fashion designers may spot an opportunity for a new style of dress (i.e., at the moment, due to recent shifts in the political climate, women won't be lynched for wearing this) but external events can never be said to have dictated the shape of the garment, which might always have been anything.

So, is fashion really all just arbitrary? In his 1948 paper "Aggressivity in Psychoanalysis" Lacan refers to the "arbitrariness of fashion". This might easily seem to chime with the idea that what's interesting about fashion is its language-like structure rather than its role in the drama of the individual wearer. But his mention of fashion immediately follows an indexing of the "imagos of the fragmented body"—a list that pre-empts Bergler's "septet of baby fears". Lacan cites "the images of castration mutilation, dismemberment, dislocation, evisceration, devouring [and] bursting open of the body" (2006, p. 104). And he doesn't just mention the arbitrariness of fashion, but the Procrustean arbitrariness. He says:

> There is a specific relation here between man and his own body that is manifested in a series of social practices—from rites involving tattooing, incision and circumcision in primitive societies to what, in advanced societies, might be called the Procrustean arbitrariness of fashion, a relatively recent cultural innovation, in that it denies respect for the natural forms of the human body. (2006, p. 105)

So, what can we make of this? Procrustes, whose name means "he who stretches", was the last of Theseus's challenges. He was a robber who kept a house by the side of the road, where he would invite travellers to eat and rest. Over a nice dinner he would tell his guests about his magic bed. The bed was exactly the same length as whoever slept on it. What Procrustes omitted to mention was that this was because he would either stretch the person or amputate their heads or legs in order to ensure a good fit. And not only that, he would first secretly adjust the bed to make it as different as possible to the person's natural height in order to ensure the maximum amount of mutilation.

So, we might conclude that the arbitrariness Lacan is referring to here has less to do with the abritrariness of the signifier as with the radical disregard for the limits of the body. One might note the ways in which fashion has emphasised various zones of the body over the centuries. As Flügel tells us: "During the later Middle Ages and the Renaissance much interest was devoted to the abdominal region, which was made as conspicuous as possible. In the eighteenth century this abdominal emphasis was abandoned [...] only to give place to an increasing emphasis on the bosom and hips." He goes on to mention the focus on the bottom provided by the bustle in the late nineteenth century, followed by the early twentieth century's love affair with legs. Flügel attempts to make sense of each fashion in relation to its cultural context, the curving belly of the Middle Ages signifying the idealisation of pregnancy, the padded hips of the eighteenth century also being equated with childbearing, etc. But if this was so, why should the large hips be accompanied by painfully restrictive corsetry? And why would one's propensity for motherhood one minute be signified by a round tummy, the next by a wasp waist and love handles? (This shift may ring a bell with anyone who has read a fashion magazine recently, and will have had firmly impressed upon them the burning importance of emphasising one's waist, not to mention urgent warnings against the crime of continuing to wear a belt on one's hips.)

This leads us to a paradox operating at the heart of fashion. On the one hand clothes cover up our unfortunate biological features and promise us a more complete body-image, just like the one we saw in a magazine, a shop window or at a party. On the other hand, fashionable clothes disregard our biological form, they pull us in at the middle, lever us up at the heel, flatten our breasts, pump them up again, accentuate curves, obliterate them, make us look like this woman, then that one, and generally treat our bodies like prime cuts of meat in an ever-changing butcher shop display.

Although shopping for fashion has been dubbed retail therapy, as if acquiring new clothes will have a tempering effect on the psyche, it can also be linked to a profound anxiety. Many of the commentaries on Lacan's recently published seminar on anxiety explore the different relations of man and woman to anxiety. Colette Soler, for example, argues that men experience less anxiety than women at the sexual level since they have something to cede in the form of their phallic detumescence. This transitory giving up of a part of the body is seen as a barrier to the desire of the Other. But couldn't we extend this notion to fashion itself? Could it be that part of the gravitational pull of fashion for women is less the acquisition of clothes—the famous retail therapy— than the giving up of clothes. Isn't fashion, in part, all about the clothes we have to stop wearing and hate?

To conclude, we have the notion of fashion as a means of organising the body, but also as a means of disorganising it. If we return to Lacan's phrase it might also be worthwhile pausing to consider the etymology of the word "arbitrary", which comes from the Latin words *ad* (to) and *baetere* (come, or go). Arbiter literally means "one who goes somewhere (as a witness or judge)", someone who settles disputes. In the fifteenth century arbitrament meant "deciding by one's own discretion", from the Latin *arbitrarius*. But by the seventeenth century the original meaning had gradually descended to "capricious" and "despotic", presumably due to anger at the various arbiters for their failure to make decisions that made everyone happy.

Perhaps this gives us a clue as to why someone might be pleased at the sight of a sweat stain on a pair of £3,000 trousers, or a lump of smouldering tobacco on the toe of an exquisite boot. No matter how much clothes promise to arbitrate between men and women, between women and women, between different psychical agencies, between who we are and who we'd like to be, they can never fully placate all the warring factions. Maybe clothing could be said to have suffered a similar shift in meaning to the word "arbitrary" itself. From its original promise as a friendly agency sent in to make everyone feel better, dress has evolved into something more like a wayward go-between, whimsically deciding this and then that with no concern at all for rectitude or fairness.

And doesn't this point us towards the idea that there's a violence in the signifier itself? Perhaps with clothing and fashion, just like other external powers—our parents, the law, language—we each have to invent our own ways of enjoying our acquiescence—or resistance. For some this will be nudism, for others an unquestioning obedience to the dictates of Vogue, and for others yet it will be little moments of revenge on the garments themselves.

Gender

Centre for Freudian Analysis and Research, 2010

In *Seminar XX, Encore (1972–1973)* (1999), Lacan tries to provide some kind of answer to Freud's question, "What does a woman want?" The seminar is packed with famously provocative statements: "The Woman doesn't exist", "There is no rapport between the sexes" or, perhaps most extravagantly of all:

> A woman can but be excluded by the nature of things, which is the nature of words, and it must be said that if there is something that women themselves complain about enough for the time being, that's it. It's just that they don't know what they're saying— that's the whole difference between them and me. (1999, p. 73)

So far so bad. But how do you know whether someone is a man or a woman? Already in Freud, sexual difference is a slippery concept, as this footnote from his *Three Essays on Sexuality* (1905d) shows:

> It is essential to understand clearly that the concepts of "masculine" and "feminine", whose meaning seems so unambiguous to ordinary people, are among the most confused that appear in science. It is possible to distinguish at least three uses. "Masculine"

and "feminine" are used sometimes in the sense of activity and passivity, sometimes in a biological, and sometimes, again, in a sociological sense. [...] Observation shows that in human beings pure masculinity is not to be found in either a psychological or a biological sense. Every individual on the contrary shows a mixture of the character traits belonging to his own and to the opposite sex; and he shows a combination of activity and passivity whether or not these character traits tally with his biological ones. (Footnote added 1915)

In *Seminar XX* (1999) Lacan takes up the ideas of masculine and feminine, grappling with the problem of how a baby becomes a sexed subject. As Dylan Evans puts it in his *Introductory Dictionary of Lacanian Psychoanalysis* (1996): "For Lacan, masculinity and femininity are not biological essences but symbolic positions, and the assumption of one of these two positions is fundamental to the construction of subjectivity: the subject is essentially a sexed subject. 'Man' and 'woman' are signifiers that stand for these two different subjective positions" (p. 178).[1] But how do you become a sexed subject? For both Freud and Lacan, it's via a tortuous inter- and intra-subjective process—the Oedipus complex—that a child begins to take up a gendered identity. Put a little over-simply, according to Freud a boy fears being castrated by his father for his sexual interest in his mother. In order to hang onto his penis he accepts his father's rules, tries to be a bit more like him, and eventually starts looking for new female love objects. A girl is initially in love with her mother and jealous of her father too. She then discovers that her mother doesn't have a penis and is so upset and disappointed that she transfers her affection to her father, identifying with her mother on the grounds that they are both missing something.

For Lacan, the Oedipus complex is split into three phases. In the first phase the child notices that the mother lacks something. There's something she desires—the imaginary phallus—so the child tries to be this thing for her. In case the idea of being the phallus for the mother sounds a little arcane, you might just as well say "be everything for the mother", or "be a perfectly good and satisfying child". In the second phase the father intervenes and separates mother and child, putting into effect the incest taboo. The mother is deprived of her object. In the third phase the father demonstrates that he possesses the phallus, causing the child to give up on the idea of being the phallus for the mother.

This involves a relinquishing of jouissance on the part of the child, which he or she can then spend the rest of his or her life trying to recover. These three phases would be the same for both boys and girls.

While Freud and Lacan agree that the taking up of a masculine or feminine position happens in relation to the Oedipus complex, they disagree about precisely how. For Freud it's to do with identification—boys identify with dads, girls with mums. But for Lacan the Oedipus complex necessarily involves a symbolic identification with the father, no matter whether you are "male" or "female", therefore identification can't determine gender. Instead, it's the relationship with the symbolic phallus that's decisive. You either "have" it or you don't. Or, at least, being a "man" means not exactly not having it. Needless to say, the phallus and the penis are not at all the same. The penis is fallible and fleshy and worryingly detachable while the phallus isn't a thing but an idea. The assumption of a gendered identity is therefore a symbolic act. Having a vagina or a penis may hold some sway over which way things go—it may even be very important—it just isn't the deciding factor. It's up there with other considerations, like whether your parents wanted a boy or a girl, what they—and you—think boys and girls are, your ideals and identifications, who you think you are, and who you want to be. The phallus is a signifier with no signified, which leads logically to the conclusion that a woman might just as well have it as a man. A subject's sexual position needs to shift from the realm of the imaginary to the symbolic, and it's as a result of this shift that a viable sexual position can be taken up. Still, having said all that, it's impossible to attain a fully "normal", finished position. (Parts of this paragraph are so heavily influenced by Dylan Evan's dictionary entry on "sexual difference" (p. 178) as to fall just short of quotations.)

In case it all sounds a bit confusing Lacan has drawn a little diagram that explains everything:

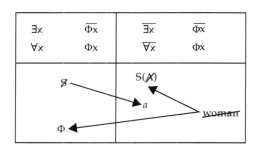

The figures in the top boxes are known as the formulas of sexuation. The left-hand side tells us what a man is, and the right-hand side explains what it is to be a woman. Underneath is another way of putting it, just in case the top bit isn't clear. Lacan writes it out at the beginning of one of his meetings (the session published under the chapter title "A Love Letter") and then says, "After what I just put on the board you may think you know everything. Don't" (1999, p. 73). He goes on to explain:

$\forall$ = the universal quantifier; "all"
$\exists$ = existential quantifier; there exists
Φ = Phi, the phallus
Φx = the phallic function, the law of castration/incest prohibition

So for men there are two related equations which, together, define the masculine position:

$\forall x \, \Phi x$: All men are submitted to the phallic function.
$\exists x \, \overline{\Phi x}$: There exists one that is not.

What kind of man isn't submitted to the phallic function? According to Freud's myth of the primal father, there was once a man who had access to all the women and didn't let the other men have sex. All the less powerful men got together and killed him. After that the men had to agree between themselves not to try to be too powerful or they'd be faced with the same problem all over again. In other words, in order to be able to experience enjoyment *at all* they had to concede to experiencing it in a limited way—they would never be allowed to enjoy fully in the manner of the primordial father. In order for the law of castration (i.e., the law of limited enjoyment) to function, there has to be something outside it, an exception. You would only agree to submit *because* of the possibility of the exception. Lacan's equation formulates this idea at the level of logic, thereby doing away with Freud's somewhat problematic invention of a myth.

Lacan's two logical statements together form an idea like:

All men are submitted to the phallic function, but only on the condition that there exists a man who isn't. Or in Lacan's own words, which may or may not help, "It is through the phallic function that man as a whole acquires his inscription, with the proviso that this function is limited due to the existence of an x by which the function Phi x is negated" (p. 79).

For women:

$\exists x \ \overline{\Phi x}$: There does not exist any woman that is not submitted to the phallic function. i.e., all women are castrated.
$\overline{\forall x} \ \Phi x$: Not all of a woman is submitted to the phallic function.

Women can either submit entirely to the phallic function or not—there is even the possibility of both submitting *and* not submitting simultaneously. This is what Lacan seems to be getting at with the idea of the "not-all". The formulation "$\overline{\forall x}$" is inconceivable in terms of formal logic as it's structurally ambiguous. It may not mean "not all women" so much as "not all of any woman". But this very imprecision is the point. It's why, for Lacan, there is no such thing as "woman" or "the Woman", because there is no single concept that covers "woman". Lacan abandons essentialist definitions and situates "woman" on his schema between Phi and S($\cancel{A}$). In other words, femininity is defined not as an essence but as a relation. As he tells us:

> Any speaking being whatsoever, as is expressly formulated in Freudian theory, whether provided with the attributes of masculinity [...] or not, is allowed to inscribe itself in this part [of the graph]. If it inscribes itself there, it will not allow for any universality—it will be a not-whole, insofar as it has the choice of positing itself in Phi x or of not being there. (p. 80)

Moving onto the lower section of the graph we see sexual difference being explained in terms of the type of enjoyment one attempts to get. The arrows represent attempts at a relation, or at experiencing enjoyment. The barred subject tries to have some kind of relation with the *object a* (on the same line as the crossed-out woman, although it's not at all the same thing—maybe you could even say it gets in the way of her). The crossed-out woman attempts to access the phallus, but at the same time she is aiming at the signifier of the barred Other. This is on her side of the graph, and is also something impossible. The signifier of the barred Other stands for the inconsistency in the symbolic order, the non-existence of the big Other. This type of enjoyment—getting satisfaction through a relation with the gap in the big Other—is also called Other jouissance, as opposed to phallic jouissance. Like "the Woman" it doesn't officially exist but, like God, people talk about it enough for us to have to look into it. How can you think about something that can't be described? Lacan suggests the only way to approach is it through logic. Using his formulae, you can at least designate a place for it, even if you can't say exactly what "it" is. There's the often-quoted moment in the seminar where he almost seems to bait women for having so little to say on the subject.

> The plausibility of what I'm claiming here—namely, that woman knows nothing of this jouissance—is underscored by the fact that in all the time people have been begging them on their hands and knees—I spoke last time of women psychoanalysts—to try to tell us, not a word! We've never been able to get anything out of them. (p. 75)

Luce Irigaray's work, especially *This Sex Which is Not One* (1977), has something to say back. Hers is certainly a very inventive theory but, speaking as (at least) a biological female, it seems to contain a large element of wishful thinking. The idea that a woman can exist in an ongoing state of arousal without any need of external stimulation because her vagina has two lips which rub together—meaning that she doesn't need to have sex, or even masturbate, because her anatomy alone provides her with so much satisfaction—is surely too good to be true. This anatomical theory is used to prop up further ideas about women's different use of language; we don't need to speak so much because we're happy to sit around in our auto-erotic state of bliss, apparently, but when we do talk it comes out all fascinatingly non-linear because we're beyond dreary phallic, patriarchal systems of signification. Despite having its roots in Lacanian psychoanalytic theory, Irigaray's theory of femininity not only relies heavily on anatomy, but could also be said to be quite homogenising, as if all biological women experience their anatomy in the same way.

Lacan himself tries to point us towards the writings of the mystics in search of some sort of evidence of this Other jouissance. Not because they have anything to say about it—they don't—but because they have a way of pointing at it without actually describing it. In Lacan's words: "It is clear that the essential testimony of the mystics consists in saying that they experience it, but know nothing about it." There's a point at which their testimonies break down, where they can no longer describe whatever it was that happened, and it's perhaps here that a space opens up, hinting at the existence of a form of jouissance that isn't phallic, that doesn't fail or finish too soon but that really goes the whole way.

Do you believe in women?

In Slavoj Žižek's essay, "Woman is One of the Names-of-the-Father, or How Not to Misread Lacan's Formulas of Sexuation" (1995), he talks about Spinoza's criticism of the notion of God as a kind of super-person. More specifically, a super-person who is called into being at the moment when all causal connections break down. When you can no longer say what happened before what happened before—before the big bang, before the grapefruit-sized hyper-dense matter (or whatever the big limits were in the seventeenth century)—God is invoked in order to give form to this unthinkable limit. Instead of a big, scary nothing you suddenly have a man with a beard. The reason this figure becomes so fascinating is that he stands for the hole in the structure of our knowledge; he gives it a positive shape.

According to Žižek, the impossible God figure is homologous with the feminine not-all. This isn't to say that woman is just like God because she doesn't exist either. It's rather that the phallus comes to fill the gap in the Other—to prop it up. A woman (in the sense of Lacan's formulae) can see through the phallic function at the same time as being entirely submitted to it. She can spot the fact that the signifier of the phallus is put there in order to prop up the inconsistency of the Other, while simultaneously investing in it. Similarly, according to Spinoza, one might acknowledge the fictionality of God while still believing in Him. In order to do this, one has to do away with the idea of God being a man and make him into something far more integral to everything so that, while God as he's generally conceived (with a beard, masking a limit) doesn't exist, God (in this new sense) is the *only* thing that exists. Likewise, the phallic function doesn't exist, and is everything.

A good test for ideas in philosophy is to see whether they pop up anywhere in popular culture. If they appear in simple form elsewhere, without having been reached through reference to other philosophical ideas, or via complex speculative logic, then maybe there's hope for them. Gene Pitney's 1961 hit, *Every Breath I Take*, written by Carole King and Gerry Goffin, is about God, and also ostensibly about a woman. (Actually, the lyrics are non-gender-specific but Gene Pitney was, by all accounts, heterosexual—perhaps surprisingly to those of us introduced to him through Marc Almond.) Who knows whether the songwriters had read Spinoza, but they certainly came up with a very similar idea. The singer tells us that he hardly ever thanks God for his incredible romantic good fortune. He never says a prayer, nor "thanks to someone way up there" for delivering such a lovely person to him. He never stops what he's doing in order to be grateful, but instead exists in a permanent state of thankfulness, permeating every single breath with cosmic appreciation. Similarly, he never fears losing his loved one if by "fears losing" you mean having marked pangs of terror at the idea of her not being around anymore. Instead, every single particle of his being is constantly infused with a continuous awareness of the awful possibility of her absence. While the song appears to be Christian, in the Spinozistic sense, in its boundlessness and invocation of the possibility of endless suffering you could also say it echoes the tradition of Sufi poetry.

As for the title of Žižek's paper, "Woman is One of the Names-of-the-Father", the author points out that the figure of the woman in courtly love has a lot in common with the figure of the primordial father—she's capricious and wants to have it all. She makes impossible demands on the poor knight who admires her. In this sense, the idea of woman as exception is the perfect crystallisation of the male phantasy—she's peculiar, and she doesn't lack. Žižek claims that the usual problem with readings of Lacan's formulas of sexuation is that men are put on the side of the universal phallic function and women are posited as an exception, something that spills out and can't possibly be contained. This is something you will find in all sorts of Lacanian commentaries, but perhaps Luce Irigaray's work is an extreme example. Here the phallic function is seen as something rather boring and limiting, while women are portrayed as creatures who don't need to be bothered with it because they're having so much fun chattering and rubbing labia with themselves, being generally better and happier than men.

The problem of what a woman *really* is has been every bit as troubling for women who call themselves feminists as it has for men who don't. If we say women are caring, unselfish and good at understanding other people's needs, is it because men have somehow caused us to be like that, or because that's our nature? Famously, there are feminist arguments on both sides. On the one hand, we have the idea that a woman is constructed to suit men, as Simone de Beauvoir argues in

The Second Sex (1949), not to mention the idea that the notion of women as Other is a male phantasy and a form of oppression. Or, much earlier but still in the same vein, we have John Stuart Mill's idea that we don't even know what a woman is because no one's ever had the chance to find out. On the other hand, there is an idea that women are essentially different, as seen in the work of Helene Deutsch and Luce Irigaray. For Deutsch, the "inferiority" of the clitoris in comparison with the penis causes women to turn in on themselves and become less assertive. Putting a more upbeat spin on things, Irigaray argues that instead of there being a dominant sex and a subordinate one—men, and women as defined by men—we have two positive and entirely separate categories. Thanks to the physical form of a woman's anatomy—something hidden, a hole, divided lips that touch each other—woman's psyche develops differently. According to this theory, while men are interested in looking, women are interested in touching; we have blurry boundaries and are better at making real contact with others. To extrapolate further: if only men could learn from women there'd be no property or alienation and everyone would love each other. So, all the lovey-dovey, caring, non-materialistic qualities put in question by feminists like Beauvoir might be seen by the other camp as essentially feminine features and given a positive value. We are invited to consider the possibility that these qualities might undermine patriarchal systems rather than simply support them.

Because there is no chance of rolling back thousands of years of human history and seeing how things might have panned out differently, the only way we can possibly answer the question of which side is correct is by saying they both are: women are like we are because we have had a certain set of feminine ideals inflicted on us, and because we really *are* fundamentally different. The essentially feminine and the culturally feminine can't be separated. Femininity is both something "in itself" and "for the other". According to Žižek, this makes Woman the barred subject par excellence—she is cut through with the impossibility of ever deciding whether she is real or fake. The human subject, aka the barred subject, is divided by its entry into language—as soon as we begin to speak, our access to being, and to jouissance, is limited. Any experience that follows will be mediated by language, a logical system that pre-exists us and that we have no choice but to submit to if we want to join in with human life. None of us, men or women, can ever know whether we really are what we think we are, nor how much we are just a jumble of things made possible by the words and rules externally imposed on us. All of us has to struggle with the question of what in us is actually *us* and what we have been made into by the Other.

Which brings us back to the problem of the difference between men and women. If what we call a woman is just a special kind of barred subject, how is it different to the type of barred subject we call a man? If, as Žižek says, the thing that defines a woman is a "pure topological cut that forever separates the 'for the other' from the 'in itself'" (1995), then what defines a man, who is also divided in terms of what he is and what the Other makes him into? If a woman is marked out by her masquerade—her way of *appearing* to be something—then men, too, notoriously *pretend*. To borrow a clichéd example, they want the world to believe that they are strong and confident, whereas actually they feel weak and fallible. How is this not exactly the same as feminine masquerade? Žižek argues that, in the case of a man, we know more or less what's behind the mask; he wants to look big and macho but actually he's flakey. In the case of women, the relationship between the mask and whatever's behind it is more ambiguous. It's as if women hold up the mask as a mask and say, "Isn't this a charming disguise and I bet you can't guess what's behind it?" The façade is held up in order to instigate the search, to make people curious, whereas with men the idea would actually be to fool people.

In case this seems to reduce men, yet again, to the generic position of "the basic sex" it's good to remember John Travolta's performance as Danny Zuko in *Grease* (1978), beloved among drag kings for its kitsch presentation of hyper-masculinity. Zuko, the coolest boy in school, is so hard at work on his macho performance that he almost appears feminised, like a woman parodying masculine behaviour. "Masculinity" appears here as a series of postures, but the effect isn't to make us think that Danny Zuko is secretly pathetic. Travolta is so brilliant at playing a man he gives the impression that he may be hiding something *more*, rather than less, behind this spectacular exterior.

Hommosexuality and object a

It's also perhaps worth mentioning homosexuality in relation to Lacan's formulas—both hommosexuality (as Lacan spells it in order to high-light something about the masculine position) and homosexuality as it is popularly conceived, i.e., a relation between two people of the same biological sex. Lacan's play on words—hommosexual—uses the French word "homme" to suggest the way in which a man loves. Everyone on the masculine side of the diagram is hommosexual in this sense; what he wants is not exactly the other person, but the other person reduced to *object a* (see chapter on the Object). He locates the cause of his desire in them—a hair type, the timbre of a voice, a body shape—and then has to put up with the rest of them because of it. According to Lacan's account of gender, this would be the masculine way of loving, or attempting to extract enjoyment from someone else.

Homosexuality, as in a relation between two people with the same reproductive organs, is something else. It's not that some homosexuals aren't hommosexual, it's just that, in Lacanian terms, one's homosexuality or not makes very little difference to how you love or get sexual enjoyment from other people. Because there is no natural affinity between the positions on either side of the graph, your own stance in relation to either phallic jouissance or the signifier of the barred Other would have no bearing whatsoever on the position of your partner. A homosexual certainly couldn't be defined as someone who chooses a partner who sits on the same side of the graph. But neither is it someone who chooses a partner with the same genitals but who is situated on the opposite side of the graph. One's sexual position is simply a mode of obtaining jouissance. So, to be situated on the masculine side of the graph just means one attempts to reduce the other person to *object a*. It certainly doesn't mean that this person whom one believes contains the object is therefore a woman. A man might fall for another man because he has a beautiful face, an elegant walk or a huge penis (whichever particular brand of part-object interests him) irrespective of this love object's sexual position. Homosexuality and heterosexuality are no different in this respect.

In spite of Freud's outspokenly non-judgemental stance, homosexuality became a fraught subject for early psychoanalysts. Even Wilhelm Reich, who was supposedly in favour of unrestrained sexuality, is reputed to have refused to treat a homosexual on the grounds that he didn't want to deal with "such filth". Alfred Adler even believed that laws should be introduced requiring the compulsory treatment of homosexuality. In 1921 Karl Abraham and the Berlin group of analysts proposed that homosexuals shouldn't be allowed to undergo psychoanalytic training due to their pathological object choice. Otto Rank and Freud objected, as did Sándor Ferenczi. Ernest Jones, president of the IPA in the 1920s and 1930s, was another homophobe, and it was largely due to his unfortunate influence that the exclusion of gay people became the official IPA position, with homosexuality being considered a pathology by many psychoanalysts long after it had been dropped from the DSM.

You can perhaps see that Lacan's formulas would make the pathologisation of homosexuality ludicrous, hence he had no problem with applications from openly gay analysts at a time when they were excluded by the main training organisations. He also had no problem training people who believed in God—even nuns, which many Freudians would have baulked at—perhaps because believing in God is not so different from believing in the phallic function. If, for many Freudians, serious religiosity suggested a foolish tendency to hang onto comforting fictions, for Lacan, the fiction of God is no less reasonable than the fiction of the law of castration.

To go back to Lacan's graph, the disparity between the two sides is what Lacan is referring to when he says there is no rapport between the sexes. Men and women don't complete each other. In fact, they seem far more designed to upset and annoy each other. But luckily, we have an ingenious invention called love that promises to make things marginally better (at times). So, what is Lacan trying to tell us about love in *Seminar XX*? Is he anti-love? Is he trying to debunk the myth? Or is it a paean to the unstoppability of love? A testament to the fact that, whatever love is, you can't get rid of it. There may be no sexual relation, but that doesn't mean love is a bad idea. Perhaps it's a rather brilliant response to the problem. Love is a strategy for dealing with the other person, and it has to be constantly reinvented in order to work. In Lacan's words; "All love [...] 'doesn't stop being written', doesn't stop, won't stop" (1999, p. 145). He certainly doesn't suggest it's an idea we should give up on.

Down under

Baz Luhrmann's *Australia* (2008) is an extraordinarily thoughtful, supremely ill-reviewed film about men and women. It's the story of a man, woman and child who come together to make a kind of family. The question is whether they can make their different impulses and wishes function together, or whether their varying needs will break them apart. At the beginning of the film the man and woman meet and, in the manner of so many classic romances, hate each other. He seems to her to be a stupid, Aussie macho whose main aim in life is to exploit females. He thinks she is a vain English idiot who imagines all men must necessarily be in love with her because she's pretty and well-dressed. They get to know each other in the Australian outback, where she has come to fetch her husband only to discover that he's been murdered. On the dead husband's farm there are a number of Aboriginal people, and a small mixed race boy called Nullah.

Some viewers asked why the film was called *Australia*. Obviously, it was set in Australia, but it was just about a handful of people at one very particular moment in history (WWII). Perhaps they had failed to notice that the film was also about the co-existence of two very different cultures. Of course, that could also be said of plenty of other countries, but the clash between white Australians and Aboriginals has been particularly painful and entrenched because of their radically different ideas about time and space. You can't give Aboriginal people bits of land belonging to their ancestors, or fence off areas where no one will go and bother them, because they don't treat land in that way. They have to be free to move around. The two cultures can't just separate and ignore each other because they will always inevitably cross paths (as if separation is any kind of solution anyhow).

Baz Luhrmann has set the two aspects of the story up so that they overlap, informing and problematising each other. On the one hand, you have the Drover and Lady Ashley, who appear to have radically conflicting needs and wants, and then you also have these two cultures with precisely the same problem; they don't fit together. As it's told in the narrative of the film, the Drover needs to do the work he loves (and for this he has to be away herding cattle for months at a time) while Lady Ashley needs to be loved and valued, and to have a home. She also successfully runs a farm—it's far from old-school sexist. She even fights a man when she catches him mistreating Nullah.

Nullah's mother dies, so it's left to the Drover and Lady Ashley to look after him. He doesn't want to be brought up like a white child, but to be allowed to go walkabout with his grandfather. Over the course of the film, the Drover and Lady Ashley, having fallen madly in love, start to drive each other nuts. He feels trapped and she feels undervalued. Nullah runs away because he doesn't want to be cooped up, but is immediately caught by the authorities and shipped off to an island to be educated by missionaries. Having all come together for a brief spell, it becomes apparent that functioning as a family is far from simple. The man goes droving, the woman tells him not to bother coming back, the child disappears into the outback, and it looks like it's all over. The only problem is that they are all now extremely unhappy. While it was difficult for them to be together, it's also hard to be apart.

Into this sad scenario crashes the Japanese bombing of Darwin, a truly dreadful event with more deaths than Pearl Harbour. The Drover realises he's running away from Lady Ashley because he's so afraid of having something to lose. He tries to find her but hears she's been killed in the attack. Worst of all, she died believing he didn't love her. To try to make amends he goes and rescues Nullah from the missionaries. When they get back to Darwin it turns out that Lady Ashley is actually alive. The Drover can love her again, and risk losing her again, but this time with a little more self-awareness. In a way, nothing's changed, but he can now make slightly more informed choices. He'll still do some droving, while also making sure to appreciate lovely Lady Ashley. He's castrated, but in a nice, beneficial way. All these changes are made easier for him by the fact that Lady Ashley has changed too. She agrees that things are better with him in the picture, but this doesn't mean he has to be there all the time. She doesn't need to be the constant focus of his attention; he can go and pay attention to bulls and horses too. She gives up on the idea of being everything for him, but it's taken a very serious brush with death and the temporary loss of everyone she values. She can also now let Nullah go walkabout without being in a temper. They can be separate and still love each other. Everyone's happy.

But are they *all* happy in a castrated, realistic way? Or is there some Other jouissance floating around? Perhaps Lady Ashley has stumbled across a mode of loving that's much more all-inclusive. Instead of clinging to Nullah and the Drover, she now loves *everything*. Throughout the film she stops being cross with Australia for being dry and inhospitable. Nullah points out that she finally seems to have realised what a brilliant place she's in. At the end of the movie we watch her in a field with the Drover behind her, and Nullah disappearing into the distance in front. (Lady Ashley is on a locus between two arrows, like in Lacan's graph.) It seems that she's found a way to love all of it: the rocks, the sky, the mobile love objects. She doesn't have to worry about losing things anymore because everything's joined up. We are left with the sense of a fragmented harmony between the characters. They all find ways to love each other that seem to work. It's vital that the story isn't about a simple falling in love, but that it has two phases. The characters fall in love initially because people seem to like doing that. They all have their little fantasies about whom they're dealing with, treating each other as objects of satisfaction until it starts to become annoying. At the point of total meltdown, they either have to give up, or to rewrite the codes in order for it to become possible to love each other again. The film is exemplary in the way it shows not only the absolute disparity between the things people might want from one another, but also the "won't stop being written-ness" of love. The fact that it's impossible isn't a reason to give up.

Note

1. This might appear to some to be offensively normative and restricting, as if Lacan is saying you need to have a firm masculine or feminine identity in order to qualify as human, or at least *not* to qualify as mad. While there might be people who read his work in this way, it's also possible to find a more nuanced position; that gender is intrinsically confusing and unsettling, and *any* livable stance is hard won. See *Please Select Your Gender* by Patricia Gherovici (2010).

Jokes

Centre for Freudian Analysis and Research, 2011

Three men go into analysis. One is a comic actor, another is a sketch writer, and one says he'd like to be a stand-up comedian. Funnily enough, this isn't a joke. Each has the idea that if they can be professionally amusing "the problem" will somehow be solved. "The problem" is one of being loved and ensuring one's lovability. In each of the cases the ideas of being unloved or unloveable are very important in the person's history. For all three, making people laugh on a grand scale presents itself as a form of salvation.

It seems that good stand-ups do very particular things with audiences in order to bring about enjoyment, thereby making themselves lovable, popular, and sometimes even rich. Freud talked about a kind of double entry system whereby, when narcissism (or "self-love" or "self-esteem") is reduced, it can be supplemented by love from the outside. But maybe you have to hate yourself quite thoroughly in the first place in order to imagine you need such huge incoming supplies, and of course you can read about precisely this phenomenon in countless celebrity autobiographies.

Narcissism, for Freud, is related to species survival. It's the libidinised component of the will to live. It isn't pathological in itself. For the species to thrive we need to be capable of loving ourselves and other people. We have to be able to look after ourselves in order to stay alive to breed, then to be able to attach ourselves to other people, at least for a while, in order to make this happen. So, human life is a constant balancing act between narcissism and object love. Freud makes an analogy with single-celled-organisms who might, at times, send "pseudopodia" out into the world (i.e., fragile fronds of themselves would extend outwards) before retracting again into blob-like wholeness.

Stand-up comedy is part of a long tradition that's currently in a bit of a boom. People like to say it's the new rock and roll, or even a new religion. West End theatres are full of stand-up acts, perhaps in part because one-person shows are cheap. Twitter and Facebook mean that comedians are in close virtual contact with huge numbers of fans. Airport bookshops are full of comedians' autobiographies. Some reveal childhood trauma, upset, deprivation, early signs of "being a bit different" (Russell Brand's *My Booky Wook*, 2007). Others talk about the craft of comedy (Frank Skinner's *On the Road*, 2008).

So, the common features of a modern stand-up comedian are that they stand up on their own in front of lots of people (some, like Eddie Izzard, can fill Wembley arena). They appear on TV, write exposing autobiographies, and communicate constantly via the Internet. What sort of person would be able to bear that quantity of attention and exposure? And why do audiences seem to like it so much?

Comedians are among the most feted, but also the most abject of celebrities. They tell jokes about farting, shitting, wanking, and violence. In other words, they're associated with the most shameful aspects of being human, but are also admired, rewarded, and special. They're not normal, narcissistic stars like Keira Knightley or Bruno Mars; comedians' work involves being very much in contact with what's usually repressed or disavowed.

There are certain odd features you come across over and over again in live comedy—primarily, the comedian being horrible to audience members, treating them like they're stupid, boring or somehow lesser beings. Having an ordinary-sounding job often comes up as a subject for ridicule, as does having a weird one. Ricky Gervais is perhaps at the apex of this, not just picking on single spectators, but goading entire auditoriums for supposedly being poorer and having more boring lives than him. He presents himself as a singular, special person while everybody else is just a miserable member of a mass. Of course, it can sometimes be funny, but why are variations on this scenario repeated so often in comedy acts? Where's the enjoyment? It can be like watching a despot. Sometimes it's hard not to think that we could all rise up and overthrow him. (I say "him" here at the risk of sexism, but the only "female" comedian I've seen behave in this way is Dame Edna. Some women in comedy, perhaps most especially Sara Pascoe, are extraordinarily brilliant at being "nice" while still finding plenty of things to make jokes about.) Audiences, however, are mostly very well behaved, singing when they're told to sing, and calling out answers when asked. Except, of course, the hecklers, who are very much part of the whole scheme or tradition. It's their job to try to puncture the comedian's narcissism, while the comedian must retaliate, punishing the heckler for his envy, and re-establishing himself as king of the room. The audience, in the presence of a talented comedian, are totally under control. There's an excellent description of it in Russell Brand's biography: "'Make people laugh'—I even love the idiom—there's no choice. The person making them do it has the power." Live comedy is a fascinating and disturbing spectacle where a single person has a huge number of people under a kind of spell and can actually affect them physically; laughter is a bodily affect. You sometimes see films of preachers making members of their congregation fall over just by tapping them on the forehead, and there's no reason to think that comedy is any less unnerving. Perhaps it's even stranger as there seems no question that the people are laughing involuntarily, whereas the fainting people might be faking. There's something shockingly real about an arena full of ten thousand people convulsing over a few words. (Of course, this reveals my prejudice. Not only do I have no direct experience of hellfire preachers, I also like to think I couldn't be affected by one, while knowing very well that a comedian can make me laugh. Even a horrible one.)

Freud talks about narcissistic women and their importance in the erotic lives of men. They've refused to give something up, apparently, so are very interesting to the people who've caved in. Likewise, with a stand-up comedian, male or female. They can seem impressively self-contained, able to appear in front of a crowd and speak without visible fear, holding everyone in their power. Perfect narcissistic leaders, they have the added charm of being largely against powerful institutions and generally a bit outsiderish. In this sense, they are easy for neurotic people to identify with. Comedians can put on a very good show of having the phallus, at the same time as ripping apart other people or organisations who pretend to. This is obviously very disarming and stops people hating comedians in the way they might hate politicians or big business people. Perhaps it also helps to explain why it's apparently such an appealing psychic solution for certain people. If the *femme fatale* is the classic embodiment of the fascinating narcissist, then the stand-up comedian is another kind of apparently self-contained being—albeit more active and less objectified.

No joke

People sometimes speak about changes in comedy from decade to decade, and while it's clearly true that we laugh at different things at different times, it also seems clear that Freud's ideas about the unconscious mechanisms at work in humour continue to hold true. The jokes people tell still involve exposing obscene material:

> Why does Santa have such a big sack?
> Because he only comes once a year.

Expressing aggression towards an individual or institution:

> A busload of politicians rolled over on the motorway and crashed into a farmer's field. The farmer stayed up all night burying the bodies. Next morning, on finding the burned-out bus, police questioned the farmer:
> "Are you sure they were all dead?"
> "Some of them tried to say they weren't", he replied, "but you can never trust those bastards."

Or opening up questions about language, truth, and signifying systems:

> Last night I had sex with two Brazilian guys.
> Wow, you must be sore—how many is a brazillion?

In this last category you also have Freud's rather complicated Jewish joke:

> Two Jews met in a railway carriage at a station in Galicia. "Where are you going?" asked one. "To Cracow," was the answer. "What a liar you are!" broke out the other. "If you say you're going to

Cracow you want me to believe you're going to Lemberg. But I know that in fact you're going to Cracow. So why are you lying to me?" (1905c, p. 161)

(See p. 193 for the appearance of exactly this type of joke in *Zoolander 2*.)

Freud describes a release of tension when an inhibition is lifted. But you can't just bluntly come out and say the unspeakable thing; there has to be a build-up and an element of surprise. Each of the jokes above have a moment of uncertainty followed by something unexpected. Jokes say things without naming them directly. The best ones can lift an inhibition very enjoyably because it also somehow stays intact. The disavowed idea gets a bit of airtime, but in a way that sits nicely with the ego. You might be turned off by someone who spoke seriously about their fantasies of murdering politicians, but you probably wouldn't hold the farmer joke against them (unless you took comedy *extremely* seriously).

A comedy audience can turn up and have some of their bottled-up aggression, perversion, and perplexity-in-the-face-of-the-symbolic lanced, and then go away feeling relieved. The comedian has had the courage to go into some scummy material and craft it in such a way as to make it a communal pleasure. Comedians have to be brilliant at tapping into the hidden forces at work in people, and at addressing them in such a way that they can be exposed and enjoyed in public. If they get it right they will be very much loved. But if they get it wrong they risk "dying".

In Frank Skinner's autobiography, he describes spending ten years away from live stand-up and coming back to find that certain things have changed. People no longer laugh at jokes about paedophiles, homosexuals, and terrorists. He goes onstage expecting to be loved because he's now a big TV star (he hasn't been doing jokes about all these things because TV is more censorious) but keeps finding that his audiences aren't amused. He obsessively tracks what people laugh at and what they don't, trying to hone his act so he can take it on tour and be adored. Meanwhile he keeps finding his narcissism dashed on the rocks because everyone thinks he's a jerk. He begins to feel absolutely disgusting. He can't tap into other people's psyches in the same way he used to. He's lost touch with certain cultural co-ordinates dictating what's funny, and perhaps also what a person can be seen by others to laugh at. As he says after one of his gigs, "There was a lot of hate in the room."

Because Frank Skinner is a crafty comedian he turns all this into a book about having one's narcissism dashed on the rocks. In this way gets people's sympathy back. He finds himself number one in the bestseller list for writing a forthright book about the management of his own self-love. The thing that comes through very strongly when you read this book is the absolute urgency of the project. The management of the rises and falls of the subject's sense of value is a deadly serious process.

In a way, stand-up comedy—and its counterpart, the comedian's autobiography—is a grand, public dramatisation of the vicissitudes of narcissism, and of the complex tricks people develop in order to manage their self-esteem. As such, you could say it performs an amazing social service. Or you could say it allows people to be horrible without taking responsibility. In either case, it isn't hard to see why comedy is everywhere.

Mirror

Turps Banana Art School, 2016

The mirror phase is one of the few bits of Lacanian thinking you might have a hope of explaining to a stranger at a bus stop. It's a theory that's potentially mind-blowing in its complexity and reach, but is also comfortingly simple. You can perhaps start by saying that human babies are born in a pitiful, flailing state. At the age of six months or so, it comes as a great surprise and source of satisfaction to them to realise that the cohesive entity they see in the mirror is somehow them. Still, they're disappointed and frustrated that it's also somehow *not* them—just because they look coherent, it doesn't follow that they feel it. They're doomed to spend the rest of their lives trying to work out what to do with this mismatch.

What can we do with Lacan's theory? Is it meant to be read as a statement of fact? "This is what happens with children between the ages of six and eighteen months … and that's why people are like they are …" Is it a poetic theory that some people just happen to like because it resonates with something? Or is it barely justifiable speculation? According to chief Freud-basher, Richard Webster:

> It is difficult to avoid the conclusion that the theory of the mirror stage expresses the emotional distress of its creator more clearly

85

than it represents the realities of childhood. For it seems to be the
product of an alienated intellectual who hugely overvalues his own
intellect and cognitive skills, and has become almost completely cut
off from the world of ordinary human relationships. (1994)

Webster's objections to Lacan's theory are many, varied, and passion-
ate. From the hectoring style of Lacan's presentation, to the ideas themselves, to the accusation that even these flawed ideas were plagiarised,
Webster finds little to admire in Lacan's best-known contribution to psychoanalytic theory. To begin with this last objection, Webster attributes
the theory to Henri Wallon, the psychiatrist and philosopher who had
encouraged the young-ish Lacan by commissioning an encyclopaedia
entry on the "family" from him. Webster's angle is certainly different
from that of fully paid-up Lacanians, like Elizabeth Roudinesco. ("The
Mirror Stage: an obliterated archive", *Cambridge Companion to Lacan*,
2003). Roudinesco finds that Wallon had put forward a rather plodding
theory showing a child going through a series of stages with regard
to its mirror image, ultimately culminating in sorting out the problem
and fully being able to understand the relationship between reality
and representation. Webster, however, finds Lacan's theory thoroughly
prefigured in Wallon's writing. Still, he adds that Wallon's work isn't
exactly brilliant either, containing swathes of speculation over a thin
quantity of empirical data, peppered with quasi-spiritual thinking.
Wallon's essay, "Les Origins du Charactère Chez l'Enfant" (1931) starts
with descriptions of animals' reactions to their own reflections, and follows with hypotheses about human babies. He dates the beginning of
the mirror relationship earlier than Lacan; for Wallon, it all starts at the
age of four months. Then, by ten months, apparently, children actually
locate a part of themselves in the reflection while experiencing their
own bodies as fragmented. Finding itself forced to come to terms with
this relationship between the whole image and the fragmented body,
the child is driven to try to bring about some kind of conceptual unity
between the reflection and its experience of corporeal existence. The
image is so utterly compelling that lived experience becomes subordinated to an idea. In this way, the child ties up the problem and enters
into the next, symbolic, developmental stage. Once it has locked down
something in the relationship between the body and its image, it can
get on with other representational systems, like language. So, for Webster, Lacan hasn't added anything to Wallon's theory, hence Lacan's

infamous reluctance to name him as a source (which isn't at all a fair accusation; Lacan refers to Wallon's essay in "Aggressivity in Psychoanalysis" in the most glowing terms (2006, p. 91)). But Webster isn't just annoyed with Lacan for stealing. He also argues that Wallon's paper was obscure enough to steal from in the first place precisely because it wasn't very good. The thing Webster hates, and which so many other people understandably take issue with in psychoanalysis, is the slippage between observable fact and wild speculation, without proper markers in between. Wallon begins his essay with a load of testable data and then glides into fantasy with ideas about what a pre-linguistic child might be thinking or experiencing. Freud obviously put a lot of effort into explaining precisely why this sort of conjecture might be necessary, but one can still see that it poses a few logical and ethical problems. Still, as Webster is fair enough to point out, there's also a problem with only allowing oneself to stay within the realm of empirically observable facts. Nonetheless, he doesn't think this sub-clause saves the mirror phase from being a bad theory.

One of the problems Webster finds with Lacan's theory of the mirror phase is that it doesn't line up with "reality", as he sees it. He takes an argument from Raymond Tallis's *Not Saussure; a critique of post-Saussurean literary theory*, 1988. Tallis thinks it's unlikely that such an important moment in human development should be stumbled across by accident. What if there were no reflective surfaces in a child's environment? Or what if it happened at a later stage? The development of subjecthood and language surely can't be contingent on catching sight of oneself in a mirror at a pre-determined age. This would mean that people born blind were unable to develop a sense of self. In a sense, he makes a worthwhile point. The problem is that his literal-mindedness prevents him from extrapolating. It's clearly right to say that the weakness of Lacan's theory is in its exclusive focus on the visual register. The entire operation is described using the ideas of seeing and being seen. It completely ignores the aural register and the possibilities of hearing and being heard. Developmental psychologists, when talking about identification and mimicry, take the aural and the visual equally seriously; sameness of sound carries the same weight as sameness of appearance. But even without that, you can still read Lacan's theory in terms of a mirroring that needn't involve an actual mirror. It's hardly an unlikely accident that a child will see another human being in the course of its development. If it doesn't, this will have serious implications for its development of language and sense of self (as Harry Harlow's immensely cruel isolation experiments on baby monkeys would suggest). For children who are born blind, echoing can do the job of mirroring. Complications arise when you don't have either hearing or vision; with a child born deaf and blind one has to call on other senses, especially touch.

A bug's life

Perhaps uppermost among Richard Webster's objections is the way in which Lacan bullies his readers or listeners by citing articles and writers as if everyone must surely know all about it; if they don't they're obviously not very well-informed. In his essay on the mirror phase, Lacan introduces an obscure text like this: "We need but recall Roger Caillois (still young and fresh from his break with the sociological school with which he trained) illuminated the subject when, with the term 'legendary psychasthenia' he subsumed morphological mimicry within the derealizing effect of an obsession with space." (2006, p. 96) There's absolutely no reason now or then why anyone should know what he's on about. Caillois's essay, "Mimicry and Legendary Psychasthenia" (1935) is still available, but is hardly seminal. You can find it easily enough, largely because it's been translated and preserved by people who have an interest in Lacan. Originally published in the surrealist magazine, *Minotaure*, it was re-published in *October Magazine* in 1988. It's a very fascinating and elegant piece of writing, but maybe doesn't do exactly what Lacan suggests it does. Before mentioning the essay, he also lays into people's "ridiculous attempts" to reduce imitation to the laws of adaptation, as if it's been totally disproven. It's rather like the sort of thing you might find on a creationist website.

In his article, Caillois talks about distinctions being extremely important; for instance, day and night, or real and illusory. But what about creatures that blur the distinctions between themselves and their surroundings? He's interested in mimicry, but particularly "defensive" mimicry; not animals who pretend to be more dangerous than they are, but ones who try to look like stones or to blend in with bark. Why would they do that? Caillois insists that it can't just be to avoid predators, the mimicry having come about accidentally over thousands of years by natural selection. The reason it can't be simply this, apparently, is that, "Generally speaking, one finds many remains of mimetic insects in the stomachs of predators". According to Caillois, as a defence it simply doesn't work; the predators are onto you. His statement leaves the reader with lots of questions. Are there are more mimetic butterflies in the first place because they're better adapted, meaning that a smaller *percentage* of them gets eaten? Are the predators adapting too, so that what used to work no longer does? There's no discussion of specifics, he simply references two books (one from the late nineteenth century, one from the early twentieth) that ostensibly support his statement, before going on to talk about instances where the insects' mimicry actually works against them. He mentions those that get cut in half by gardeners' shears because they blend so well with the foliage, and others who look so much like leaves that they end up eating each other. In the first case, garden shears come rather late in the planets' evolution so it's perhaps not a good counter-argument. In the second case, he names a book by Dr L. Murat, *Les Merveilles du Monde Animal* (1914) supposedly documenting the phenomenon of accidental cannibalism in mimetic bugs. This, it turns out, is a purely fanciful idea, long since consigned to the entomological dustbin.

The aim of Caillois's essay is to persuade the reader that mimicry has little to do with adaptation and lacks a utilitarian function. Instead it's a luxury, an unnecessary extra, but one that appears all over the place in nature. In place of the notion that insects who blend the best with their surroundings are most likely to avoid predators you have the idea of a fascination or will to imitate. Caillois ultimately puts mimicry down to a "temptation by space". Rather than living as if one is separated, or distinct, from one's surroundings, imitation opens up the possibility of blurring the borders between the world and oneself. Caillois comes up with the term "legendary psychasthenia" to mean "a disturbance in the relations between personality and space".

Psychasthenia is a term coined by Pierre Janet in order to get away from "neurasthenia", which suggests a neurological problem. Psychasthenia would be characterised by terrible anxiety states, disordered thinking, disruptions to the sense of one's physical self, and phobias. It's likely that many of Janet's cases of psychasthenia would now be diagnosed as schizophrenia, both conditions featuring a disruption of the subject's sense of space and a blurring of the distinctions between inside and outside. In relation to this, Caillois talks about fear of the dark (and the related idea of there being no perceivable edges), experiencing oneself as if from the outside, and lacking a stable sense of a body in space. He relates these states to an insect-like blending with one's surroundings, or of letting your surroundings make you what you are.

Caillois calls it an "attraction by space"; space sucks you out of yourself, or lets you suck it in. In either case, you're transformed. (Another good example might be people who absorb a discourse so thoroughly that they are subsumed within it. Lacanians who speak mainly in jargon could be likened to mimetic bugs.)

Lacan introduces Caillois while speaking about the transformative power of the image. He mentions the example of the pigeon that becomes fertile when it sees another pigeon, or even if it catches sight of itself in the mirror. A similar mechanism operates in the case of locusts who might be solitary or gregarious; one can switch a locust from one type to the other by showing it another of its species at a key point in its development. Lacan argues that the image is similarly affecting for human beings; it has a formative effect. "The function of the mirror stage thus turns out, in my view, to be a particular case of the function of imagos, which is to establish a relationship between an organism and its reality—or, as they say, between the *Innenwelt* and the *Umwelt*" (p. 96). Engaging with an image enables one to begin to map the relationship between one's insides and one's outsides. The problem is that the gap between the unity of the image and the chaos of the body is so huge that it sets up a permanent schism between the two in the psyche. One is condemned to be haunted by the mess of the infant body, and compelled by images of corporeal unity.

To recap, the beginning of the mirror stage is marked by an identification with one's own reflection. At the end of mirror stage one identifies with the imago of one's peers. Once you reach this point you're on the way to having a socialised ego that will allow you to be jealous, competitive, courteous, or accommodating depending on how you want to play it. You could say that Lacan has quite a roundabout way of saying something quite simple. But his theory does at least answer an important question that gets left hanging in Freud: What gets added to primary narcissism in order to produce secondary narcissism? How do we move from self-preservation to self-love? It's a persuasive theory, and objections to it aren't very profound; they're more problems with his mode of presenting it, or weak criticisms like Raymond Tallis's argument about blindness.

I feel for you

"Empathy, Its Development and Prosocial Implications" (Martin L. Hoffman, 1978) is an essay with considerably less swagger than

Lacan's, but it arrives at similar conclusions. An overview of the contemporaneous literature on the subject, rather than focusing on the cognitive conception of empathy—people being aware of one another's feelings and intentions and trying to understand them—it looks at what Hoffman calls "affective empathy", i.e., vicarious responses. Why do we cry in movies? Or read novels? Why might we be upset if we see someone being hurt? Or be cheered up by another person's happiness? According to Hoffman you can't untangle the cognitive and the affective. Your ideas about "what" and "why" regarding other people's feelings will clearly have an impact on your gut reactions. Having said that, babies cry when they hear other babies crying, so it seems that you can have an affective response without elaborate cognitive reasoning.

Hoffman first discusses some of the neural mechanisms that bring about empathic responses, describing a limbic system divided into two halves, one that's concerned with self-preservation, the other with expressiveness and feeling states linked with sociability and preservation of the species. The limbic system is linked to the pre-frontal cortex, a later development in our species' history that processes information cognitively. It's linked to the limbic system, meaning that primitive affect can be processed in a more sophisticated way. So, the limbic system is older than the neocortex and mediates emotions, and may very well provide the neural basis for empathy. Hoffman suggests that we are hardwired to be affected by things that happen to other people as well as to ourselves. (This is all in the decade before the "discovery" of the mirror neuron.)

Unlike Lacan, Hoffman is happy with the Darwinian idea of natural selection, suggesting that altruism must have been an advantage in terms of survival. Sticking together and co-operating was surely good for humans, and empathy may have made that possible. We are not *just* inclined towards rivalry, but co-operation too. Hunting in groups and staying awake to look out for predators while others slept was perhaps better than going it alone. And if that's so, then people who could empathise would have been more likely to survive than selfish egotists, at least under certain conditions. In support of this we are pointed towards George R. Price's work of the early 1970s in which he draws up mathematical equations in order to prove the value of altruism to species survival. These calculations were soon followed by further equations that supported the idea of heritable horribleness proliferating when circumstances require it. What seems most likely is that a combination of altruism and egotism works best, as an individual must ensure his or her own survival in order to breed (see also Freud on narcissism in the previous chapter, See p. 79–80). All of which is to say that the tendency to help people in trouble may form part of our biological inheritance. In humans one doesn't find a fixed altruistic pattern, like you might observe in some bees, wasps and ants, who always help each other. Humans have to weigh up egotistical and altruistic motives and make choices. This seems to be linked to reproduction; altruistic insects, like worker bees, don't have to reproduce, but selfish ones, like queen bees, do. Their functions are portioned out, whereas humans have to weigh up both tendencies. In humans, it seems we have an automatic empathic response, and a system in place to keep an eye on that response and to decide how to act; to help the other or not. Altruism isn't a certain outcome of affective empathy; you may empathise without doing anything about it, perhaps if it would cost you more to help the person than you deem it to be worth. Aside from instantaneously weighing up whether it's a good idea to fish a terminally ill person off a live train track, decisions are constantly being made at a micro level. In 2011, J. Santamaria and D. Rosenbaum published the results of their research around the polite habit of holding doors open for other people ("Etiquette and Effort: Holding Doors for Others", *Psychological Science*). They measured the average distance from the door for the second person—too far away and either it's not worth it or it embarrasses the other person into hurrying. They concluded that door-holding altruism benefitted society by preserving resources; the time spent holding the door was unconsciously weighed against the effort of the other person to start opening the door from scratch. One isn't separate from the other person—you are both somehow parts of the same organism.

All this takes us quite far away from Lacan's essay. On the one hand, it's all getting very Darwinian and functional, but on the other hand you do have this idea of an inadvertent impulse towards empathy and mimicry. If they cry, you cry. If they're afraid, you're afraid. If they're hungry, you're hungry. And, separate from that, there's the possibility of doing something about it. The ideas that you find in Caillois, of a mindless temptation or attraction to similarity, are there; the mindful/useful bit comes later.

There are serious questions about the cues in the other that elicit empathy, and whether feelings arrive untransformed. (See p. 151 on projection.) Do we read other people right or wrong, and does it matter? Do we decipher facial expressions? Or is it the entire situation that tells us what another person is feeling? If it's the face, then why might we be affected by reading a letter? If it's the situation, what about people who react oddly? Those who are miserable at their own birthday party, or who *like* being beaten up? Hoffman's study breaks empathic reactions down into five modes:

1. The reflexive crying of newborn babies (who *don't* cry after other loud noises). Distress in a baby produces distress in a newborn. Still, there's a question of whether it's learned or innate—but even if it could be learned extremely quickly this would still be a notable fact.
2. Classically conditioned empathy. A child gets stressed when its mother is stressed. This may be due to different handling, or the facial expression of the mother. Her mood affects the baby. Empathy is seen here as a kind of contagion.
3. Learned experiences of pleasure or pain activating empathic experience. A child falls over and cries, then cries later when she or he sees another child fall over. This wouldn't just happen in cases of physical distress, it would cover any affect or experience with which the child can identify.
4. "Objective motor mimicry" (Theodor Lipps, 1906). Doing the same thing as the person you're speaking to, maybe blinking when they blink, moving your lips more if they stutter, or simultaneous itching. (This last phenomenon is something psychoanalysts often have to watch out for. However hard we might work to separate ourselves out from the people who come to see us, we often end up inadvertently mimicking their small itches.)
5. Imagining what it would be like to be in the other person's place. The most cognitive, thoughtful from of empathy. The difference between trying to imagine what a person is feeling, and something more inadvertent. In 1969 Ezra Stotland performed experiments showing that people felt more anxious, and exhibited greater palmar sweating, if they were told to imagine themselves in the place of a person undergoing a heat treatment. If they were simply told to imagine what the other person might be feeling the effects were less pronounced. In either case, subjects were more affected if the person experiencing the heat treatment was somehow similar to themselves.

So, there you have five empathic modes, not in particular sequence apart from the fact that the first two are in place from infancy while the last three develop later. A person may, of course, experience different modes of empathy at the same time. For instance, objective motor mimicry might intensify cognitive processes.

How do these different modes of empathy develop in the child? And what are the differences between "mature empathy" and "infantile empathy"? The key distinction is that mature empathy involves the knowledge that whatever's happening is happening to the other person; you're just affected by proxy. Infantile empathic responses fail to distinguish between self and other. One child sees another child get a cut and cries, or it sees a child fall over and needs to be comforted. One needs to be able to distinguish between self and other in order to develop more elaborate cognitive responses. Empathic experience depends on the level at which you cognise others. This is something that changes greatly over the course of a child's development. For the first year there's no real distinction between inside and outside, but at twelve months or so a child would be expected to have established "person permanence", a term from Jean Piaget meaning that the baby understands people don't stop existing when they're out of sight. Then, by two or three years old, they begin to have the idea that other people have thoughts and feelings independent of their own. From here they can go on to develop more and more complex empathic responses.

Hoffman draws up a four-stage system showing how the two strands of empathy—what he calls infantile and cognitive—develop and affect each other.

1. For the first year you have a state where the child has no real notion of what's them and what isn't. Cues from the other can illicit a distress response, like crying. This first stage he describes as a "primitive, involuntary response based on the 'pull' of surface cues …".

2. The child begins, at twelve months, to develop a sense of self and other. At this point it's in a volatile state, and these distinctions may seem unclear. A child friend of Hoffman's would, for his first year, suck his thumb and pull his ear when upset. Seeing a sad look on his father's face, he pulled a sad face and sucked his thumb, but pulled his father's ear. This is exactly as Lacan describes it when he talks about the end of the mirror phase, referencing transitivism in the work of Charlotte Buhler. She speaks about a confusion between self and other at the beginning of perceiving oneself in socially elaborated situations. When Lacan talks about the end of the mirror phase he

doesn't mean it's all sorted, just that something has been laid down which will then be constitutive for the psyche, and will continue to inform social relations. While children might no longer cry if they see someone else get hurt, their sense of themselves will continue to be reliant on the other. Henceforth a person will always rely on the image of the other for coherence and stability.

3. By the age of two or three a child will generally be aware that other people have different thoughts and feelings to their own. When they are upset, for instance, they may need different things. A younger child might offer their own teddy, or bring their own mother to someone in distress, but by their second or third year they will try to think what the other person might need or be comforted by.

4. During late childhood a child begins to grasp the bigger picture. They don't just experience reactions in the moment, but have a broader understanding of a life lived over time. They might see that a person is happy today, but may worry about the fact that the person's partner is ill, or that they don't have a job. They are able to enter imaginatively into the life condition of another human being.

(In case it's all starting to sound like empathy is "all good", it's perhaps helpful to look at recent studies, like that of Anneke Buffone and Michael Poulin at Buffalo University (2014) who conducted experiments to demonstrate that higher empathy levels are closely linked with higher aggression.)

Hoffman is talking about some of the same phenomena as Caillois and Lacan, albeit in very different ways. His work is certainly more plodding, but the things that perhaps seem problematic in Caillois and Lacan are interestingly elaborated in Hoffman's paper. Lacan attacks "the ridiculous attempts made to reduce these facts [of mimicry in nature] to the supposedly supreme law of adaptation" (2006, p. 96) using Caillois's anti-Darwinian stance as support. But their objections to evolutionary theory start to seem a bit unnecessary, and even ridiculous, in the light of this later research. If they're arguing against Darwinism, what do they propose instead? And what do they think the laws of adaptation *are*? It appears that they are quite confused about what Darwin was actually saying. Darwin was very clear that evolution was non-teleological, that there was no ultimate goal or aim. Each living thing might try to sustain its life for long enough to reproduce but nothing more elaborate than that. Any developments, longer legs, poison, looking like a twig, are just accidental mutations produced over enormous periods of time—much bigger than Darwin estimated. If mutations produce a situation whereby an animal lives for longer and breeds more, then great, in a sense, but even this may not save it over time because another creature's mutations might catch up. Your species might come to look exactly like twigs, fooling everyone and allowing you to breed up the place, and then humans might mutate in ways that allow them to invent garden shears and chop you up. Alternatively, a certain type of bird might get really good at spotting you. Or you might get so bad at spotting each other that you start to bite each other—it's theoretically possible although I can't find any evidence of this actually happening. Still, even if it did, this wouldn't be a problem for evolutionary theory, or natural selection. It would just be an example of a bad adaptation. Unless, of course, cannibalism turned out to be somehow good for the species. In other words, "bad" adaptations are not a point against evolutionary theory.

Nonetheless, Caillois and Lacan object to this supposedly crass, utilitarian theory, suggesting something else in its place; a senseless inclination to mimicry, a luxury, something non-functional, completely different to sucky Darwinian utilitarianism. People sometimes pick up on this in Lacan and commend his noticing that there were some problems with Darwinian theory. But the problem he brings out using Caillois isn't the one. Of course, we now have genetic drift and the modern synthesis and all this stuff that wasn't in Darwin—"the ridiculous attempts made to reduce these facts to the supposedly supreme law of adaptation"—but none of these later developments are saying that natural selection isn't a good theory, they're just noting that there are other factors influencing evolution as well. Factors to do with chance and mathematics, not the survival of the fittest. None of this was particularly well pinned down when Caillois published his paper in 1935. Julian Huxley's first paper on the modern synthesis came out in 1936. But Huxley's linking together of natural selection with genetics was well established by 1949 when Lacan gave his second version of the mirror phase paper. While in 1935 it may have been tenable to be grumpy about natural selection; there certainly was "something else", although it was as yet unknown what this "something else" was. But by 1949 Caillois's critique of Darwinian theory maybe doesn't look quite so clever, unless you forget about specifics and treat it as a general attack on empiricism and functionality, all of which would still fit perfectly well with neo-Darwinism, a theoretical perspective that very much includes the possibilities of bad design and superfluous features in nature.

To return to Hoffman's paper on child development, he claims that there is something like a primitive temptation to mimicry in humans, but that this has turned out to be useful for survival. Of course, it would have come about as something completely senseless, but it made later developments possible. So Caillois, and Lacan, appear to be onto something with this idea of a senseless compulsion to imitate, although not in the way they represent it. It isn't at all something mysterious outside the system, but something very much inside it, bearing in mind that the system of mutation and survival is an extremely complex one that involves both random swerves and functional honing.

Perhaps it's a red herring to have made an analogy between camouflaged butterflies and human beings' tendency to copy and identify. In the first case, you have physical changes that make a creature less visible, and in the second case you have a strange behaviour that lends an advantage. (Copying is senseless at first but gradually opens up onto other possibilities.) A better analogy in nature might be a mimic octopus who actively reflects its background.

It might be most generous to say that Lacan is right, but for the wrong reasons. The phenomenon he describes fits very well with evolutionary psychology, in spite of his essay being presented as an attack on that very same theory. It seems important to try to unravel that sort of problem in Lacan in view of the things Richard Webster talks about—the bullying style and mystifications: "*Of course we all know about Caillois*"—as if that's proof in itself. Lacan makes reference to the "ridiculousness" of the laws of adaptation without saying why they're ridiculous. The teaching of Lacanian theory can sometimes align itself with all of that. Students may be browbeaten or made to feel stupid if they don't "get it". They may also be given the idea that they are part of the most important project in the world. All of which adds up to a classic brainwashing technique.

There is a funny quote from Elizabeth Roudinesco:

> Lacan's texts were sacralized, his person was imitated; he was made into the sole founder of the French psychoanalytic movement. Subdued, an army of barons spoke like Lacan, taught like Lacan, smoked Lacan's cigars ... If that army had been able, it would, like

Lacan, have carried its head inclined to the left or had the carti-
lage of its ears stretched in order to have them, like his, stand out.
(1990, p. 103 in the French version)

One might want to resist being one of those people, but the fact that they
exist at all is perhaps a strong reinforcement of Lacan's ideas about the
necessity and intensity of identifications, and how fundamental they
are to the construction of any kind of self. You could say that a carica-
tured, brainwashed, jargon-spouting Lacanian is a fool, or you could
say that they are living proof that Lacan is correct in everything he says
about the construction of human subjectivity, and are therefore sensibly
following him in his excellence.

Neurosis

Centre for Freudian Analysis and Research, 2012

If Lacan famously insisted on a "return to Freud", what made him feel this was necessary? How and why had psychoanalysis moved away from the theories of its forefather? In order to attempt to answer these questions I'll look at the writings of some of the post-Freudians from the 1930s to the 1960s. I'll focus in particular on ego psychology (Lacan's big *bête noir*) to see how this group's theoretical developments had drifted away from distinguishing the different forms of neurosis (hysteria and obsession), overwriting Freud's clinical categories with the idea of the defences. In the writings of the ego psychologists we find long lists of various styles and strengths of defence, with a continuum ranging from pathological to normal. Delusional projection would sit at one end (aliens or the FBI are after you and you must save yourself) while having a good sense of humour resides at the other.

I'll also look briefly object relations theory and ask whether both this and ego psychology risk tending towards a limiting idea of cure. On the one hand, you have the idea of "good object relations" and on the other the notion of the robust and well-functioning ego (and often the two together—good object relations are very much included in the aims of ego psychology) both of which seem to lead too often to the idea that to be "healthy" is to be able to sustain a monogamous relationship, with a stable income, without wanting to jump out of a window.

Helene Deutsch, who became a member of Freud's Vienna Psychoanalytic Society in 1916, provides us with an example of the ways in which things were being conceptualised before these two schools of thought took hold. The term "neurosis" is very much in use in her work, and the aim of her writing often seems to be a precise study of different forms of neurosis. In her book, *Neuroses and Character Types* (1965) you have chapters on hysteria, phobia, and obsession. She starts the book with a particularly ingenious device for getting at the difference between the various forms of neurosis. Three female patients each face the same real-life problem. All three are married and have fallen in love with another man. None of them has chosen to have an affair or to leave her husband; all three have instead renounced the object of their affections and fallen ill. The question for Deutsch is why their illnesses take such different forms. Why does one suffer from convulsions, one become agoraphobic, and one develop bizarre, time-consuming rituals involving the contents of her husband's pockets? Deutsch looks at the various psychic mechanisms by which the symptoms are brought about. In the case of hysteria, convulsions are a perfect compromise in that they fulfil the wish at the same time as defending against it. The patient's fits are orgasmic re-enactments of her fantasy scenarios, at the same time as being symptoms of an illness that stops her going out and having an affair. In the case of the phobic woman, Deutsch shows how she uses her symptom as a demonstration of fidelity to her husband. If she goes out of the house she's overcome by anxiety, so she stays in, thereby blocking her freedom to do what she wants. The obsessional woman is characterised by a death wish against her husband. She'd seen him pull a knife out of his pocket while he was undressing and had turned her wish to harm him into a wish to protect him. She has to look through his pockets before he leaves the house to make sure he has everything he might need. She also opens and closes her cupboard doors obsessively, the opening being linked to a wish to dress up and see the man she likes, and the closing being a rejection of this idea.

The actual conflict in each patient's life is transformed into a neurotic symptom whereby they can't act on their wish *or* completely renounce it. They're stuck between the two possibilities. Deutsch looks at the background conditions that might bring this about. Each conflict is considered in the context of the repetition of infantile prototypes, i.e., in terms of the patient's oedipal constructions. Psychoanalytic treatment would then aim to bring out the nature of the situation they are repeating and to show how their childhood responses to disappointments and frustrations—specifically in relation to questions around love and sex—are informing the current situation.

The tone of Deutsch's book is humane and non-judgemental. The idea of "cure" goes something along the lines of showing the patient the roots of the conflict so they can get on with trying to solve it non-neurotically. They may decide to have an affair or end their marriage if that seems the most bearable solution. Or they might realise that the idea of an affair is somehow doing something for them, and that it's not really about the individual guy at all. This is very much in line with Freud's idea of what cure might be—to try to untangle the threads of the patient's neurotic suffering in order that they become better able to get on with their lives and make difficult choices. (Deutsch herself was in analysis with Freud, where she evidently discussed at length her extra-marital affair with the appropriately named Herman Lieberman, so perhaps it makes sense that they should be in accord on this subject.)

Deutsch's book came out in 1965. The first section consists of an entire older book, *Psychoanalysis of the Neuroses*, first published in the 1930s. There was apparently a suggestion that she revise this book to bring it up to date with advances in psychoanalysis, particularly the revisions of theory put forward by the ego psychologists. In the introduction, she explains that she tried, but that she really couldn't see the point—nothing in the new theories threw any extra light onto her cases. It's funny to read if you're used to hanging out with Lacanians, because Lacan's take on ego psychology is so vicious. It's refreshing to see Deutsch's calm rejection. She simply shrugs the whole thing off because she can't see what's useful or interesting about it.

What's the difference between the sorts of things Deutsch is doing in her work, and the ideas being developed by her contemporaries, Heinz Hartmann, Ernst Kris, Rudolphe Lowenstein, and Anna Freud, amongst others? On the surface, you could say that it all looks quite similar. The ego psychologists, too, were interested in analysing their patients' defences with the aim of affecting the symptom. They believed they were following on from Freud, taking his theory and pushing it to its logical conclusion. Their work makes great use of a late paper of

Freud's, *Inhibitions, Symptoms and Anxiety* (1926d [1925]). Throughout the early 1920s Freud had been developing his structural model of the mind, i.e., the notion that the psyche consisted of three agencies or components, the id, the ego and the super-ego. He discusses this in *Beyond the Pleasure Principle* (1920g) and then three years later in *The Ego and the Id* (1923b). In the 1920 essay the ego is envisaged as being rather helpless with regard to the id. The drives are seen as being extremely hard to contain; the id runs wild with the ego chasing around after it trying to keep things in check. In other words, the ego is a bit flaky (which would also be the Lacanian position, albeit differently conceptualised). In Freud's 1926 essay things are somehow made to look slightly more dignified, with the ego doing a very important job mediating between the id and the superego. In the earlier text you get a kind of Basil Fawlty model, whereas in the latter it's all a bit more James Bond. Of course, things can still go wrong; the deals between the agencies can break down and then the ego will be flooded with anxiety.

The big idea in ego psychology is that you need to have a well-functioning ego in order to be healthy. It's there to limit the id impulses, and to have some effect on the pleasure principle, thereby making way for the reality principle. The plan for reducing psychic suffering is to give the ego better options than simply to throw up its arms and succumb to illness. To this end you would analyse the ego's defences, and maybe replace unhealthy defensive strategies with better ones. A great deal of conceptual work revolved around defining the functions of the ego and drawing up lists of various defences the ego might use, categorising them according to some idea of their level of pathology.

The functions of the ego would be reality testing (i.e., being able to distinguish what goes on with you from what goes on in the outside world), controlling aggressive or sexual impulses, making sure you don't get too upset ("affect control"), judging situations and responding appropriately, ensuring good object relations, bringing together conflicting functions, and engineering a sense of synthesis and coherence. If your ego's good at doing all that, you'll be fine. And of course, the ego psychologists are right. If your ego can do its job well enough then you probably won't be rushing off to the nearest analyst's office. The question is whether treatment *should* aim to make everyone like that, or whether there are other ways of dealing with psychic conflict. And that's not to mention the question of whether you even *can* do that. Is it possible for anyone to develop a strong, realistic, ingenious ego? Or is that just a wishful fantasy?

Number neun

The clinical technique developed by the ego psychologists is known as defence analysis. It involves confronting/explaining/interpreting the kinds of defence mechanisms a patient uses with the aim of giving them greater control. You can track how the theory is developed in Anna Freud's *The Ego and the Mechanisms of Defense* (1992 [1936]). Whereas Freud had very much privileged repression, he also acknowledged that there were other forms of defence. Anna Freud tries to systematise these other forms—and also perhaps to play down the primacy of repression a little. She draws up a list of nine types of defence: regression, reaction formation, undoing, introjection, identification, projection, turning against the self, reversal, and sublimation. These can be used in pretty much any combination. Added to these are other defences, such as rationalisation and intellectualisation. This list in turn became organised into different levels of defence mechanism. Level one would be the mechanisms we might normally associate with psychosis: denial, distortion of reality, and delusional projection. Level two gives us the kinds of defence we might commonly see in adolescents. When used by adults they appear extremely immature: hypochondria, acting out, passive aggression, fantasy. Level three is still definitely problematic, the sorts of defence that can get you through a small problem but, if used constantly, tend to lead to trouble in love and work: displacement, intellectualisation, reaction formation, and repression (which, as you can see, has been quite seriously demoted to a fairly lowly, boring position as just one defence amongst many, and not even a very serious one). Level four defences are the "healthy" ones. These would-be things like altruism, humour, sublimation, and suppression, which is far milder than repression and simply means deciding not to think about something for a while.

To go back to Deutsch's women; her question certainly revolved around the kinds of mechanisms that were producing these different symptoms, but the aim of the work was to bring out something of the unconscious ideas being activated by the present situation, making it possible for the subjects to choose something other than a symptom—even if that meant having an affair, leaving the husband, and being despised by mutual friends. You can see how, according to ego psychology, the idea might instead be to replace the symptom with a "healthier" form of defence. In the case of Deutsch's women this might be to develop altruistic feelings for one's husband, see the funny side and get a hobby. It's not necessarily a bad analytic outcome, the problem is not being given a proper choice. If analysis can only aim towards so-called good object relations (i.e., the kinds of relation supported by conventional society) and "healthy", "realistic" life choices then it's a very limited and limiting practice.

To go back to the question of what happened to the concept of neurosis, we're still seeing the after-effects of ego psychology's blurring of clinical categories. George Eman Vaillant based his continuum theory of defence on Anna Freud's list. The division into four levels of defence—psychotic, immature, neurotic, and mature—forms the basis of the diagnostic categories found in the *DSM*, with everything bundled together under notions like "personality disorder" and its subcategories (narcissistic, borderline, histrionic, antisocial, paranoid, schizoid, avoidant, dependent, and obsessive compulsive) and checklists to help psychiatrists distinguish one from another.

An ego psychology manual from 1974 (*Ego Psychology, Theory and Practice*, Gertrude and Ruben Blanck) starts with a critique of brief therapies, saying they don't work and aren't even necessarily brief as they generally have to be repeated over and over again; nothing has time to be consolidated in the treatment. The irony is that treatments like cognitive behavioural therapy, and especially now cognitive analytic therapy (which supposedly takes the unconscious into account, just very quickly) are actually based on many of the same theoretical premises as ego psychology; they've just done away with analytic notions like repeating and working through. The idea that you can take the ego seriously and equip it, James Bond style, with the latest devices for keeping things in order is very much the same. To a contemporary Lacanian psychoanalyst, it can be strange to look back at the texts Lacan was so furious about and to discover them, in places, to be far closer to their psychoanalytic origins than the coercive regimes that pose as psychotherapy in contemporary life. If Lacan thought his colleagues were bad one can only wonder how apoplectic later developments might have made him. A quick spot of CBT before you claim your benefits, sir?

Objects

Centre for Freudian Analysis and Research, 2008

The *objet a*—or *objet petit a*, or *object a*—is a difficult idea to define as it keeps changing throughout Lacan's work. I'll try to talk about it in relation to "the agalma", a concept that appears in *Transference, Seminar VIII (1960–1961)* (2015), where it's used to say something about what a patient might see in their analyst. Here you could say that the agalma and the *object a* are analogous. So first I'll try to explain what Lacan might mean by "agalma" as it's not necessarily what Greek people or historians might mean by the same term, and it's also not a word you can look up in the English dictionary.

Although the word "agalma" doesn't itself appear in translations of Plato's *Symposium*, the idea that Lacan builds his concept out of does. It comes near the end, when Alcibiades arrives and launches into his drunken rant about Socrates's all-round excellence. Alcibiades is a statesman and a general and, by his own estimation, incredibly good looking. He is madly in love with Socrates and has been for a long time. The subtext seems to be that it's slightly odd that this younger, handsomer, very successful man is in love with some old guy; it's a fact that maybe needs some explaining. Although it's clear everyone understands that Socrates is a bit special, there's also the fact that there's something almost brutally ordinary about him. He letches after young boys and acts like a bit of an idiot. It isn't easy to pin down this thing that makes him stick out, that causes him to be an object of fascination for other people. Alcibiades tries to explain it: "My claim is that he's just like those statues of Silenus you see in sculptor's shops […] when they're opened up you find they've got statues of the gods inside." Silenus was the tutor of, and companion to, the god Dionysus, and was generally portrayed as being a bit portly and shabby. Inside these statues of this unkempt, flabby figure (which would have been made of clay, or some other non-precious material) you would find a little treasure trove of shiny figurines. It's to these golden figures that Lacan applies the word "agalma", meaning something ineffable and precious somehow located inside someone else. In Modern Greek, the word means something far more general, simply "a statue" or, in Ancient Greek, "an artwork dedicated to the Gods". To quote Alcibiades again, "I don't know if any of you have seen the statues inside Socrates when he's serious and opened up. But I saw them once and they seemed to me so divine, golden, so utterly beautiful and amazing, that—to put it briefly—I had to do whatever Socrates told me to." In the *Symposium* this treasure inside Socrates is equated with philosophy; not any dry idea of what philosophy might be, but something truly staggering. Alcibiades compares his experience of philosophy with being bitten by a snake and driven into a frenzy by its poison. He wants to access the treasure he perceives as residing inside Socrates, but doesn't know how to go about it. He has the idea that if he offers his fit, handsome body to the older man they will be able to perform some kind of transaction. Socrates will use him for sex and in return he will be given access to the philosopher's inner marvels. But Socrates blocks him, basically saying, "what you're trying to get from me is much better and more valuable than what you're offering, and how can you be sure I possess it anyway?" They spend the night together and nothing happens, but Alcibiades is left completely smitten. He continues to believe in the presence of the agalma, perhaps even more so because Socrates has refused his offer.

If it's not exactly a golden statue, what is it? If the agalma and the *object a* are basically the same thing, then how can we understand this object psychoanalytically? Obviously, it has its precursor in the Kleinian part-object. But, of course, this is exactly what it *isn't* like.

As the Kleinian idea goes, the breast (the primary part-object) is a fragment of a whole person. The infant attaches to this part object and experiences all sorts of satisfactions and frustrations in relation to it, splitting the object into good and bad in order to deal with its different qualities. Somehow the baby has to get from these split relations to part-objects onto more moderated relations to whole objects. In other words, it has to understand that the breast is part of a human being who is both a bit good and a bit bad. Once it's got the hang of that it's basically on its way. It can have friends/boyfriends/girlfriends without wanting to kill them.

In Lacanian psychoanalysis, no one's going to hold their breath waiting for a full relation to a whole object. If you must talk about breasts and object relations you might say that the breast-object is the remainder of the oral demand. It's not important as a *thing* at all, merely as the trace of a relation that has been interrupted. As people sometimes like to say, the object is more of a hole than a whole. It's what's left over or excluded when the relation to it is problematised. Apart from the separations and physical frustrations that problematise our relations to objects, the key thing that breaks into and alters our early relations to our objects of satisfaction is language. Hence the idea that the *object a* is what's leftover when the subject enters into language.

You'll also sometimes hear that the *object a* is like the Kantian object, in that it's characterised by a kind of schism. (Darian Leader has spoken about this in one of his lectures here.) You have the idea of the Kantian object of intuition as a disorganised blast of sensations, which has to be coupled with the concept of the object. Then these two things—the intuition and the concept—have somehow to be synthesised in order to give us the sensation of a real object. The Kantian object could be said to exist in three registers, the real, symbolic, and the imaginary. The intuited object is something like the object in the real, the concept of the object is the symbolic object, and the synthesised object is imaginary. To take it further, you could say (indeed Darian *has* said) that the real object is overwhelming, while the symbolic object provides a limit, and the imaginary object is a fetish.

Already that's quite a number of definitions that don't necessarily add up, or aren't quite the same. Lacan apparently saw the *object a* as his main contribution to psychoanalysis, but others might beg to differ. Even if people agree it's important, they might have very different ideas about why. Still, one thing about the *object a* you probably *can* say, is that if you accept it as a concept then you are bound to start noticing its effects (like God again?).

Love story

This is a story which I found quite amazing in terms of what a person might be trying to do with a love object. Since first hearing it I've heard it again many times, in different forms, most famously in the film *Catfish* (2010), and in the unfortunate case of Manti Te'o, the American footballer who fell in love with a girl who didn't exist. It's about a divorced man in his early forties who has a small son. One day, three years after his parents' separation the son said to his mother, "Guess what? Daddy's got a girlfriend." A few days later, when dropping her son at the father's house, the woman noticed that the entire flat had been cleaned and repainted. Her ex-husband told her he'd met someone and that she would soon be moving in. This new woman was a model, but was sick of modelling and wanted to study. The man also let slip that she was a little crazy, and that she had earned enough not to have to worry about money for a very long time. The ex-wife asked whether it might not be better for the son and the new girlfriend to get to know each other before anyone started talking about sharing a living space. The man explained that it had been complicated as his girlfriend currently lived between Canada and Paris. It hadn't been possible so far to arrange a meeting.

The next day, as the woman collected their son from school, he said, "I met Daddy's girlfriend and she was lovely." It transpired that he'd "met" her on Skype. "That's not exactly meeting her," his mum told him, and the little boy said, "Well, Daddy hasn't exactly met her either. She's his friend on Facebook and they only know each other through the computer." The Mum didn't hide her horror but the little boy said, "It's OK, she's a friend of some of his other friends and she really is very, very nice."

The mother found herself more and more worried by the idea of an unfamiliar "crazy" person suddenly descending on her son's life. She rang her ex and told him she was concerned. He said, totally calmly, "I know it seems like a weird situation but, trust me, it's OK." He repeated what the son had said, that the woman was a friend of some of his other friends, not just a random stranger.

The next day the ex-wife gets an email from her ex telling her he's going to go and meet the girlfriend in Paris that weekend. Two days later she gets a short text saying that the trip is off. She rings her ex who explains that he got an email from the model's agent that morning telling him she'd died of an aneurism on the flight from Canada to Paris. Her flat had been cleared, and she'd already been cremated. Something sounded fishy. The man rang whoever you ring in Paris to find out about deaths and cremations only to be told that they had no record of anyone by that name. He googled the model and couldn't find any trace of her. The girlfriend's face hadn't been visible during the Skype conversations—she'd been able to see him, but he hadn't been able to see her. He'd literally been talking to a blank screen. The only images he had of her were the ones on her Facebook page, which were all magazine shots, not informal snaps. He said, though, that the con-versations had been incredibly intense, that he'd never in his life had the sense of having such an intimate and obstacle-free exchange. One story she'd told him seemed to him to somehow form the backbone of his attachment to her, and he described it as a real Greek tragedy. It involved a big mess between the woman's mother and father, which culminated in her seducing the father's mistress's husband to get revenge on her mother's behalf. Somehow this seemed to him to form the heart of his attachment. Between the girlfriend's disturbing story, with its oedipal crossings over, and the idea of a woman generally prized for being beautiful, it was possible for this man to think about overturning his entire life.

It's hard to say what kind of object this woman may have been for the man, but I think we can safely say that he wasn't enjoying a full object relation with a whole person. But whatever she seemed to con-tain, it really got him going. As he said to his ex-wife, "It was definitely love." But as his son apparently said to him, "Next time you fall in love, make sure the person is in front of you" (maybe the son is a Kleinian).

In Lacanian terms, you might say that something got added to this "person", and this something made things happen. It's a strange kind of limit-case example as the woman could barely be said to have existed in the first place. She was somewhere between a photograph, a voice, and a story. She wasn't quite a *thing*, and to her was added this other non-thing, the combination somehow resulting in the perfect love object. It's like a fairy tale where the main character falls in love with someone who doesn't fully inhabit the real world; they can only take on human form between midnight and dawn, or they can only appear three days a year. The hero or heroine desperately tries to hang on by throwing away their animal skin, or by tricking them into staying until daylight, and in this way they lose them.

All of which brings to mind Lacan's formula of phantasy: $\$ \Diamond a$. The subject is doing something with this *thing*. This is the paradox of the object: it doesn't exist, but still somehow promises to be more real than reality. If it's a remainder, the thing that's left over when one enters into language—the thing that's excluded when the whole world becomes artificial—then it's surely the most real thing in the world. Or at least that's the promise, which might go some way towards explaining why it can seem easier to attempt to access it through people who don't exist. They are less likely to get in the way. They won't feel like they're being valued for the wrong reasons, or be constantly trying to find out what it is you like about them, or just be irritatingly different to whatever you want them to be. Maybe the special kind of love that people feel for celebrities is important in this sense. On the one hand, you're not crazy for overvaluing the person because lots of other people do too. With luck, it's very unlikely that you'll ever meet them. Whatever you want to imbue them with can appear to exist with less interference. (For this same reason it's important that you don't "know" your analyst.)

In *Paris Hilton's British Best Friend* (2008) a line-up of people competed to become Paris's BFF in the UK. All of the contestants claimed to be great fans of Paris, and to love her. It would be a dream come true for each of them to actually become her best buddy. But Paris, who devised the show herself, seemed to know that this was the last thing any of them really wanted. She invited them to go and live in a heavily surveilled house together, only making contact with them occasionally. The idea was that she would watch the CCTV footage, sussing out who was the nicest person. Having said that, she didn't seem particularly interested in any of them. Whenever she met them they would mainly gush, "I love you, Paris," and, "We're so alike," so you could see why it might not be very exciting for her. (She would sometimes complain about this in the voiceover.) Still, she seemed to be very good at managing her relationships with these people so that they could maintain whatever precious fantasy they had of her.

You could say that Paris Hilton is very phallic; she is brilliant at appearing to have, or be, something. This perhaps provokes the question of the difference between the phallic object and the *object a*. Is there one? One way of answering this might be to say that sometimes the object takes a phallic form, and sometimes it doesn't. Or the phallus is just one form the object might take. Paris Hilton is very phallic, in that she's apparently not lacking—and perhaps that's the secret of her appeal. Alternatively, you could argue that whatever agalmatic object she appears to contain is different in the case of each fan. You would have to look at each of their histories in order to find out what they were trying to do with her.

The Rapunzel man

I'd like to give a very brief clinical example where the subject seems to be trying to access the object in a very different way to the man in the *Catfish* story. If his tale was too much about nothing, then this one is too much about something. The man is utterly obsessed with long haired women, and has been since about the age of five (he's now in his late twenties). It makes him feel incredibly guilty and he tries as hard as he can to hide his fetish from the world. The man follows long-haired women down the street, but is sure they would be shocked and disgusted if they ever caught him looking. It's hard for him to be in relationships as he feels he's sexually interested in all the wrong things. With girlfriends, he tries to act like his idea of a generic man, but soon finds it unsustainable and has to leave. He has been single for a while now, occasionally going to visit prostitutes. He is convinced that no one would want a man like him, and that every bit of satisfaction he gets involving hair-play is somehow snatched in the face of incredible unlikelihood.

Recently, on a regular dating site he found a woman with hair down to her waist. He contacted her and found out that she expected to be paid for a meeting. Still, she was different to the prostitutes he usually visited in that she would actually be expecting him to be interested in her hair. He made an appointment and then became more and more nervous during the two-week wait. Would he really be able to enjoy himself? Was this really what he wanted? What if it was just rubbish? If it turned out that it wasn't about hair after all, then what *was* it about?

When the appointment finally came, the main thing that bothered him was time. If he only had forty-five minutes, how should he spend it? If he was plaiting her hair, then he was losing time which could have been spent smelling it, and if he was smelling her hair, then maybe he would have been better off brushing it. He told himself to calm down and stick to one thing, but then noticed that what he was really enjoying was her chatter. As she told him small details about her life he got the sense that friendly speech was what he *really* wanted from her; it was much easier to enjoy than all the other stuff.

When he came for his next psychoanalytic session he told me it was going to take him a long time to process what had just happened. He couldn't quite piece it together. Was it a success? A failure? The best way he could think to describe it was that "there was liking in it, but not the liking I'd expected". Whatever he was trying to get at in this other person seemed very elusive, not at all what or where he expected it to be. If what he was trying to access seemed far too embodied by a *thing* (hair) then how could this thing continue to be desirable when it was suddenly a brute physical presence right there in front of him? Either it was too overwhelming and exciting, or it was totally stupid and disappointing. He seemed to have found a way to stop it being either by turning the presence of the hair into an absence by constantly fretting that he was missing out on some other part of the experience. Was it the look of the hair, or the smell of it? Did he want to touch it or look at it? In the end, he could only enjoy the object by allowing himself to be distracted by something else about the woman, her speech.

Oedipus

Centre for Freudian Analysis and Research, 2012

In her autobiography, the actress Dorothy Dandridge (2000) describes dating in Hollywood in the 1940s. She tells us that everyone in the movie business was in analysis. A typical conversation over a supposedly romantic dinner might go something like this: "You've got an Oedipus complex", "No, you're the one with the Oedipus complex", and then there would follow a batting back and forth of the accusation, as if it was something some people had and some didn't. The implication was that if you had one you were a slightly lesser being, or at least a bad person to sleep with.

Perhaps the idea has since been subject to a cultural downgrade. Everyone still knows about it—it's arguably the most famous Freudian concept—but it took quite a beating, first from anthropologists and then from feminists, to the point where it might seem surprising that anyone bothers to mention it at all any more.

To cite a well-known quote about Oedipus from *The Interpretation of Dreams* (1900a):

> [Oedipus's] destiny moves us only because it might have been ours—because the oracle laid the same curse upon us as upon him. It is the fate of all of us, perhaps, to direct our first sexual impulse

towards our mother and our first hatred and our first murderous
wish against our father. (p. 280)

It's perhaps a useful statement to bear in mind because it shows how
generally applicable Freud initially thought the complex was before all
the later business about penis envy crept in. In the quote from the *Interpretation of Dreams* he lumps men and women together, and maybe we
can return to that idea, having had a look at what Lacan has to say.

We should also glance over the Malinowski debate, and the idea
that the Oedipus complex is culturally relative and therefore not as
important as Freud thought it was. Lacan concludes that the Oedipus
complex as Freud understood it *is* culturally relative, but the fact that
a child must use its carers in order to structure its psyche is universal.
There's something so nice and obvious about the Lacanian rethinking of
the Oedipus complex that it could probably be summed up in a single
sentence. But then again, it's also so complex that it'll be impossible to
do it justice in an hour and a half ...

As well as being one of the best known, you could say that the Oedipus
complex is one of the least understood ideas in psychoanalysis. If you
look at the kinds of condensations of the theory presented in psychology
A Level textbooks, the simplifications often seem to increase the incom-
prehensibility. If you search out a quick definition you will be told that
boys fall in love with their mothers and want to kill their fathers, and
that girls love their fathers and want to get their mothers out of the way.
In the course of their development, both girls and boys either get over
these feelings or they don't. To make things worse, you will often be
presented with Jung's "Electra complex" (Oedipus for girls) as if it's a
Freudian idea.

On top of the subhuman straightforwardness of these kinds of explanation there's also the persistent idea that the Oedipus complex was
"disproven" by the anthropologist, Bronislaw Malinowski, in 1915.
Malinowski claimed to have found that there was no such thing as
an Oedipus complex among Trobriand Islanders, whose society was
ordered along matrilineal lines. He claimed that the totally different way
in which the family was organized, coupled with the fact that Trobriand
Islanders had no knowledge of the man's role in procreation, meant that
boys didn't grow up fearing punishment from their fathers for loving
their mothers. The classical Freudian Oedipus complex might apply
to nuclear families with stern patriarchs of the sort typically found

in nineteenth century Western capitalist societies, but not necessarily to anyone else. Even if you grew up in one of those societies, but in a differently structured family, you might be exempt. So, particularly later on, people often took this to mean that if you grew up in a single-parent family, or you had gay parents or you grew up on a commune, then you'd necessarily dodged the curse. Perhaps because the Oedipus complex is quite an unsavoury idea, it seems like there was a huge temptation to jump on studies like Malinowski's and say, "Phew! That's the end of that then." But there are two big problems with this. One is that the Oedipus complex and the theory of infantile sexuality are not the same thing. Just because your family isn't organised according to the norms of Viennese society at the beginning of the twentieth century, it doesn't therefore follow that your development will be free from sexual or destructive phantasies about the people who bring you up. Whatever your family configuration, you'll still have to develop ideas and phantasies to get you through the obstacle course that is growing up.

The other problem is that Malinowski's findings turn out to be somewhat open to question. There's the business of paternity and what the Trobriand Islanders *actually* knew, which is problematised by the question of what you mean by "knowledge" (*Oedipus in the Trobriands*, Melford E. Spiro, 1992). Apparently in the Trobriand Islands it was unforgivably bad manners to say that a child looked like its mother. You had to say it looked like its father if you wanted to be liked. This would suggest that there was some understanding of the part the man might have played in conception. There were also various stories about how babies were made, and you'd get a different answer depending on whom you asked, and on what they thought of you. Women and children would be told one thing, while "men's talk" was something else. But even the children's stories would involve things like the mixing of semen with menstrual blood, suggesting that the people knew very well that men's ejaculations had something to do with it.

Another key part of Malinowski's argument was that, in the Trobriands, the important figures weren't mothers and fathers, but sisters and uncles. Boys would be expected to have sexual ideas about their sisters, and these, it was hoped, would appear in dreams. If you had a sexual dream about your sister it was thought to be a good thing, although it was acknowledged to be extremely anxiety provoking. Instead of fathers, it was uncles—or, more specifically your mother's brother— whom you would supposedly feel hostility towards. As people who continued to believe in the importance of the Oedipus complex were quick to point out, sisters and uncles aren't *so* far removed from mothers and fathers. What's more, unlike in Viennese society, you were all but encouraged to experience those difficult feelings towards your relatives. Sister incest dreams were classified as "official" as opposed to "spontaneous" or "ordinary" dreams. They were prescribed by tradition, and hoped for and awaited.

When Sophocles's Oedipus discovers that the man he killed was his father, and that the woman he's married to is his mother, he's so appalled and remorseful that he immediately gouges his eyes out. At some level Oedipus is totally innocent, but he takes the punishment nonetheless. You might say that the way in which the story is told by Sophocles, and then preserved and retold in Western societies, is quite removed or displaced. It's not about a man who wants to kill his father and fuck his mother—it's about someone who unwittingly does just that and is totally mortified when he finds out.

Melford Spiro (who is an anthropologist, not a psychoanalyst) points out that the conscious and culturally backed-up ideas that the Trobriand Islanders had about sisters and uncles may be a form of displacement. If it's just too disturbing to think of having sex with your mother, you can perhaps soften the blow by replacing her with your sister. Likewise, with fathers and uncles. In the same way that Sophocles makes the story more bearable by causing Oedipus to do it by mistake, perhaps the Trobriand Islanders make their Oedipus complexes more bearable, or at least presentable, by substituting the main characters with slightly more tolerable ones. (This is also what you often see in fairy tales—the terrifying maternal character is generally a step-mother.) Holding these alternative figures up as people whom you might be expected to have difficult feelings towards might actively help you *not* to think about the people at whom these impulses are more readily directed.

There is a fascinating book, *Oedipus Ubiquitous* (Allen W. Johnson & Douglass Price-Williams, 1997) written jointly by a psychiatrist and an anthropologist. They approach the question of the universality of the Oedipus complex by looking at folktales from around the world that deal with the themes of maternal incest and patricide. While they concede that the Oedipus story as constructed by Sophocles isn't particularly common, there are lots of stories where a hostility develops between an older man and a younger one, or where a young man develops an erotic attachment to an older, motherly woman. The first half of the book is an analysis of what they call "family complex folktales", and the second is a collection of one hundred and thirty-nine Oedipus-type stories from around the world. In the first section, they come to the conclusion that in smaller societies people are more liable directly to represent aggressive and sexual acts occurring inside families, while in larger, more complex societies people tend to learn to hide their impulses better. Higher levels of politeness/deceptiveness mean that these impulses appear in far more disguised forms in the stories these societies tell. The authors decide that a story told by the African !Kung is the most violent and directly sexual representation of an Oedipus-style family story: a son chops his father in half in order to be able to have sex with his mother. In contrast, we see eighteenth-century French and Japanese stories where the characters apparently have no idea what they're doing—and *if* they find out they suffer horribly over it. While the authors of the book don't try to make any big claims about universality, they conclude that the story of the man getting his father out of the way in order to access his mother has something about it that "likes to be told", and that it appears in various forms all over the world.

One might argue that in our complex, neoliberal society the story appears in all incarnations, from the ultra-ciphered to the brutally blunt. Hitchcock's *Psycho*, for example, depicts the horrifying effects of a disavowed incestuous phantasy, while a book like Mackenzie Phillips' *High On Arrival* (2009) tells the story of her consensual sexual relationship with her father, John Phillips of The Mamas and Papas, which began on the eve of her wedding and continued for ten years.

Myth-making

Before going on to talk about feminine development and penis envy—and the problems Freud gave himself with all that—I should perhaps briefly say something about *Totem and Taboo* (1912–1913), which some have come to see as a necessary counterpart to the story of Oedipus (for a fuller account of Freud's myth, See p. 66). In Paul Verhaeghe's book *New Studies of Old Villains* (2009) he talks about how Freud invented the myth of the primal father as if to back up the role of the father in the Oedipus complex (See p. 31). This myth was perhaps necessary for Freud to reinforce the role of the father in the family. If men are often actually a bit weedy and fallible—not at all strict and authoritarian—there's good reason for it. In order for society to function, there has to be a pact among men to be less powerful and libidinous than they might otherwise like. In order for all this to make sense, you need the figure of the primal father lurking in the background. The primal father is the guarantor of masculinity. *There was once a man who really was a man, but he was impossible to live with, so now we have all these slightly lesser men instead.* The Oedipus complex, in the sense in which Freud installs it in Little Hans, is the perfect neurotic solution. A big man is put in place in order to bar the way to total, overwhelming enjoyment with a woman/mother. The actual father clearly isn't that sort of man at all, but the primal father stands somewhere as some kind of back-up. Using this myth, Freud sanctions the classic neurotic solution; belief in a father who can actually do the job of protecting you from your mother. As Claude Lévi-Strauss said about Freud's myth of the primal horde:

> In the one case, the progression from experience to myths, and from myths to structure. In the other, a myth is invented to explain the facts, in other words, one behaves like the sick man instead of diag-nosing him. (1949)

So, the myth is invented in order to prop up an idea that clearly needs help. In this sense, Freud behaves just like Little Hans.

This idea of propping up the father appears in both Freud and Lacan, but in slightly different ways. Freud does it by acting as though the father really is in charge, while Lacan sees that he isn't, but still seems to wish (at least in his earlier work) that he could be. But does Lacan really prescribe a return to authoritarian fathers who rule the roost at home and keep the women in their place? If so, how come he is the darling of certain feminist theorists?

Penis envy and the feminine resolution of the Oedipus complex

"Penis envy" is an idea that appears in Freud's writing quite early on. He mentions it in his *Three Essays on Sexuality* (1905d) where he says it comes as a big surprise to children to realise that girls and boys have different genitals. When boys notice that girls don't have a penis they're likely to resist this knowledge, but are forced to recognise the facts after some kind of internal struggle. Girls are apparently "immediately [...] overcome by envy for the penis" and wish that they were boys.

Later on, Freud uses the idea of penis envy to explain how women go from loving their mothers to loving their fathers and identifying with their mothers. The problem for him was that women appeared to have it a lot harder in that, unlike men, they had to shift the focus of their libidinal impulses from one parent to another (see his later work, "The Dissolution of the Oedipus Complex" (1924d), "Some Psychological Consequences of the Anatomical Distinction Between the Sexes" (1925j), "Lecture 33: Femininity" (1933a)). In "The Dissolution of the Oedipus Complex" boys are said to love their mothers, then their dads get in the way. They have to identify with their dads, learn how to be men, and then to go off and find other women (who will be a little bit like their mothers, but not *too* much). The end of the Oedipus complex was decisively put in place by the threat of castration. Or as Freud more colourfully phrased it: "It is literally smashed to pieces by the shock of threatened castration." Boys are apparently so afraid of losing their penises that they will do almost anything to make sure it doesn't happen. Hence, they give up their mothers as their primary objects of affection. But what would make female children suddenly detach from their mothers and start getting excited about their fathers? And *then* what would make them give their fathers up? Famously (and infamously) the answer Freud came up with hinges on penis envy. When little girls discover that they are lacking, they are supposedly very disappointed. Then, when they also work out that their mothers are similarly castrated, they turn away from them in scorn and disappointment, focusing attention on their fathers. They begin to phantasise about receiving a baby from their father, as if this would be the thing that would compensate for their lack of a penis. They might identify with their mothers—insofar as the mothers clearly had *something* going for them if the fathers were so interested in them—but the basic wish was to get them out of the way. If boys resolved their Oedipus complexes by fearing castration and becoming like their fathers, girls would resolve them by gradually getting over the idea that they might one day receive a baby from their dad. According to Freud, they never *really* got over this, at least not in the unconscious, so the resolution of the Oedipus complex was far more difficult for girls. Because girls had no precious organ to lose, there would be no decisive resolution, no "smashing to pieces"; it could just drag on until ... until what? Freud never came up with a conclusive answer.

Another knock-on effect of all this had to do with women's relation to the law. When a boy let go of his mother in order to become like his father, the result was the arrival of the super-ego. Now, thanks to his fear of punishment, he had a built-in psychic agency to keep him in check. But because women weren't obliged to sort things out in quite the same way—they didn't fear castration—then they wouldn't have quite such well-established super-egos and would therefore be less bound by the rules of society.

Feminists have traditionally taken this in either of two ways. One is to say that Freud is an idiot and that penis envy is a total fiction. Another is to say, yes, isn't it great, women are less law-bound, and therefore more subversive and interesting than men. Freud himself proposes a third way of thinking about it at the end of his essay on anatomical sex distinction, and one that is perhaps more in keeping with contemporary ideas about gender-fluidity. Although, he explains, it looks like his theories seem to back up the age-old idea that women are less rational, more prone to emotion, and have "less sense of justice" than men, you have to bear in mind that most men fall very far behind the masculine ideal, and that no one is either purely masculine or feminine.

Now we can go back to Lacan, and his persistent idea of the terrifying mother, to show how things change in his later work. To return to the case of Little Hans, we see the way in which Hans is saved from his terrifying mother by the installation of his father in a slightly propped up role; it's a perfect illustration of the Name-of-the-Father being instituted in order to save the subject from the desire of the mother. So far so old fashioned. Women are scary and weird, and men are called in to be rational and sort out the mess they make, just like it says in the Bible. But you can see that, on the way here, there have been a number of shifts. In early Freud, the Oedipus complex looks like a set of relations between real people. You love your mum because she's lovely and you hate your dad because he's cold and strict. Later on in Freud there are all sorts of other, more complex, ideas—although still involving actual relations to real people. You might be erotically interested in your father's punishments. Equally, your mother might be very seductive, which you might hate. Then, in early Lacan, you have the potentially devastating pre-oedipal relation with the mother, and a paternal function that comes along to ameliorate the situation. It does this by introducing a symbolic dimension, allowing the subject to separate him or herself from the mother, who wants to gobble them up.

This, of course, begs the question of whether mothers actually want to consume their children, in the same way that Freud's theory forces us to ask whether all fathers are actually authoritarian. Perhaps it's possible that this all-consuming mother is an imaginary construction in much the same sense as the Freudian father. But why would children *want* to make their mothers so frightening? How might it help them? Some possible answers to this can be found in Lacan's *Seminar XVII: The Other Side of Psychoanalysis (1969–1970)* (1993d), where parents are depicted as something like living dolls, used, manipulated and phantasised about by the child as it tries to organise its existence.

As psychoanalysts are so often inclined to remind us, babies are born in a totally helpless state and have to struggle with their own drives and the sensations in their bodies. Anyone who's spent any amount of time with a baby knows that they're frequently upset; they scream, cry, and make a fuss. If you're the person looking after that baby you have to try to work out what they're getting at. The way in which you interpret their suffering will inevitably say more about you than it does about them. You might imagine they're hungry whereas they actually have a pain in their body. You think they're too hot but actually they're thirsty. You act on the baby until it stops screaming. (Or you leave it to scream because you believe that screaming is what it needs to do.) The baby tries to tolerate the unbearable fact of its existence while you respond to it in whatever way you think is appropriate. In this way, you inevitably become bound up with whatever the baby is feeling. The things you do form its experience of the world. You put your marks on the baby, touch it, speak to it, clean it and abandon it in whatever combination you choose. In this way, you begin to inscribe jouissance on it. By responding to the baby, you help it to tame and order its drives. You teach it to inhabit its own body, to turn the hideous sensations into enjoyment, although this enjoyment is never easy; it's always in relation to the horror, discomfort and helplessness it's formed out of. The baby comes to access an enjoyment of its own body through the signifiers of the mother, or primary carer. The carer becomes so intimately bound up with this jouissance that they appear to be the cause of it. The child's suffering is somehow outsourced. The baby externalises the problem by holding the mother/carer responsible for the sensations it experiences. She becomes scary, because the baby needs her to be like that. Better that *she's* scary than that the scariness is intrinsic to existence. Having made her into something dreadful, it then just needs to make its father into a person who can save it. Abracadabra, all the badness is gone.

You can see that, when viewed in this way, there's no need for the so-called mother to be a woman, and no need for the "father" to be a man. The "parents" might even share the childcare equally, meaning that the child will have to come up with another entity, or logical configuration, to sort things out. The point is that the person, or people, who look after a child in it's very early existence will become tied up with—you might even say, blamed for—its drives. With luck, the child will come across some other person or thing who can get this invented monster off their case. The Oedipus complex, as Freud appears to have understood it, is just one way things could go. It may very well go this way quite often in a culture where men go out to work and women stay at home. But even then, you see (as in the cases of Little Hans and the Wolf Man) that all sorts of other people—maids, sisters, professors— might get dragged in to help tidy up the mess.

It seems that the most far-reaching application of the Oedipus complex is as an equation where the x's and y's could be anything or anyone; what's consistent is that relations need to be conceptualised and organised by the infant in order for it to grow up and take up a position in the world.

Suicide

Alton Counselling Service Conference, 2013

Sometimes people come to therapy in order to choose between life and death. There are guidelines regarding suicide, both in law and in psychotherapy organisations' Codes of Ethics, but these don't always help in individual cases. At what point should you break confidentiality and involve third parties? Might you lose the trust of the person—if, for example, you call their GP—and make the situation worse? If you sit tight, how will you live with it if they kill themselves? And are they telling you about it because they want you to act? Or because they trust you not to?

Suicide became illegal in UK in the thirteenth century, the idea being that God was the only entity with the right to decide when a life should end. By committing suicide, you were disregarding the will of God. This would seem hard to argue logically. Why should the will of God not include suicide when it includes war, disease and accidental drowning? Nonetheless, Thomas Aquinas thought it didn't, and the people safeguarding the law carried on agreeing with him for hundreds of years. A person could be prosecuted if they failed to die in a suicide attempt, but there were also were legal consequences if they succeeded. Their estate would be forfeited to the Crown, and their immediate family could face fines. The UK was unusually tolerant in this regard; in other countries, terrible things might be done to the body after death, ostensibly in order to act as a deterrent.

Suicide was finally decriminalised in the UK in 1961 when it was agreed that it made no sense to take people who were already in a vulnerable state to court. (A tactic which had possibly made it even more important to suicidal people to make sure they actually died rather than just gave everyone a fright.) The church argued that we should be kinder and more understanding towards those who were already suffering, and to help rather than legislate against them. The new laws were rather complex as they opened up questions around assisted suicide. If killing yourself wasn't a crime any more, did that mean other people could help you? Apparently not. Suicide is unusual in that it isn't a crime in itself, but helping someone commit this non-crime—at least in the UK—is illegal. Even accompanying someone to a country where assisted suicide is legal is currently in the balance, with changes to the law under discussion. In 2009, Debbie Purdy won a case stating that the law was unclear on this point, and that this very unclarity was a breach of her human rights. She'd wanted her husband to come with her to a country where it would be possible for her to commit suicide in a painless, controlled way (she had multiple sclerosis) but the law was unable to tell her whether or not he would be prosecuted after her death.

The laws of some countries acknowledge that suicide might be a valid response to certain situations, for instance if you have an incurable disease which will leave you in unbearable pain until you die. And perhaps now we are beginning to see a more tolerant attitude towards people who feel suicidal for other reasons, such as emotional suffering—although physical pain still appears to carry more weight than psychological pain in the context of the law.

In terms of therapists' Codes of Ethics, if someone is thought to be a danger to themselves or others then therapists are licensed to breach confidentiality. You can talk to the patient's doctor, a family member, close friend, or to the police. Like many guidelines that purport to be commonsensical, it can actually be a bit paradoxical when you attempt to put it into practice. There's not much concrete to be said about the precise moment at which someone officially becomes a "danger to themselves". People often come to therapy to speak about their suicidality, rather than just going ahead and acting. The very fact that they turn up to sessions means they are trying out something other than killing themselves, although they might be saying in the actual sessions that they can't see any other way, and may argue forcefully against you if you ever suggest they have alternatives.

When might you decide that someone is such a danger to themselves that you would be prepared to jeopardise the therapeutic relationship in order to involve a third party? Would it be at the moment they say something like, "I'm definitely going to kill myself tonight"?, or sooner, like when they're just generally stating that they can't see another way out of their predicament? This is a question of tact and personal judgement. One might expect a therapist to panic at a slightly later stage than a friend. Still, therapists might also be thought to recognise the real risks sooner than friends, and to have more ideas about whom to approach and what to say. There can't be a precise, correct moment to intervene, which can obviously be very anxiety-provoking for practitioners who might want to preserve a space for the person to come and speak freely, but who also want the person not to die.

Why should we insist so much on the continuation of life on behalf of other people? It's a question that seems to go beyond reason. Thomas Aquinas and, much earlier, St Augustine try to use logic to argue the case. Some of that "logic" might appear to be built over a chasm, and all of it relies on a belief in God. For instance, why can't suicide be an act of repentance rather than a sin? St Augustine's arguments may seem even more tenuous than Aquinas's, depending, as they do, on the subtleties of the wording of the Ten Commandments. "Thou shalt not kill", is broad and non-specific while, "Thou shalt not bear false witness against *thy neighbour*", has a particular victim in mind—somebody other than oneself. Therefore, according to Augustinian logic, "Thou shalt not kill" implicitly includes an injunction against suicide. Still, it apparently doesn't include a ban on killing animals. St Augustine wasn't vegetarian himself and argued against the idea that Christians ought to be vegetarian. Apparently, veganism was the norm in the garden of Eden, but after the Great Flood, God said it was OK to eat meat. All of which is to say there are very serious inconsistencies in some of the historical arguments against suicide …

Much of our daily existence is at the service of the continuation of life and defence against death: eating, drinking, breathing, working, sleeping. The will to the continuation of life is perhaps so ingrained in living beings that going against it can't be taken lightly. In ancient Greece, the bodies of suicide victims were treated differently; they were given unmarked burials outside the city walls. Perhaps it's understandable, not just in terms of broader ideas about *all* lifeforms, but also in relation to the particular lifeforms who brought about your existence: your parents (or whoever's hands you fell into after birth). Babies who are loved and wanted appear to fare better than those who aren't. It's far more likely that newborns will live if they are spoken to, looked at and touched. Even the most premature babies require an interlocutor, somebody to engage them. It's not just a matter of receiving the right medicine or surgery, but something else. It might sound fanciful, but it seems we need to be welcomed into being by someone who wants us to exist. Healthy, full-term babies, too, require constant care and attention. Somebody else has to will you to live, and their will has effects on your organism, helping it to develop. Research into genes shows that genes are "switched on" by experience. External events affect the body. And, of course, life itself is the result of someone else's act. Maybe it's not so much about whether *you* want to live, but whether someone else wants you to. Until you're able to support yourself, your life is thanks to other people's wishes. In this respect, humans are different to many other animals, some of whom need no parenting, others very little. In a sense your life really isn't your own, or certainly not at birth. It's absolutely someone else's business.

In *The Myth of Sisyphus* (2005), Albert Camus famously says, "There is but one truly serious philosophical question and that is suicide." Everything else is just quibbling. Who cares, really, about how to prove an event took place? Or endless wranglings about the true meaning of "goodness"? All of this pales into insignificance in the face of the question: "Is life truly worth living?" We get into the habit of living before we are able to start asking questions about whether or not we want to do it. The question is whether habit is enough to carry us through. In the words of Camus: "Beginning to think is beginning to be undermined." He starts from the assumption that human life is extremely difficult, often uncomfortable, unjust, and a huge amount of work. Worst of all, it involves a great deal of senseless labour. It doesn't matter whether you're a banker, a road sweeper, or a make-up artist, you're basically just pushing a rock up a hill. If you expect life to make sense or be fair you're liable to be extremely disappointed. Camus concludes that living is an absurd task and that accepting the absurdity might compare favourably with expecting life to make sense and be fair, and killing yourself when things don't go your way. He talks about the big, serious causes of human unhappiness, describing an apartment manager who lost his child but kept on living for five years before finally killing himself. What is it that finally makes people choose to stop living? For Camus, it's often a small thing—an unfriendly look or an unreturned phone call.

So, there's the enormous question of whether life is worth the bother or not. Answering "no" implies an insult to existence, and perhaps to all those who keep going with it. Then there's the problem of how on earth this question could be answered. What would make you come down on either side? By choosing life, perhaps you could be said to be aligning yourself with habit, carrying on the existence that was given to you without your consent, and which you senselessly find yourself sustaining. By choosing death, at least you break that habit. Alternatively, you could choose to live in an undermined, questioning state, acknowledging the absurdity of existence and seeing what you can do with it. Given the fact that death is a certainty, why not try out a few other things first?

The miserable cure

Jacques Lacan designated "subjective destitution" to be the aim of analysis. It's something very different to the cohesive, largely happy individual that other forms of therapy or analysis might strive towards. In a state of subjective destitution all of the ideals and identifications that have previously sustained a person, holding them in place and giving them a sense of identity, fall away. In this condition, without the imaginary supports that promise to make life bearable, a person may very well be confronted with the question of whether or not they want to carry on. Lacan's idea isn't that your analysis stops there, at which point you're flung out onto the street to deal with the horror. The idea is more that, having done some analytic work, you can then undergo a labour of reconstruction, but from a different perspective. You are no longer trying to double-guess what the Other wants from you, placating or frustrating them accordingly. You acknowledge the external forces that transpired to make you *you*, and can see how driven they are by chance and contingency. You're no longer looking to anyone else to guarantee or authenticate your existence. It's a state that is liable to be both extremely frightening, and a tremendous relief. What, in Lacanian jargon, is known as "traversing the fundamental phantasy" means loosening your grip on your phantasy of who/what you are for the Other.

It's hardly a jolly idea to offer to people in order to buck them up, or talk them out of suicide, but it may sometimes help in that it frames a state of abjection as a starting point from which a person can begin to make choices.

Happy non-endings

A man came to see me, tormented by thoughts of killing himself. Suicide was, for him, a romantic idea. It would strike him very strongly in certain situations. On a mountain road he would think about driving his car over the edge. If he'd had a good evening he'd think about departing from life on a high. He had lots of important relationships tying him to the world: a partner, three sons, a mum, a dad, a sister, plus a circle of close friends. Still, death appeared to offer itself as a constant temptation. He felt his suicidal thoughts were a terrible betrayal of the people who loved him and who would be deeply affected by his death.

He worked over plenty of apparently relevant material during his time in analysis. He spoke about the frustrations and schisms in his relationship. He and his partner never quite arrived at a stable sense of union, and it seemed he was always at risk of getting into battles with her. He was also blocked from doing anything with other women because of his domestic commitments. Added to his romantic and sexual frustrations was the fact that his partner, a City lawyer, was the main breadwinner (she also paid for his analysis).

This man had an early memory of being ferociously told off by his mother for borrowing some of her underwear for some kind of proto-masturbatory game. After this he described going into a kind of lifelong sulk, expecting only frustration, prohibition, and rejection. He had the idea that part of the appeal of death was perhaps the promise of being undivided and unbroken.

While he made amazing progress in terms of making sense of the phenomenon, this didn't appear to help him deal with the effects of it. In fact, he reported thinking about suicide even more. Things became difficult at home and the man decided he was no use to his family—he was constantly grumpy, a bad influence on his children. His partner would be better off paying for a professional nanny and having him out of the way. If he killed himself he'd be doing them all a favour. At this point I resorted to running through a couple of the more commonplace arguments for staying alive, i.e., that his partner and children would be traumatised for years to come, if not permanently, and that he couldn't pit that sort of unhappiness against the calm efficiency of a nanny. He wasn't impressed. He ploughed on with his supposedly logical idea that his suicide would be for the best. Arguing against him was pointless, it just made his position more entrenched. An alternative to getting into a fruitless row seemed to try to go back to linking his ideas about killing himself with his fantasies of a perfect sexual and romantic union, and to keep going with the idea that human relationships weren't really like that. It was hardly inspired, just something to resort to in desperation.

Parallel to the suicide idea grew the notion that he could walk out of his life and cut all contact. He also started regularly cancelling sessions at the last minute. When I questioned him as to why, he became extremely defensive, saying it was to do with events entirely beyond his control. Still, he never tried to reschedule when a cancelled train or school meeting got in the way of his appointments. After a few weeks he sent an abrupt email to say that he wouldn't be coming any more. I replied with a friendly invitation to say he was welcome to change his mind at anytime, but heard nothing back.

It can be tempting to hope for happy endings in analysis, although it's hard to say exactly what kind of ending would qualify. *All* endings might be considered complex or difficult, even ones where the person says, "Thank you so much, I feel better now." An as analyst, you have to get used to sudden stops, or weird reasons for pulling out suddenly, and not to see them as necessarily any worse than neater, more "ideal" conclusions. You sometimes hear from people that it was the way in which their analyst let them go that was worth as much as anything said during the course of the treatment. All of which risks sounding foolishly self-justifying because the last thing you *want* is to be alienating your suicidal patients just when they're threatening to go off the rails.

So, what do you do when something like this happens? Do you freak out and break confidentiality? Or do you let the person go? I chose to do the latter because the former felt inappropriate, even though the latter seemed unsatisfactory and *laissez-faire*. The man had spoken about his suicidal feelings to his family doctor, so he was "in the system" in some sense and would go in from time to time for check-ups (where he flatly refused to take anti-depressants). I even wondered whether his ending the therapy might be a good thing; if he wasn't going to walk out on his partner and kids, he could at least walk out on me without it having dire consequences. I tried not to flap, but to see it as a lesson in not panicking, not letting the very serious question of life or death push you to act in equally drastic, black and white terms. Perhaps it's possible to let people speak about suicide, even with some urgency, without invoking the law, emotionally blackmailing them out of it, coaxing them with common sense, or any of the other reactions that might make it frustrating to speak to friends and family. While this kind of work can be hard on the therapist, there's a hope it might not be a total waste of time. Still, I didn't *at all* like the way the work had ended.

Two years later, I received an email from the man asking for an appointment. I could hardly have been more pleased to hear from anyone. He was still with his family, but continued to be plagued by suicidal thoughts. This time around, he was more deeply immersed in questions about himself, the world, co-existence, work, politics, meaning, satisfaction. His questions were always pithy and well-formulated, philosophical in the most immediate and pressing sense. His pull towards death was as urgent as ever, and my wish to "save" him was as gut-wrenching and pathetic. Still, however Sisyphean the task might appear, on both his side and mine, it seemed worth keeping open a space to speak, with no guarantees, and to see where it took us. So far, we're both still here.

Time

Centre for Freudian Analysis and Research, 2015

In *Harry Hill's TV Burp*, a popular Saturday night show summing up the week's television, the host would find two incommensurable things and ask, "Which is better, A or B? There's only one way to find out: Fight!" Babies or cats? Mermaids or boobs? Pasta or nothing? At this point two actors would appear dressed as babies, cats, fusilli, or whatever, and slug it out into the ad break.

In the psychoanalytic world, there is the pressing question of which are better, fixed-length sessions or variable ones. The variable-length session has been a fraught subject in the history of psychoanalysis, with plenty of aggression mobilised around it. Central to Lacan's exclusion from the IPA, he was constantly in trouble over it with certain of his fellow analysts. He said he'd stop doing it but didn't, and then bought a very nice holiday home in 1951, which may have aroused colleagues' envy. There's the unfortunate coincidence of his doing visibly very well financially at the same time as making his great "theoretical breakthrough"—shorter sessions ostensibly meant more cash. Given that psychoanalysis is a bit weird, paradoxical, and messy, perhaps it seems comforting to some people to think that one thing about the process can be certain: even if it's a load of rubbish, it should be fifty minutes of rubbish to ensure fair play.

131

So, which is best? On the one hand, we have the well-known Freudian idea that "there is no time in the unconscious". Then, on the other, there's the much-repeated idea that the unconscious needs time to reveal itself. (Fight!) There appears to be a total impasse, with intolerance and ignorance imputed to each side. Lacanians stand accused of greed and unanalysed countertransference. Non-Lacanians are allied with envy and theoretical rigidity. To demonstrate the deadlock more clearly, perhaps it's helpful to look at the way Lacan introduces the idea in his "Rome Discourse" (2006), and also at André Green's treatment of the subject in his book *Time in Psychoanalysis* (2002) where he seems to be responding to the passage in the "Rome Discourse", although he doesn't say so directly. Reading both texts, one gets the impression that there's something utterly non-negotiable on each side.

Institutional time

André Green attended Lacan's seminar during the sixties, even though he was affiliated with the the Society Psychanalytique de Paris (SPP), the organisation that Lacan had been "manoeuvred" out of. Lacan had previously been the vice president of the SPP, and had been very highly thought of by many of its members. Much later, in the eighties, André Green became the president of this same organisation. Before that, he had been vice president of the Institute of Psycho-Analysis (IPA). So he and Lacan were very much on opposite teams, although Green had played it down the middle, at least for a while, going to Lacan's seminar at the Société Française de Psychanalyse (SFP). (Apologies for all the acronyms, but anyone interested in Freud's notion of the "narcissism of petty differences" might at least get a laugh out of it.) What all this seems to have meant, ultimately, is that André Green was well-positioned to become a kind of super-enemy. He fell out with Lacan in 1970 over a theoretical point, after which he seems to have made it his mission to demonstrate to the world why Lacan was wrong about everything. Still, reading Elizabeth Roudinesco's *Jacques Lacan and Co* (1990)—a forensically detailed study of the French psychoanalytic scene—it appears that things were already complicated before this. Green was a protégé of Lacan's, partly because he was smart and subtle, but also, apparently, because he was elegant. Green himself had trouble choosing between the SPP and SFP and momentarily straddled both, despite being warned off each side by the other.

The problem was that, because of all the ill feeling evidently generated between the different psychoanalytic factions, there was very little cross-pollination. Members of the SPP (affiliated with the IPA) tended to take it on trust that Lacan was very bad. Roudinesco speaks of a culture of castrated "artisans" on the IPA side, very much opposed to charismatic narcissists like Lacan. In this adversarial context, the practice of short sessions was enough in itself to justify taking up a position against Lacan. Of course, they demonstrated that he was a terrible, unethical practitioner who just wanted to grab people's money and spend it on country houses and good suits, all the while rambling on about things that didn't make any sense.

André Green was a gift to people who didn't like Lacan but couldn't argue against him. Green had actually been to the seminars, and could therefore construct counter-arguments that sounded plausible if it suited you to find them so. For instance, he "proves" Lacan's absolute idiocy by stating that the unconscious can't possibly be structured like a language. The reason for this is that, according to Freud, the unconscious is constituted by "thing presentations"; words only appear in the preconscious. This is an extremely problematic argument for anyone who's read Freud's *Interpretation of Dreams* (1900a). In this book, he describes how thing presentations can be ordered into a sentence, or rebus, which then needs to be decoded, taking into account the syntax and grammar of the individual parts. In his famous statement, Lacan very purposefully says, "*like* a language", because he's talking about language in the structuralist sense. According to Freud, thing presentations in the unconscious can be linked, exchanged, replaced, and opposed, just like words. He's not saying they *are* words, and neither is Lacan. So, it's a shaky argument from André Green, who pitches himself as Freud's true defender. Perhaps because people were so thirsty for any argument at all that would help them write Lacan off without thinking about it too much, he nonetheless seems to have been fêted for it. Green was the man who came back from the other side and lived to tell the tale.

In the passage in *Time in Psychoanalysis* (2002) where Green deals with variable sessions directly, he refers scathingly to Lacan's "so-called technique of sessions of variable duration" (p. 48), bemoaning the fact that "discussion has very little effect; for the deep reasons for adhering to such a technique are so powerful that no argumentative treatise would overcome them" (p. 48). He invokes the Freudian question, why would anyone give up a satisfaction? According to Green, Lacanian

psychoanalysts' material greed and love of power is supremely well
supported by this technique, so what could possibly persuade a person
thus indoctrinated to throw it into question? Again, in the words of
Green, "… he [would] find it too difficult to give up the position of
omnipotence …" (p. 48). Green insists on variable sessions being bad for
the analysand: "the moment of interruption emphasises precisely the
issue he needs to be thinking about, the analyst choosing to disappear,
leaving behind him an empty space so that the signifier can wander in
dereliction." (p. 48) You could argue that this is rather patronising to the
analysand, who is apparently lost without an analyst to guide him or
her. But it also provokes the question of the analyst's self-interest. If variable sessions are really so terrible for the analysand, leaving them bereft
and clueless, then this technique may not necessarily help with building
a busy practice and buying a country house. Unless, of course, one concludes that most psychoanalytic patients are gullible masochists …

Lacan's Rome discourse

If for André Green it's all about the unthinkable—or at least what can't
be thought by the analyst—so it is for Lacan too. Let's take a passage in
the Rome Discourse where Lacan mentions the taboo surrounding the
subject of variable length sessions. Here he speaks about the "[…] scru-
pulous, not to say obsessive, character that observing a standard takes
on for some if not most analysts—a standard whose historical and
geographical variations nonetheless seem to bother no one—is a clear
sign of the existence of a problem that analysts are reluctant to broach
because they realise to what extent it would entail questioning the analyst's function." It's a typically dense and tangled quote, referring to
the idea that the standard fifty minute hour was arrived at somewhat
arbitrarily, and that forty-five minutes was actually the norm in France.
Lacan's mention of scrupulousness and obsession seems to appeal to
Freud's portrayal of the anal character; one wants to appear impeccable
because one's unconscious is bursting with filth. While Green claims
Lacanians can't put themselves in question over variable sessions because
it would interrupt their satisfactions, Lacan says pretty much the same
thing about the supposedly orthodox Freudians, whose satisfactions
might, according to this account, consist in feeling safe, authoritative,
and self-righteous (not to mention the phantasmatic anal satisfactions,
which amount to the same thing). This is in keeping with Lacan's

characterisation of the opposition as stultifying types who are mainly interested in ensuring their continued existence (and income—it's still an economic argument) by making sure they have a rigid set of codes and orthodoxies to adhere to, which will protect them, like armour.

One has to remember that this runs alongside the idea, seemingly accepted by all psychoanalysts, that one can't know in advance how long an analysis will be. On the macro scale, there's a fairly unanimous agreement that you can't dictate the amount of time it will take in advance, but on the smaller scale (each session) certain people think you can, should, or even *must*.

In his Rome Discourse, Lacan has already been extremely disparaging about most sections of the analytic world by the time he gets onto the subject of variable sessions. The people who disagree with him are portrayed with a sarcasm worthy of Jane Austen: "The unconscious, it is said—in a tone that is all the more knowing the less the speaker is capable of justifying what he means—the unconscious needs time to reveal itself" (p. 257/313). Lacan goes on to say that he agrees with the basic premise, the problem is how one measures that time. Is it clock time, bearing in mind that units of clock time are a fairly recent invention? Can it really be the case that the human unconscious can be discussed in relation to a machine? Why should the unconscious be able to reveal itself in fifty minutes, but not twenty?

There seems to be an uncrossable divide between the two schools of thought. If you can see the point in one, you supposedly can't see the point in the other. But of course, there are plenty of people who practise in both ways and who can see the upsides and downsides of each. Still, we might be accused of theoretical sloppiness by those who are strongly identified with either argument. Nonetheless, there seems no good reason to be pushed in one direction or the other just for the sake of appearing consistent. At least uncertainty can give you space to think. Green writes about Lacanians being "enjoined by the force of the group ..." to exercise their power (p. 48) and end sessions "early", and actually I recognise the idea that, in some Lacanian circles, if you give fifty minute sessions you risk as being seen as either a wimp or a square, or somehow otherwise suspect. Still, this is nothing compared with the pressure on people affiliated with the IPA to give fixed-length sessions. They're simply not allowed to do anything else.

In terms of what people in analysis, or going into analysis, say they would prefer, it's clear things go both ways. Of course, you meet people who say they'd hate to be slung out by their shrink when they feel they're just hitting their stride, or when they feel they haven't quite got their money's worth. But you'll also find the opposite. I saw one person who said he'd despised previous therapists for being "clockwatchers". One is reminded of the therapist in *Little Britain*, slyly looking at his wristwatch, hoping his patient won't notice. As Lacan points out in relation to Huyghens' clock, "the discontent of modern man precisely does not indicate that this precision serves him as a liberating factor" (p. 313). Clocks have not made our species any happier.

In 2009, an ultra-clockwatchy management of time in psychoanalysis was proposed by government-backed regulators. A draft document was produced as a result of a "Skills for Health" consultation. It put forward four hundred and fifty-one guidelines for therapists. Part of the aim was to reduce patients' uncertainty around their therapy and to make sure they felt OK at all times during treatment. According to this document, people in therapy need to know exactly what their therapy *is*, what its aims are, and where they are in the process of achieving those aims. It advised that no interpretations should be made less than twenty minutes before a session ended. This would give both sides just the right amount of time to clear up any unfortunate misunderstandings. In other words, the last twenty minutes of the session ought to be devoted to making sure the unconscious *didn't* reveal itself, or at least that any hint of it was very thoroughly tamed by going home time. Many therapists resisted—at the risk of being accused of anti-regulatory villainy—and the document never progressed from draft status.

The Zeigarnik effect

In perhaps his most famous quote on the subject of variable sessions, Lacan sounds extremely certain: "I would not say so much about it if I had not been convinced—in experimenting with what have been called my 'short sessions', at a stage in my career that is now over—that I was able to bring to light in a certain male subject fantasies of anal pregnancy, as well as a dream of its resolution by Caesarean section, in a time frame in which I would normally still have been listening to his speculations on Dostoyevsky's artistry" (2006, p. 315).

Why should this "cutting short" have such a potent effect? The reason often put forward for this, although not by Lacan himself, is the "Zeigarnik effect". He mentions this phenomenon elsewhere, at the very beginning of his "Presentation on Transference" (1951), where he discusses "Dora", Freud's great, interrupted case. The theory, dating from 1927, is named after Bluma Zeigarnik, a psychiatrist and member of the Vygotsky Circle, a network of doctors, psychologists and educators active in the Soviet Union between the 1920s and 1940s. Apparently her professor, Kurt Lewin, had noticed that waiters tended to forget the details of an order once it had been paid. At least, the waiter at the café in which he and his students would regularly meet did exactly this. He didn't write orders down, but held them in his head until the bill was settled. If you loitered at your table after payment, and then asked him what you'd had, he apparently had no idea, and might even respond quite rudely (perhaps understandably to anyone who's ever had a waiting job). Lewin's particular area of interest was motivation, and his curiosity about the waiter grew out of his research into what caused people to care about one thing and not another. Did the waiter forget the order as soon as there was no longer a pressing reason for him to remember it? Bluma Zeigarnik latched onto this puzzling phenomenon and devised a series of experiments to demonstrate this particular configuration of remembering and forgetting (*An Introduction to the History of Psychology*, B. R. Hergenhahn, 2000, p. 479). She asked forty-seven adults and forty-five children to complete between eighteen and twenty-two tasks. The tasks varied from the manual to the mental. Some of these would be interrupted and some wouldn't. This would all happen in no apparent order, and without prior explanation. Many people found the interruptions annoying, some even objecting quite strongly. Subjects were then quizzed on what they had been asked to do. Zeigarnik concluded that, overall, interrupted tasks were remembered far better than uninterrupted ones, although this varied greatly from subject to subject. One person apparently demonstrated five hundred times better recall for uncompleted tasks, while another was found to be twenty-five times worse. Tired people, apparently, tended to remember completed tasks better. Still, in the tradition of statistics-based research, the general tendency has come to be presented as an overall fact: interrupted tasks are remembered better (Zeigarnik, 1927).

Citing the Zeigarnik effect as the reasoning behind "short sessions" has the apparent force of science and empirical proof behind it, but this wasn't Lacan's point at all. His mention of Zeigarnik focuses on the effects of transference revealed in her experiments; subjects apparently fared differently according to how much they hoped to please or impress the experimenter. Lacan doesn't *at all* suggest that experiments of this sort should help to inform psychoanalytic practice. Quite the opposite. For Lacan, psychoanalysis "preserves a dimension that is irreducible to any psychology considered to be the objectification of certain of an individual's properties" (2006, p. 216). There's also the fact that the Zeigarnik effect was seriously put into question by experimental psychologists who repeated her experiments in the late sixties and got a very different set of results. One of the key variables seemed to be whether or not the person had a personal investment in the task, making the simple binary "interrupted/completed" too reductive to be useful, even for people persuaded by empirically testable psychological theories.

Rather than "interrupting" for the sake of it, what if variable sessions don't even begin with a notion of a fifty-minute session that may be curtailed, but simply with the idea that the session will end as soon as something odd or surprising appears? Afterwards the analysand will go away and live with this until the next session, seeing what other thoughts it might provoke.

Prisoners and birthdays

In his essay, "Logical Time and the Assertion of Anticipated Certainty: a new sophism" (2006 [1945]), Lacan presents us with the prisoners' dilemma. We have three prisoners and five discs, two of which are black and three of which are white. A single disc is placed on each prisoner's back. If, without saying anything to one another, they can work out what colour their own disc is, they can go free. Only the first one to do this will be released, while the others must remain in jail. Each prisoner is then given a white disc. After a pause, they all leave at the same time and give the same explanation. Why?

Each prisoner sees two whites, and has to work out whether he has a black or a white. He imagines what would happen if he had a black disc: each of the other prisoners, on seeing a black and a white would be able to establish instantaneously what their own colour was; if no-one had made an immediate bolt for the door, each could assume that they themselves were white. It's the lengthy pause that gives the game away, followed by the continued stopping and checking, suggesting uncertainty across the board.

Lacan's essay goes on to elaborate the problematic nature of this conclusion. The answer can't be reached using straightforward mathematical logic, which presumes simultaneity and doesn't offer a place for the distorting feature of time. Without the element of time, the problem can't be solved, throwing the supposed purity of mathematics into question. It's not just logic, but logic in time, and time taken up with intersubjective calculations; the solution relies on seeing what the other people appear to be thinking.

Lacan divides the time of the solution into three parts: the instant of the gaze (or glance), the time for understanding (comprehending), and the moment of concluding. You see what you see, you pause, and your pause alongside the other prisoners' pauses, gives you the solution. In other words, you get to know something about yourself in the presence of the enigmatic gaze, perplexity and silence of the others. Having laid out the problem, there is the time one takes to see it and to process its implications, followed by the moment for making something of it. This is played out on a micro and macro level in analysis, inside single sessions and drawn out over years. The pauses, blanks, and hesitations are part of the work. As with the prisoners, one can't say in advance how long it will take to find a solution.

A strange mathematical problem, which came to be known as "Cheryl's Birthday", appeared in the newspapers in 2015. It had been set as a question in a Singaporean maths olympiad, aimed at fourteen-year-old students. In it, Albert and Bernard have to work out when Cheryl's birthday is using only a minimal set of clues. There are two possible, mutually exclusive, outcomes. Both are correct, although the people who set the question hadn't predicted the second answer so initially believed that only one was right. The problem is as follows:

> Albert and Bernard just became friends with Cheryl, and they want to know when her birthday is. Cheryl gives them a list of ten possible dates:
>
> **May**
> 15, 16, 19

June
17, 18

July
14, 16

August
14, 15, 17

Cheryl then tells Albert and Bernard separately the month and the day of her birthday respectively.

Albert: "I don't know when Cheryl's birthday is, but I know that Bernard doesn't know too."

Bernard: "At first I don't know when Cheryl's birthday is, but I know now."

Albert: "Then I also know when Cheryl's birthday is."

So, when is Cheryl's birthday?

Two ways of setting off give two different solutions. The difference hinges on the second half of the first statement, and how come Albert knows that Bernard doesn't know. Perhaps it makes poetic sense that a riddle involving birthdays should point to an unthinkable schism or gap. Birthdays mark the transition from not being there to being there, life and death. In this sense, the "Cheryl's Birthday" problem has something in common with the riddle of the Sphinx; it's all about beginnings, middles, and endings.

First solution

Albert: "I don't know when Cheryl's birthday is, but I know that Bernard doesn't know too."

The first part of the sentence needn't be there at all. Of course, Albert can't work it out on his own, given only the month. Bernard, however, *might* have been able to work it out on his own if the number had been either eighteen or nineteen. But Albert knows that it can't be either of these numbers (without being told) because he evidently doesn't have May or June. He must therefore have July or August.

Line 2) Bernard: "At first I don't know when Cheryl's birthday is, but now I know."

Bernard is clever and realises that Albert has one or other of the latter two months. The fact that he now knows the answer means he *hasn't* been given the number fourteen. If he had he'd still be in the dark. So, the number must be fifteen, sixteen or seventeen, each of which would give away which month it was, as these numbers only appear once.

Line 3) Albert: "Then I also know when Cheryl's birthday is."

Albert has worked out that the possible dates are July 16th, Aug 15th and Aug 17th. If he now knows the answer, it can only be because he has July. So, the answer must be July 16th.

Or must it?

Second solution

1. Albert knows that Bernard doesn't know. But how? Perhaps Bernard pauses and looks perplexed. Albert therefore realises that Bernard doesn't have eighteen or nineteen, which are both unique numbers. Albert teases Bernard about the fact that he doesn't have the answer.
2. Bernard sees what Albert sees, which is that he hasn't got eighteen or nineteen. If Albert had June he would immediately know the answer, because there is only one date left in June: the 17th. So, because Albert pauses or is stuck here, Bernard deduces it can't be June.
3. Bernard now knows the answer.
4. If Bernard is so sure, it can only be because he has a number that only appears once. So, it can't be eighteen or nineteen. What's left? There are two fourteens, fifteens, sixteens and seventeens. Bernard knows it's not June 17th, so that leaves August 17th.
5. Albert growls to himself, then imagines himself in Bernard's place and follows the logic outlined above. He concludes that Bernard can only have seventeen. Albert announces he knows the answer too.

So, August 17th is also a valid answer (pieced together with massive help from, "How to Solve Albert, Bernard and Cheryl's Maths Problem", Alex Bellos, *The Guardian*, 13th April 2013).

The mathematics, or logic, is affected by a very subtle difference at the beginning. In the first solution, Albert deduces that Bernard doesn't know because Albert is holding a month that doesn't have a unique number in it. In the second solution, Albert *sees Bernard's perplexity,* so begins by crossing off numbers eighteen and nineteen. From each starting point you get a different solution to the same mathematical problem. The first solution was the one designed by the examiners, and considered more "correct" because it relies on pure mathematical reasoning. The second could be considered more suspect as it relies on two moments of perplexity from the people involved; as in Lacan's prisoners' dilemma, the confusion itself informs the logic. It's less purely mathematical because it includes the element of time—and what is communicated wordlessly between humans during that time.

So, you have two ways of solving a problem, with something like an unthinkable schism—how can both solutions be right but also exclude each other, or make each other wrong? One is more purely mathematical, one draws on subjectivity.

In terms of psychoanalysis, it's a commonplace to say that your starting point will warp the outcome. That's why you don't generally step in with leading questions at the beginning of a session, but let the person decide how they want to start—even if it means floundering a little. Of course, your analytic orientation will inevitably affect what you find in the person's discourse. A Kleinian may conclude that their patient has failed to progress through the depressive position, while a Lacanian may find that the same person refuses to accept the fact that the sexual relationship is asymmetrical. There is no such thing as analytic neutrality.

Love, hate, and money

Perhaps it shouldn't come as a surprise that such a terrible theoretical schism has arisen around the idea of endings; the psychoanalytic world has had a great deal to say about loss and separation. There are beautiful theories around mourning, eloquent ideas about attachment, separation, love, and hate. But, as we know, theory can't vaccinate you against experience. Just because we ramble on about death, endings, partings, and voids, it doesn't follow that we actually know how to deal with them. The beginnings and endings of sessions are a very real enactment of the game of *fort/da*. No wonder psychoanalysts have got themselves into trouble over it.

There are other important schisms within the psychoanalytic world regarding how analysts ought to work with separations from patients, perhaps as a holiday approaches. Object relations people would tend to tackle the situation with pre-emptive words, trying to bring out the potential emotional impact of the break and name it. "You're angry/

you're upset/you want to withdraw first." The loss is named in an attempt to deal head on with the feelings it provokes. Lacanians might be more inclined to allow voids to hover, seeing what gets produced in those spaces.

On a smaller scale, individual session endings might very well unleash a great deal of anxiety in the analyst. In *Money Talks: in Therapy, Society, and Life* (2011) we hear a great deal about session endings in relation to money. In Arielle Farber Shanock's essay about money and gender she talks about the ways in which concluding sessions can become complicated, especially if this is the moment at which the person pays. In particular, she discusses a male client who regularly causes her to keep going beyond the allotted fifty minutes. It turns out that the man hates his job and doesn't like the idea that his thera- pist, too, is doing a job and might also hate it. He wants her to see him for love, not money, so drawing out the ending of the session is a way of getting something for free. She colludes, she feels, partly thanks to social conditioning around women and caring. She thinks a male therapist would find it easier to end the sessions, and perhaps also that he wouldn't be expected to love his patients like a good, caring mother, giving without expecting anything in return. The endings of this patient's sessions become fraught with anxiety for the analyst, and perhaps for the patient too, or at least he knows how to exploit his analyst's discomfort.

All of which is to say that going by the clock doesn't save you from difficulty. Having the idea that your session *ought* to be fifty minutes long doesn't guarantee that it will be. The fact that the clock supposedly dictates the conclusion may even introduce a new layer of difficulty. In this case, the patient insists on making a division between the analyst and the clock—he won't let her be a clockwatcher.

Donald Winnicott speaks about session endings in his essay, "Hate in the Countertransference" (1949), explaining how they can be a place for analysts to subtly exercise their hatred of their patients. Just because the ending isn't decided capriciously, it doesn't therefore follow that you can't exercise your countertransference through it. Like a mother sweetly singing a lyrically violent lullaby, an analyst can conclude a session correctly and punctiliously, and still get a kick out of kicking the person out. As Winnicott puts it:

> [A]s an analyst I have ways of expressing hate. Hate is expressed by
> the existence of the end of the "hour". I think this is true even when

there is no difficulty whatever, and when the patient is pleased to go. In many analyses these things can be taken for granted, so that they are scarcely mentioned ... (1958, p. 197)

The ending can appear to pass undramatically, but this very "quietness" may mask something darker.

Can endings ever be routine and meaningless? There are analysts who use alarms in order to appear to remove themselves from the equation, but it doesn't take years of reading Freud to see that this, in itself, might mask a great deal of aggression. Money, too, is a place where analysts can be surprisingly unstraightforward. Some have discreet tables where money is left rather than being handed directly to the analyst, or even assistants who chase up payments so the analyst herself doesn't have to be personally involved. While one might take it for granted that psychoanalysts will lack prudishness around the subject of sex, they might occasionally retain a strange reticence around money in spite of Freud's explicit advice that one should always be up front about it. Could it be that time, like money (with which it is so often conflated), might also trigger a certain squeamishness?

End games

André Green criticises Lacan over the idea that the unconscious will appear in a kind of lightning flash, leading to the session being cut in a dramatic moment. Green points out that the unconscious doesn't reveal itself in this way at all, or at least only rarely, or certainly not once, twice, three times a week, on cue. He describes the unconscious as "a continuous bass following its sinuous path ..." (2002, p. 49). as opposed to "a clap of cymbals". But might there be things one can do to shake the unconscious out into the open?

The Oulipo, a group of writers and mathematicians formed in 1960, used mathematical formulae to warp the writing process. They might write a poem only including words with a certain number of letters, or in a fixed numerical relation to other words in the dictionary. These limits would, in theory, force invention. Raymond Queneau, one of the group's founding members, was a student of Alexandre Kojève's and friend of Georges Bataille's, both of whom were well known to Lacan. The Oulipo were therefore very much a part of Lacan's milieu. The group shied away from romantic ideas around inspiration, opting instead for a more machine-like approach to literary production. This, of course, could be said to be a further development of the age-old principle of beginning with a structure or rhythm—a sonnet, iambic pentameter—and finding the words to fit. Perhaps the best known Oulipian work is Georges Perec's *La Disparition*, an entire novel written without the letter "e". By forgoing the option to fall into one's usual verbal habits, one takes the chance that strange words and ideas will inevitably form. In other words, it might be quite revealing, both of the mechanisms of language, and of the contents of one's own mind, once the customary defences are down.

The paradox is that this might just as well be an argument in favour of the fifty-minute hour. While Lacan's variable sessions have tended to be seen as radical in relation to the more conservative fixed length, another way of looking would present things the other way around; mathematical time might affect speech in surprising ways.

In his "Rome Discourse" Lacan speaks about inelegant endings:

> The indifference with which ending a session after a fixed number of minutes has elapsed interrupts the subject's moments of haste and can be fatal to the conclusion toward which his discourse was rushing headlong, and can even set a misunderstanding in stone, if not furnish a pretext for a retaliatory ruse.
>
> Beginners seem more struck by the effects of this impact than others—which gives one the impression that for others it's just a routine. (2006, p. 314)

Lacan here appears to be arguing for more "naturally" conclusive endings. *Let the patients formulate their thoughts aloud in their own time.* He suggests an ending may be traumatic if handled robotically, referring to the difficulties that newer analysts might run into over curtailing people's speech, suggesting that that older analysts risk becoming callous and inhumane. The anxiety felt by the analyst around session endings may be a sign that they are more alive to, and engaged in, the interaction. Far from being something that they need to "get over" it might even be a signal that they're doing something right. The handling of endings is liable to be quite revealing of the analyst—even just to themselves. If they give fixed length sessions do they nonetheless let people follow their final trains of thought? Do they sometimes overrun? Stop a little early? Do they let their patients push them? Are they weak or strong? If they give variables, are they impatient? Cruel? Disinterested? Overly generous?

All of which is to say that endings are difficult, but also extremely necessary. You can't merge with your analysands and have them all come and live with you. Endings are part of the work—even of the "cure". Without doubt the nature of the endings you engineer is a huge feature of that work. Do you let people go easily or with difficulty? Do you present it as an unfortunate thing, a routine thing, a relief? What effects will these differences have on the people you work with?

In "The Storyteller" (1998 [1936]) Walter Benjamin speaks about the ways in which endings retroactively inflect what came before. He reconfigures an idea of Moritz Heimann's, saying, "A man who died at the age of thirty-five [...] will appear *to remembrance* at every point in his life as a man who died at thirty-five" (p. 99). The ending of a session, or of an analysis, will surely have an effect on everything that came before. Later in his essay Benjamin goes on to say: "The novel is significant therefore, not because it presents someone else's fate to us, perhaps didactically, but because this stranger's fate, by virtue of the flame which consumes it, yields us the warmth which we never draw from our own fate" (p. 100). We like novels because they end. There is a satisfaction that comes from the very artificiality of a shaped life.

So, what might this mean about psychoanalysis, and the stories people go there to tell? One might say that the stranger in psychoanalysis is you. The multiple endings you experience there are surely fundamental to the work you do, whether you are consciously aware of it or not.

Transference

Croydon Counselling Service, 2012

In an episode of the comedy sketch show, *Smack the Pony*, we meet a young female psychoanalyst in the process of speaking with a handsome male patient for the first time. She begins to explain to him, in a deadpan tone, that there is a phenomenon known as transference. She warns him it "may manifest itself as an intense longing for … um … me!" The patient appears unfazed. After a bout of nervous laughter she continues: "You may imagine after a number of sessions that you've … uh … […] fallen in love with … *me*." After an excruciating ramble about her patient's inevitable desire for her (accompanied by more and more explicitly auto-erotic gestures) he tells her rather tersely that this isn't going to be a problem. "Are you gay?" she snaps. He says no. Evidently feeling rejected, she lets him know she's very expensive and probably out of his league.

Freud spoke very succinctly about working with transference in the twenty-seventh of his *Introductory Lectures* (1916–1917). It's an amazing essay given that psychoanalysis was still so new, and a huge leap from his work of two decades earlier. In the *Studies on Hysteria*, (1895d) people keep getting better. This later text makes it clear that analysis is laborious and fraught with difficulty, and that any benefits from it are hard won. Still, in the 1890s, with Anna O., we have the first case of transference getting in way of treatment. The work ends with her feeling extremely upset because she's fallen in love with Joseph Breuer. He's so disturbed by the experience that it puts him off psychoanalysis forever. The transferential and countertransferential effects came as a total shock to both parties.

Psychoanalysis began as a kind of sense-making practice; the patient supposedly just had to be told the real meaning of their symptom in order to feel much better. It soon became apparent that the relationship with the analyst was something that couldn't be ignored. The key clinical question is whether transference is an obstacle, or a useful tool, or both. And if it's both, then how might you best work with it?

There's the standard idea that transference means feelings towards a significant person in the patient's life being transferred onto the analyst. However, it's not as straightforward as saying that if you love your Dad you'll also love your male analyst. Transference might equally mobilise unconscious feelings so that, if you think you love your Dad, you might find yourself hating your male analyst because he has become a target for all the disavowed bad feeling directed at your father. Equally, you might form an erotic attachment to your female analyst, re-enacting the lost, loving counterpart to your hostile feelings towards your mother. And of course, your female analyst might appear to take on the qualities of your father, or your male analyst your mother. Or both, at different times, or even simultaneously. It's far from a straightforward process. To make this even worse, there's also the question of why it happens at all. Is it just because the analysand is in a semi-intimate situation with someone who shows signs of caring about them? They mistake their analyst for an important, emotionally invested person because they are somehow being "looked after" by them? Or is it something else? While Freud sees that a patient's feelings towards their analyst might be triggered by their somehow being reminded of the people who *really* matter to them—mums, dads, sisters, and so on—the key thing you've got to be attentive to is this "something else".

Freud spends a great deal of time in his lecture describing the difficulties of analytic work, the main one being that the pathogenic material is unconscious. Any treatment that aims to bring out disavowed thoughts and feelings is bound to run into all sorts of difficulties. There's the question of what would induce a person to do something that their ego fundamentally objects to. The main reason Freud finds for a person to give up their reluctance to "go there" is that the suffering caused by the symptom outweighs the unpleasantness of having to confront the suspect material. But that would, of course, be far too easy and logical, as Freud and Breuer discovered in their early work. They may have wanted to believe that their patients were so relieved to be allowed to think and feel the things they secretly thought and felt that they would drop all their nonsense and get better immediately, but this was what consistently *didn't* happen. (Although, when you read those early texts it can sometimes look like as though it did.) This put Breuer off and made Freud more interested. He noticed that you couldn't just make interpretations and expect people to accept them. Even if they accepted them in theory, the "clever" ideas might just sit there, parallel to the unconscious material, which would remain totally unaffected. You also couldn't cure people by encouraging them to act out their fantasies directly—to have anal sex, or suck toes, or whatever. If you wanted to dismantle the symptom in such a way as to make it unlikely that it would quickly re-emerge in some new form, you had to bring the repressed material to light in a much more delicate manner. You had somehow to make it possible for the patient to access it of their own free will, not as an imposition from outside. Then they could decide for themselves what to do about it.

The thing Freud noticed about transferential effects was that they were liable to take wild swerves. A person might suddenly go from hating to loving you, or vice versa, without your necessarily knowing why. As far as you can tell, you haven't done anything different but, for the analysand, everything has changed. The explanation Freud gives for these sudden and surprising effects has to do with resistance. In the initial stages of analytic work you're just trying to make it possible for the patient to speak and to think; to start finding points of access to the things they *really* need to talk about. If all goes well, they'll find you worth speaking to and will continue to produce interesting, relevant material. The problem with this is that, by trying to help themselves, and you, by doing the work well, they are liable to lay the unacceptable material at risk of being exposed. This is a very destabilising position for a person to find themselves in. The forces at work in them that keep repression in place are liable to fight against the forces that threaten to unleash the beast. Still, once the cat is halfway out of the bag it becomes much harder to conceal the fact that there's a cat in there, so one of the available options is to release the half-cat and pretend that it was only ever a two-legged creature in the first place. According to Freud, this would very likely be the exact moment at which you'd get a sudden eruption of transferential passion, whether it's love or hate. The patient has stumbled into a situation where they've found themselves obliged to deliver some of the pathogenic material over to their analyst and, at that precise moment, they become hyper-aware of the analyst's being. They may suddenly become inhibited, whereas before they were chatty and outspoken. They may find reasons to dislike or mistrust their analyst. Or they might fall madly in love with them and insist that the work has to stop so that they can pursue a relationship. Whatever form the transference takes, the flow is interrupted and the back end of the cat—the more disturbing half—is kept firmly out of view.

This idea of transference as a form of resistance is taken up by Lacan in *Seminar XI, The Four Fundamental Concepts of Psycho-Analysis (1963–1964)* (1986). Whereas in post-Freudian literature transference is generally presented as a form of repetition, Lacan insists on this other dimension—a major disruption. Instead of seeing it as a useful re-enactment of precisely the stuff you need to know about, Lacan takes up the *other* Freudian idea; that a key feature of the transference is its capacity to obscure things. This leads to a major divergence in analytic technique. If you think of the transference as a form of repetition you might be inclined to take it seriously and to investigate it thoroughly. But if you see it as interference you would be more likely to play down its importance and to continue to focus your interest on the material it attempts to conceal.

In Freud's *Introductory Lectures*, he moves from speaking about transference as interference to the transformation of a neurosis into a "transference neurosis". According to Freud, once the patient has taken this strange swerve away from the unconscious material, directing their attention towards the analyst, the neurosis takes on a wholly new form. Instead of the old configuration of symptoms and the unconscious forces that produce them, you get a new situation whereby the analyst becomes the focus of the symptomatic behaviour. If the analysand is in love with you, you analyse the love. If they're afraid of you, you analyse the fear, and so on. Freud even claims that memories and childhood events vanish into the distance at this point. You're left with the analytic relationship in whatever form it has suddenly taken. If you can properly get to the bottom of this intense manifestation of transference, the patient will be truly and lastingly cured. (Fifteen years later, in the *New Introductory Lectures*, he revises his ideas yet again, in a considerably more pessimistic direction …)

So, it would seem that Freud himself swore by interpreting the trans-ference—in fact believed that this technique was absolutely central to any kind of stable cure.

Interpreting the transference

Famously, analysts of a more British persuasion use a technique called "interpreting the transference" whereby the analyst tries to name what he or she thinks is going on between themselves and their analysand (as parodied in the *Smack The Pony* sketch). Ostensibly, one of the reasons for doing this is to reduce the patient's paranoia. Rather than wildly imagining what might be going on in the consulting room, the patient has it all spelled out for them: "You think I'm angry with you", "You think I want to get rid of you", "You're saying that because you want to make me angry". Keeping bad feeling above board supposedly stops it going underground and ruining everything.

For Kleinians, transference may not be spoken about in terms of repetition so much as "splitting" and "projective identification". The patient projects their own state of mind onto the analyst; if they're feel-ing angry and aggressive towards their analyst they might imagine that their analyst has angry and aggressive feelings towards *them*. By this same process your patients might imagine that you are in love with them, that you want to take something away from them, or any num-ber of other possibilities. Complications arose when certain of Klein's group—primarily Paula Heimann—took the idea a little further. Instead of saying simply that the patient projected thoughts and feelings *onto* the analyst, you now had the idea of projecting *into*; the analyst receives the ideas and sensations and feels them too. If the patient is boiling with rage, the analyst will be infected with their emotion. Klein evidently believed this was an unhelpful clinical direction as it meant that cer-tain practitioners might think their own feelings towards their patients were somehow thrust there from outside, and weren't in fact their own business. If they disliked their patient or were frustrated by him, it was because the patient had projected these feelings into the analyst, not because the analyst had some questions to answer for herself.

In Paula Heimann's paper "On Counter-Transference" (1950) she presents a brief clinical vignette. A divorced, promiscuous man goes into analysis. At the very beginning of the work, he tries to seduce her, but of course she doesn't go with it. He suddenly gets engaged to a woman he's just met. Heimann feels extremely anxious about it, especially when he describes his fiancée as having "had a rough passage". Of all the many possible associations to this phrase, Heimann chooses to focus on the idea of its relating to her own status as a refugee. The man has a dream about buying a secondhand car, but there's someone trying to persuade him not to do it. Heimann interprets this dream as being about her, and tells us he "spontaneously" identified her with the car. Her choice of adjective sounds disingenuous—the more obvious reading is surely that the fiancée is the car, and the analyst is the naysayer. The man explains that, in the dream, he has to confuse this other person so he can get on with fixing the car. You could argue that he very successfully confuses Heimann. In her own mind, she is the desirable (if faulty) car, rather than the frustrating advisor. She believes her anxiety is caused by the patient's capacity for self-destructive acting out. To a reader, it's hard not to wonder whether it's caused by something more like the patient's readiness to replace her with another woman. Happily, however, she doesn't believe that analysts should interpret the countertransference back to the patient, just that they should be attentive to it as it may tell them something they need to know.

Still, if the feelings are completely misattributed, how helpful can they be? In 1951 Lacan offers a damning definition of the countertransference as, "the sum total of the analyst's biases, passions, and difficulties, or even of his inadequate information at any given moment in the dialectical process" ("Presentation on Transference", 2006, p. 183/225). Reading Heimann's paper ungenerously, this seems particularly pertinent. However, Lacan isn't altogether dismissive of the idea that one's feelings towards one's patients might sometimes be relevant. In 1953 he concedes that, "it is up to [the analyst] to take [their own feelings] into account in an appropriate manner, to be guided by [them] as by an extra needle on the dial" (1988, p. 32). They can't tell you everything you need to know, but that doesn't mean they tell you nothing.

This can perhaps be contrasted with Melanie Klein's pronouncement on countertransference at a Wellcome meeting in 1958:

> [...] to be able really to accept that, now, I see very mean traits in the patient, that he really is out to get everything out of me that he can, that his attitude is really one in which he gets out of people what he can and then turns away, perhaps even maligns them—is not easy. [...] If we see such character traits worked out against ourselves, and instead of feeling, "Now I can't bear this patient, and that

proves that he is this or that". If instead I really feel, "Well I want to study him, if he is so greedy, so envious, that is part of his psychology, that is why he came to me, and is what I want to understand," then there is another element, not only empathy, and it is the wish to know. Now the wish to know, I think, is a very important thing in being analyst; the wish to explore the mind whatever the mind is like. (Klein Archive, C72)

On the surface, it might appear much like Lacan's position: there's no problem with the analyst having feelings towards the patient and acknowledging them, as long as the desire of the analyst is stronger than the wish to get little satisfactions from acting out love or hate scenarios. But Klein's conceptualisation of the problem is not quite the same. She also says, at the same meeting, "I never found that the counter-transference has helped me to understand my patient better; if I may put it like this, I have found that it helped me to understand myself better" (C72, Klein, 1958). And then again:

I cannot find a case established, that counter-transference is to be a guide towards understanding the patient, I cannot see the logic of that; because it obviously has to do with the state of mind of the analyst, whether he is less or more liable to be put out, to be annoyed, to be disappointed, to get anxious, to dislike somebody strongly, or to like somebody strongly. (C72, Klein, 1958)

Maybe her vehemence has as much to do with her relationship with Paula Heimann as anything coolly theoretical. As such, it's yet another transferential effect. Still, Klein's idea is that an analyst must put their feelings to one side in order to do their job properly; no one has been so immaculately analysed that they can be one hundred percent sure they can read situations correctly rather than through the distorting lens of their own neurosis. Therefore, for Klein, an analyst must act as though they aren't swayed by feelings, and then go and deal with these feelings in private later.

In spite of strong counter-arguments, Heimann's ideas have stuck around and are relied on by many contemporary practitioners. There are plenty of accredited therapists who believe that they receive authentic communiqués from their analysands through the airwaves. At a large psychoanalytic meeting, involving practitioners of various persuasions,

I heard a woman stand up and say that she knew when she'd made a really accurate interpretation because she could feel her internal anal sphincter open up. While it may sound outlandish to the uninitiated, the last laugh might be on us if research into mirror neurons eventually tells us that this sort of thing can be explained by hard science ...

Transference and countertransference in Lacanian clinical practice

Reading about countertransference can leave an analyst feeling paranoid about every aspect of their being. In Heinrich Racker's *Transference and Countertransference* (1988)—an overview of the various theories of transference—countertransferential effects are theorised and scrutinised. As an analyst, whoever you are, you will always fall short of the ideal. Your personal flaws and unconscious prejudices will be bound to wreak havoc in your practice. It's undoubtedly a fact that your training analysis has let you down in a number of places. Thinking about countertransference from certain perspectives is liable to lead to super-egoic meltdown. In Racker's book—much-read by training analysts—there's a huge focus on naming and interpreting the affects associated with the phenomenon, backed up by examples of analysts whose personal failings have got them into deep water.

In Lacanian analysis, one certainly isn't encouraged to work with the countertransference, but this is different from saying that you don't need to take it seriously. While you might not be using it to inform the bulk of your interpretations, you would be foolish to try to ignore the inevitable likes, dislikes, sleepinesses, and anxieties triggered in you by your analysands. The work seems to be to keep it out of the way without denying it, and also without imagining one has to strive for an unachievable level of mental hygiene. Likewise with transference. If people tell you about the feelings, thoughts, and fantasies they have about you, the idea certainly isn't to change the subject as fast as possible. It's just that transferential and countertransferential material isn't privileged over anything else a person might bring to their session.

During fourteen years of working analytically I'd say I'd only had two bad experiences, but these were extremely bad, both for me and for the other person. In each instance it was plain in retrospect that the things that finally went awry were being presented and articulated in various ways right from the beginning. I have often asked myself whether forceful transference interpretations could have saved the day.

What if I had tackled the person about this or that at the time? Would it have set things off on a different, better track? Psychoanalytic work can sometimes be extremely turbulent, but is there any super-idea that can promise to ease the terror? Transference interpretations can sometimes seem like a kind of über-technique that promises to hold things in place. It brings to mind Erica Jong's idea that there are no atheists on bumpy flights. When things get tricky, does one necessarily have to put one's faith in this hoary old trick? If everything's being brought out into the open the whole time, is it really true that it can't spring out and attack you? If the analysand's envy/hate/neediness has been named, does it therefore follow that it will be tamed?

At first glance it might seem that Freud's essay on transference in the *Introductory Lectures* (1917d) explicitly recommends the Anglo Saxon way, and that Lacan is therefore at odds with Freud. But perhaps it's not exactly like that. According to Lacan, transference appears as a key moment in the dialectic between analyst and analysand, both of whom are being altered and affected by the treatment. Isn't this rather like the phenomenon described by Freud, who speaks about the moment in the analysis when transference strikes? In *Seminar IV, The Object Relation (1956–1957)*, Lacan brings out both the helpful and unhelpful dimensions. On the one hand, you have transference as repetition, which he puts on the side of the symbolic. On the other you have love and hate for the analyst as a form of resistance, and very much on the side of the imaginary. Still, in *Seminar XI* we are told, "[…] the concept of repetition has nothing to do with the concept of transference". Just because Lacan says something in one place doesn't mean he won't totally contradict it in another.

Many post-Freudians have run into all sorts of difficulty regarding how exactly to theorise transference. Does it cover *all* feelings directed at the analyst, or just unconscious ones? Or maybe it refers only to "unrealistic" ones? Racker's book, for example, has a great deal to say about "realistic" and "unrealistic" relations to the analyst. According to more conservative conceptions of analysis (perhaps especially ego psychology and its derivatives) the analyst is there to get the patient back in touch with reality. Transference interpretations might aim at this by demonstrating to the patient that his or her ideas about their analyst are phantasies, completely at odds with the facts. You can perhaps see how transference interpretations would lend themselves particularly well to this sort of approach. Unlike the other characters in the analysand's life, the analyst has *some* knowledge of what she thinks and feels about her patient. If he wrongly imputes feelings to her, she can "correct" him, thereby bringing him round to a more realistic understanding. The problem, for Lacan, with all of this is that it relies on a naïve notion of "reality". One's own sense of reality only exists, in Lacanian theory at least, thanks to the operations of the ego, which is, in itself, a fictitious entity. Trying to induce another person to accept what you consider to be "reality" is simply to attempt to subordinate them to your ego. Therefore "acceptance of reality" can't possibly be the aim of a psychoanalytic cure.

Still, this doesn't entirely rule out transference interpretations. In Seminar I, *Freud's Papers on Technique, (1953–1954)*, Lacan speaks about knowing how to use the feelings one has for one's patients in one's practice:

> No one has ever said that the analyst should never have feelings towards his patient. But he must know not only not to give into them, to keep them in their place, but also how to make adequate use of them in his technique. (1988, p. 32)

In this section of the seminar, Lacan is speaking about Margaret Little's famous paper "Counter-transference and the Patient's Response to it" (1951). As ever, Lacan slips between remembering Little's text and misremembering and misrepresenting it. One minute he appears correctly to recall that it is presented as a semi-fictionalised story about a male analyst and his male analysand. Next minute he is referring to Margaret Little's interpretation, as if she is the analyst in the story ("Margaret Little brought the subject back to a sense of the unity of his ego", p. 31). Some years after the publication of the essay she revealed that the patient was in fact herself and that the "experienced male analyst" was Ella Sharpe, who had been her training analyst. She is quite critical of the analyst's behaviour in the case, referring to a key intervention as "inappropriate". In the disguised case study, the patient has given a presentation on the radio shortly after his mother's death. This presentation was apparently on a subject of great interest to his analyst. In spite of being in a state of deep mourning, the man managed to pull himself together and do a good job. When he turns up to his next session in a state of shock, the analyst interprets this as being to do with the man's fear that his analyst will resent him for encroaching on his precious subject area. Amazingly, the patient accepted the interpretation and quickly felt much better. It hardly takes a trained practitioner to see that this interpretation is just as likely to have named the truth of the analyst's feelings as the analysand's. Nonetheless both Little and Lacan concede that this sort of interpretation needn't be a disaster. One doesn't have to name an objective truth in order to see therapeutic effects. Little puts these effects down to oedipal resonances—which only became apparent to the patient two years later—while Lacan attributes the instant calming effect to the idea that, *"Here is someone who points out to me that indeed everything is much of a muchness and that life goes on"* (1988, p. 31, italics in the original). Neither of them claims that the analyst got it all wrong, just that they came at things from a rather bizarre angle.

So why do people with Lacanian trainings so often have the idea that the transference is an absolute no-go in terms of interpretation? It would appear, from reading Lacan, that he considers it one subject among many that might be broached in the treatment. The thing *not* to do is to impose transference interpretations systematically, refusing to give the analysand anywhere to go other than to agree. He speaks about analysts who think they should look primarily in the here and now, comparing this with certain marital discussions (ibid, p. 30). When a spouse comes home and shouts and rants about a third party, the listening partner can choose whether to take what they say at face value, or to see that the accusations, recriminations, and general ill-temper might also be directed at them. Perhaps especially if the angry spouse is telling the story largely in the second person: "And I said to Adrian, 'You're useless. You never listen. You don't care about anyone but yourself!'" and so on. One has to be careful if one chooses to take the invective personally, but equally you'd be missing a trick if you thought it was really all about Adrian. Being able to take both possibilities into account would seem to be key to a viable marriage. If you *always* think it's about you then your partner might, understandably, stop telling you things. Alternatively, the two of you might sink into an endless quagmire of "talking about us"—"us" being the only subject you seem able to take seriously. The problem isn't in seeing that a person's communications on other subjects might relate back to something nearer to home, but in insisting on this always and only being the case. As Lacan says, "What is serious is to [... believe ... oneself] authorised by a certain technique to make use of it straightaway and in a direct manner" (ibid, p. 32)

In his "Presentation on Transference" (2006 [1951]) Lacan discusses the mess Freud made of the Dora case, and puts it down to Freud's countertransference. He was apparently too identified with certain figures in the story, and too interested in Dora herself. Her negative transference—which causes her to storm out of the treatment—emerges at a moment of stuckness. There's nowhere in the discourse for Dora to go. She finds herself confronted with what Lacan calls "the permanent modes according to which she constitutes her objects", (2006, pp. 184/225) treating Freud as she would any other annoying guy. Lacan asks, "What does it mean to interpret the transference? Nothing but to fill the emptiness of this standstill with a lure. But even though it is deceptive, this lure serves a purpose by setting the whole process in motion anew" (2006, pp. 184/226).

In other words, a transference interpretation might sometimes be a brilliant thing, not because it reveals a truth to the patient, but because it might introduce an interesting idea or open up something new to speak about. It may even do this better if it's a bit "wrong". Then you'll definitely have something to talk about. But it's most likely to work if it isn't rote and systematic but instead injects an element of surprise. For Lacanian practitioners, transference interpretations can be a doubly great tactic; not only do you have the possibility of a jolt brought about by the content, but perhaps also from the person's astonishment that you're making a transference interpretation at all.

Lacan and the subject supposed to know

Lacanian commentators sometimes say confusing things like, "Freud noted that there was no transference to the subject supposed to know in psychosis" (p. 78, Jean-Louis Gault, "Two Statuses of the Symptom", *The Later Lacan*, 2007) It's easy to laugh about the anachronistic idea that Freud was *au fait* with Lacanian jargon, using it deferentially. Of course, Freud would have thought that Lacan was just wonderful, and would have swallowed his lexicon wholesale. Still, perhaps more bewildering is the idea of there somehow being "no transference".

The notion that there is a problem with transference in cases of psychosis does indeed come from Freud, who had the idea that it would be inappropriate to attempt analytic work with people who were floridly psychotic. Still, he didn't maintain that psychotic people can't experience transference. The question is whether they are capable of the kinds of transference that make analytic work possible. In the Schreber case Freud discusses the psychotic judge's transference to Doctor Flechsig. He describes how Schreber's disavowed sexual feelings for his father and brother appear to have been transferred onto his physician, and explains how this underpins certain of his delusional ideas. Schreber's friendly feelings towards his doctor, according to Freud, are built out of his feelings of fondness for his father and brother. Schreber "rediscovers" the figures of his father and brother in the doctor. At the same time, it seems, he also rediscovers something of his disavowed sexual wishes, and these are extremely distasteful to him. Instead of acknowledging his erotic feelings towards Doctor Flechsig, he turns them around so that the doctor desires *him*—and in this way Flechsig becomes his persecutor.

The moment where the physician suddenly becomes the villain is typical of psychotic transference. When you work with paranoid patients you have to be prepared to deal with the fact that one day they might very well develop the idea that you are somehow out to get them. While it would clearly be incorrect to say that there is no transference in psychosis, it would be very true to say that psychotic transference *can* be extremely difficult to work with.

While in Freud's work the word "transference" was used to mean feelings about one person being transferred to another and, later on, feelings about other people being transferred onto the analyst, for Lacan it's more to do with knowledge. The patient invests the analyst with a knowledge he or she doesn't actually have; a knowledge of the patient's unconscious.

The "subject supposed to know" is an idea that's introduced in *Seminar IX, Identification (1961–1962)* and developed in *Seminar XI, The Four Fundamental Concepts of Psychoanalysis (1963–1964)*. It refers to the notion that the patient imputes a knowledge to the analyst and that this supposition sends the patient to work. Because the person thinks the analyst knows something about his or her unconscious, it makes them more attentive to it themselves. If you have the notion that your analyst can hear something beyond the obvious meanings of the things you say, then maybe you start to listen out for it too (or try wildly to defend yourself against it).

This may not happen straight away. Or it might. The idea is just that, by the end of the analysis, the analysand has worked out that the analyst doesn't know anything more than they do. Of course that doesn't mean the analyst is licensed to be a passive idiot. They have at least to try a little to earn the role assigned to them by the patient. They shouldn't do this by being a smart aleck, trying to prove they know everything—if they attempt this they will soon get something wrong and fall from grace—but by listening extremely carefully and responding in ways that suggest they've actually heard something. One might do this by showing an interest and asking more, noting an oddity, or checking whether one has understood something well.

In analytic work, one deals with neurotics and psychotics very differently. With neurotics, in the words of Lacan, the treatment involves "inducing in the subject a guided paranoia" (2006, p. 89). The analyst appears to know something about the patient, who must get the situation back under control by coming to know what the analyst knows. Psychotics may be paranoid enough already, so you would be attempting to help them get a handle on this from the start—or at least not to make their paranoia any worse. Still, it's not simply about what you are trying to do with your patients, but what they are trying to do with you. Psychotics may insist on seeing you as the perfectly enigmatic Sphinx who inscrutably coaxes out their "secrets" (while you may think you're being quite relaxed and chatty) and neurotics might rigidly stick to sense-making and problem-solving however much you try to nudge them towards murkier waters.

The idea that there's no transference to a subject supposed to know in psychosis is completely contradicted by experience, but to try to unpick what Jean-Louis Gault might be attempting to get at, he appears to be arguing that Freud thought psychotic people wouldn't be helpfully inclined to imbue the psychoanalyst with a prior knowledge of their unconscious—in the way that neurotic people supposedly do. Apparently, while psychotic subjects might have a transference of the old-fashioned sort—Dr Flechsig is a bit like my Dad, so I fancy him like my Dad, so I hate him like I hate myself for fancying my Dad—they purportedly *don't* have a Lacanian-style transference which would involve believing that the analyst knows precisely what all their dreams and slips of the tongue mean and is sitting on the information while they work it out for themselves. Gault goes on to say, "For all that, Lacan nonetheless insists that there exists a psychotic transference, though it is of a particular kind. It is an erotomaniac and persecutory transference." In other words, psychotics won't be sent to work by the idea that they need to find out what you know. Instead they may think that *they* already know what goes on in *your* mind (that you are secretly in love with them or that you want to harm them). They may also believe you can see right into them, and try desperately to defend themselves against this. So, there might be a transference to a very literal subject supposed to know in psychosis, but you have to be careful how you work with it. You could even say that the subject isn't *supposed* to know, but *known* to know, which is far more serious.

If you behave in an overly enigmatic way with a paranoiac subject it may very well be a disaster. They will fill up any blanks with their own theories about your intentions towards them. They may feel completely invaded by your presumed knowledge and be very upset with you about it. The fact that you appear to them to know everything means you can mistreat and/or have power over them, which they might, understandably, object to. So, you see time after time that there is *absolutely* a subject supposed to know in the transference with a psychotic. It's just that you can't make use of it. To put it crudely—you can't sit there, shut up and see what they do. You might even say that Lacan's theory of the subject supposed to know *is* a theory of psychotic transference. Psychotic treatments are the ones where you might expect really to see evidence of the idea that the patient comes along believing that the analyst has intimate knowledge of them.

The uncanny

Prince of Wales Drawing School, 2014

The subject of robots has particular relevance to psychoanalysts, for reasons I'll try to explain. I hope it's also pertinent to people who are interested in drawing, especially to people who are interested in representational drawing, which I believe is a particular concern of the Prince's Drawing School. I understand that Prince Charles is worried by the idea of an erosion of tradition in contemporary art trainings. It's easy to laugh about his fusty ways. It can all sound a bit cosy—a flat rejection of art where you might not know where the work begins and ends, nor why it was made; art that might seem disturbing, pointless or confusing. In response to that, I wanted to try to speak about some potentially troubling aspects of realistic representations.

I would say I was a fairly typical product of a contemporary art training in that I think art can be pretty much anything, but I did get there from drawing as a starting point. There's a book called *Drawing on the Right Side of the Brain* (1983), by Betty Edwards, which was very popular in the 1980s. It tells you to look freshly and not make assumptions about what you're seeing. If you think you already know what a chair or an ear looks like you will confuse a generic chair or ear with the very particular one in front of you, coming up with something wonky and cartoon-like rather than accurately observed. This advice works just

163

as well for psychoanalysts and writers; don't take anything for granted and never assume prior knowledge. My experiences of representational drawing, and ways of thinking about drawing, were very helpful for the work I came to do later.

The uncanny valley

"The uncanny valley" is a term coined by the Japanese roboticist, Masahiro Mori (2012), in an essay published in 1970. Mori explores some of the phenomena Freud describes in his famous work on the uncanny: moving dolls, disembodied hands and the sense of dread evoked by anything quasi-human. Mori's essay delineates a zone between the charmingly "lifelike" and the frighteningly "deathlike", with skilful puppet shows at one end and menacing androids at the other. He argues that people enjoy seeing animated figures up to a certain point, but when they become too realistic they start to appear frightening.

The Freudian uncanny has arguably been chronically over-mined. As people at art school in the 1990s used to say: "The uncanny needs a holiday. It's been working too hard." Mori provides a new take on an old theme, at least for psychoanalysts. Maybe people who work in computer imaging have exhausted the uncanny valley as much as we have Freud's text. In the movie world, apparently, it's important to establish whether or not an animated film accidentally falls into the "yuck" zone. *Polar Express*, for example, was deemed too realistic, but also not quite realistic enough. This, apparently, makes it creepy. Pixar have consistently chosen to be "unrealistic" in their use of CGI after a bad reaction to a short film they made in 1988. Since then a number of their films have featured humanoid figures, but in each case are so stylised as to avoid any unnerving effects.

It isn't clear whether Mori read Freud or not—nor whether he read Ernst Jentsch, who wrote about the uncanny before Freud, and who is credited with introducing the term. Mori seems to be more in agreement with Jentsch than with Freud in that he's not overtly interested in sex, only death. This, one might say, is the problem with a great deal of the contemporary research going on in the areas of fright and fear. Terror Management Theory (TMT), for instance, posits the idea that the main reason people do pretty much *anything* is that they're afraid of death. That's why we eat, work, and have friends. The reason we have sex is also because we're afraid of death, so sex is secondary. (TMT theorists appear to believe that sex is primarily to do with reproduction.) This undoubtedly makes sense, perhaps too much so. By appearing unarguably self-evident these theories risk drowning out any need for complexity. At the other end of the scale, Freud's argument is so knotty as to be virtually unsummarisable.

The Freudian uncanny

Freud essay starts with an extremely long definition of the word "*unheimlich*", which literally means "unhomely" in English. He then shows that it doesn't exactly have an opposite in the word "*heimlich*"—in fact the two words can be used interchangeably. Sometimes "*heimlich*" is used to mean something hidden and a bit off limits; your "*heimlich*" parts would be your genitals. Likewise, unheimlich doesn't simply mean unfamiliar and odd, but also maybe *too* familiar.

Freud goes on to discuss E. T. A. Hoffmann's tale of "The Sandman" (1816), and the question of whether something is dead or alive. In the story, the hero falls in love with a lovely woman, Olympia, who turns out to be a life-sized doll. Dolls and automata regularly feature in tales of the uncanny. But why? Children often like the idea of their toys coming to life, and might even believe it to be possible. For Freud, however, the fact that children like it and think it could actually happen isn't an argument against the same idea causing uncanny effects—especially in later life. Still, Freud thinks Olympia is more of a comic interlude and that the really creepy thing about Hoffman's story is the way the Sandman meddles with people's eyes. Freud links the risk of loss of eyesight with castration, the Sandman being a version of the bad father who messes with the son and gets in the way of his ever having a satisfactory sexual relationship with a woman. He also discusses doubles and likenesses in relation to castration. When you have two of something, if someone takes one away then it doesn't matter so much. This needn't just apply to penises but also to your whole self, death being the ultimate castration. One way to outstrip mortality is to have two of yourself, so doubles and likenesses are linked with the wish to cheat death. Realistic portraits and Egyptian coffins also stand as testimony to this.

However, while we might think we know we don't want to die, the roots of the wish to keep living, according to Freud, are bound up with primary narcissism—an early psychic stage most of us are eventually persuaded to overcome. Hence doubles and likenesses are associated with a phase we might rather forget. You can see it's not as simple as saying that we don't want to die because we're programmed to ensure species survival. Wanting to live, for humans, isn't simply "good", "right" or "nice". This is because it's a wish informed by primary narcissism. This early state gets knocked about by the later wish to be loved and accepted, the fulfilment of which most often involves the giving up of being a megalomaniacal monster. It's never altogether clear to us whether wanting to live is simply a good thing, or whether it's also potentially deeply shameful. Plenty of stories deal with exactly this problem; what does it mean to die for love or for a greater cause? Is it good or bad to value yourself? What's your importance in relation to others? Are other lives sometimes more valuable than one's own? (See Snape in *Harry Potter*, Jack in *Titanic*, the heroic GIs in *Saving Private Ryan*.) These questions invoke all sorts of other problems around envy, rivalry, and destructiveness—the things a person is bound to feel in relation to those they've grown up around, or been socialised in relation to. Do we ever fully accept the laws that civilise us, or is there always a little part of even the most decent human being that resists? While we might consider self-sacrifice one of the most beautiful human acts, it also risks appearing comical or ridiculous, hence the much-parodied raft scene at the end of *Titanic*. Surely Jack briefly considered tipping Rose off the plank? Or was he actually getting a kick out of acting subordinate? Wasn't she just pretending not to have any space on board because she was getting a narcissistic buzz out of watching a man die for love? Human beings are fundamentally perverse, and might very well choose dying over living, or suffering over happiness, badness over goodness, and so on.

To compress the essay into something really short and stupid, Freud goes on to show how all sorts of things that might have appealed to us at one point become uncanny due to repression. Enclosed spaces are frightening because they remind us of our mother's womb (a space we might unconsciously long for). People whose wishes come true are spooky because of the long-since-abandoned infantile notion of omnipotence of thought. The idea of the evil eye is the same. So, not dying, being comfortable, and getting what you want are all, in this context, extremely problematic. Everything the pleasure principle might lead us to hope for risks being tinged with horror and disgust.

So that's the Freudian uncanny. As a theory, it's jam packed with all the things that people find annoying, unpalatable, unprovable, and counter-intuitive about psychoanalysis.

The uncanny valley

To move on to a modern and popular incarnation of the uncanny, Masahiro Mori's essay discusses what people do and don't like about robots. He designs a graph to describe it. It's quite a poetic graph, not drawn from statistical research, more a pictorial way of getting a point across. On one side, you have an industrial robot, and on the other, a human being. The "valley" refers to a deep dip in the graph at the point at which robots start to look too human, but also not quite human enough. Still, Mori does preserve a place on the far side of the valley, an ideal point at which robots might become so human that we'd start to like them again. Mori doesn't recommend aiming for this point; he thinks roboticists would be better off aiming for the high slope on the near side. This is because, in the 1970s, as now, people don't have a hope in hell of hitting the far side with a moving robot.

The same would go for prosthetic hands. If they get too good, people are shocked when they discover that the hand isn't real. Mori also states, along with Freud, that people hate to see a hand moving on its own. Mori therefore recommends that amputees use unrealistic wooden hands so they don't risk giving anyone a fright. He ends his essay saying that a living person is a lovely thing, at the peak of the moving line, but that as soon as we die we fall into the "trough of the uncanny". This is his explanation for the horror people feel on seeing realistic automata—they remind us too much of corpses.

It's a charming, humanistic essay but, as a theory, it's far more one-dimensional than Freud's. Fear of death equals fear of robots. Still, the problems really begin with the fact that the essay speaks about an area of life that has enormous financial, ethical, and political implications. It's not just the makers of industrial robots who are interested in it. The Cognitive Science Society published an essay titled "Androids as an Experimental Apparatus: why is there an uncanny valley and can we exploit it?" (Karl F. MacDorman, 2005). The author tries to work out, in the first place, whether Mori's hypothesis is correct. MacDorman takes ideas from Terror Management Theory (TMT), which was developed by a group of psychologists in the late 1990s. TMT revolves around ideas about how human beings manage their fear of personal extinction. Like all animals and plants, we mostly seem to try to avoid dying, developing life-sustaining behaviours accordingly. But, supposedly unlike other creatures, we are conscious of our own mortality. So, what do we do with thoughts about death? We either push them out of our minds, or counterbalance them with comforting stories, like that our grandparents lived to be a hundred and two, or that modern medicine is very advanced. But we also experience what the TMT people call "nonconscious" thoughts about death. ("Nonconscious" as opposed to "unconscious" to create distance from Freud, perhaps.) The responses to these are more complex because we have to deal with the unwanted reminder without our defences actually reminding us of what we're trying to forget. (Sound familiar? Of course, to anyone crazy enough to think Freud's still worth reading.) In modern psychology, these are christened "distal defences", meaning defences that are remote from the point of origin. So, a classic distal defence against a subliminal reminder of death would be something that supports the idea of existence as orderly, permanent, continuous, and meaningful, coupled with the idea that you can symbolically transcend death by aligning yourself with the forces that that support structure, permanence and stability. If your family and your country can be seen as permanent, you can somehow ensure your own continuation by adhering to the standards of your culture, and making sure your family does too.

According to the *Cognitive Science* essay, any nonconscious reminder of death will activate these distal defences. TMT people call this the "mortality salience hypothesis". One consequence of this is that if you are subliminally reminded of death you will immediately become more nationalistic, at least until you've annulled the threat in your mind. The TMTers have performed more than two hundred experiments supporting this idea. For example, the word "death" is flashed up on a screen for a split second in the middle of a film about something supposedly harmless, after which a control group and an experimental group are shown two letters from foreign exchange students, one criticising the group's homeland, the other saying how much they like it. The subjects are then asked which exchange student they prefer. The idea is that the experimental group will show a more marked preference for the student who admires their homeland than the control group. Apparently, this consistently proves to be the case. Another experiment involves the subjects being shown two politicians' speeches—one by a charismatic, nationalistic leader, and one by a relationship-oriented leader (who said he'd listen to people). The death-reminded people tend to go in for the nationalist more frequently.

Karl MacDorman's addition to all this is to see whether a human-like robot elicits the same distal defences as a flash sighting of the word "death". In order to work this out, the subjects of his experiment were shown four photographs: a head, a piece of wire, some coffee creamer, and a pair of headphones. The only difference between the control group and the experimental group was that the head in the latter case belonged to a very human-like robot, while the control group saw a picture of a real woman in a very similar pose. Subjects were then asked about the foreign exchange students, the politicians, and also to fill in words with missing letters, like COFF_ _ or MUR_ _R. Would they see COFFEE or COFFIN, MURMUR or MURDER? The experimental group would be expected to choose the death-related words more often. The results of the experiment showed that they did (although not massively more than the control group). After the experiment, participants were asked about the photos. They largely agreed that the humanoid robot was scary.

You can see it's all a little bit Freudian in the sense that "nonconscious" ideas bring about surprising results. But it's very un-Freudian in trying to homogenise these effects, suggesting that all humans react in similar ways to the same stimuli, like similarly programmed robots. The thing that's sinister about the paper is given away by the title. If you think you can establish that most people will react in a certain way, then perhaps you also think you can manipulate people accordingly. In this case, you could aim to exploit the uncanny valley effect by reminding people of death on their way into a polling station, thereby "programming" them to support a right-wing candidate. On the bright side, the results of the experiment weren't particularly persuasive—not everyone becomes a fascist on reading the word "death"—but of course we hardly need to be reminded that when people are very frightened or worried they become susceptible to submitting to terrible, authoritarian leaders.

Dead behind the eyes

Stephen Spielberg's *A.I.* is a film about a robot that aims for the far side of the uncanny valley. It's based on a short story, "Super-Toys Last all

Summer Long", by Brian Aldiss, written in 1969, around the same time as Mori's essay. The story deals with robots that promise to help out with the problem of human loneliness. They respond to you, answer your questions and, in the case of the little electronic boy in the movie, actually love you. Like Mori, Brian Aldiss and Steven Spielberg also seem to think this is probably going to end badly. The problem isn't just on the side of humans, who are unlikely to be fully convinced by a machine that has been programmed to respond to them in a particular way. The far greater problem in this story (as in Pinocchio) is on the side of the robot. If it's a properly sophisticated robot, which this one is, then it can't just say "I love you" and not expect anything back. It has to hope for some kind of return, or to register upset if its love isn't recip-rocated. If it doesn't expect to be loved back, then it isn't doing the first part properly and therefore doesn't have a hope of making a dent in the human being's loneliness. It has to be programmed to be desperately needy and vulnerable if it's to have any chance of working at all. But, as it appears in the story, the last thing any person needs or wants is a needy robot hanging about the house trying all its pre-programmed tricks in order to generate love. In the film, the woman takes the robot boy into a forest and abandons him. In the short story the couple are given permission by the state to have a real baby, making the fake child superfluous. The message is that human responses are far too complex to be programmed, and perhaps also that being human is unbearable and you wouldn't wish it on a robot.

Shrinks vs. Siri

Psychoanalysts could be said to position themselves at both extremes of the uncanny valley. On the one hand, they have to be pretty implacable. But then again, they have to be able to inject an element of surprise. One has to demonstrate a certain "aliveness" without stamping one's subjectivity all over the other person. Just following procedure can't possibly go well; you won't seem worth speaking to, but splurging all your own stuff isn't any use either. We have to learn to listen in ways that are both sub-human and superhuman.

In spite of all the warnings against, recent developments in robotics are opening up the possibility of "caring" automatons. Machines are being designed to pick up on gestures and vocal intonations, and to respond accordingly. If a person appears upset or agitated these robots will supposedly know what to do. The main proposed uses for the contraptions are as children's nannies or carers for the elderly. The problem is that children and old people appear to have very different attitudes towards robots; young people are apparently more accepting of the notion, while older people are understandably dubious. Experiments with robots seem to show that older people don't allow themselves to fall for the illusion that the machine they are speaking to has a mind (Carlson & Skubic, 2013). They refuse to "chat" to a robot, preferring to issue it with simple instructions. "Go and get my glasses from the table" is fine; "How are you?" isn't. Children, on the other hand, are more liable to imbue an intelligent, responsive robot with real feelings, going so far as to feel sorry for it if it is left out of a game (Peter Kahn, University of Washington, 2012). They are also often happy to chatter away to computer programs like Siri, leading psychologists to fear we may be at risk of eroding young people's expectations of communication and interaction. If children are content to make do with the low-grade simulation of demand and response provided by a machine, perhaps they, in turn, will find themselves both offering and expecting less sophisticated interactions (Sherry Turkel, *Alone Together: why we expect more from technology and less from each other*, 2013).

Perhaps the question for psychoanalysts is whether our tendency towards spooky unresponsiveness provokes thought and speech in the other person, or not. Will our patients shut down if they don't receive the reaction they might have hoped for? Or will they try harder to articulate themselves? We will presumably be scanning for precisely this sort of difference and adjusting our friendliness and levels of interest accordingly.

Of course, it's not just the analyst who risks being unnervingly machine-like. All people might experience themselves as bizarrely automated, set on trajectories that make little sense, like errant wind-up toys. Lacan describes being called to analysis by a real that always slips away from us. He borrows the word *tuché* from Aristotle, which he translates as "an encounter with the real", and then plays it off against the word *automaton* which is aligned with repetition, i.e., the thing that causes us to make the same mistakes or to act a certain way without really knowing why. The real is necessarily traumatic, an interruption. Through repetition we might try to master it, but always without knowing exactly what it is we're trying to do. That's what gives repetition its automated, unnerving quality. It's impossible to say exactly what's pushing us in that particular direction. Even if we come to find out something about it in analysis it can never be straightforwardly grasped. We might arrive wishing for an encounter that would break the circuit of our repetitions, but discover that the repetitions themselves are a kind of safer version of the thing we can't actually think about or name.

A prime example of this would be Freud's Wolf Man, who falls in love with women in lowly positions and is excited by seeing them on their hands and knees. Freud pushes him towards an event or construction—the "primal scene"—that provides a kind of origin for these later phenomena. The Wolf Man comes up with the idea of himself as a baby watching his father having intercourse with his mother from behind. It's not a memory, but an idea that designates a cause for some of the things that follow. The man can now see himself as "programmed" to find certain situations and images exciting. This is all very well but, as he spent the rest of his life telling anyone who would listen, it far from solves the problem.

We are not robots precisely because we experience our "programming"—with words, images, experiences—as an imposition and a problem, not as a simple state of things. There is always more to us, something that can't be named or tamed, and however much we try to crack the codes of our own existence, the more we are faced with the impossibility of the task.

War

Sana Gallery, Singapore, 2015

The first time I spoke to the artist, Issa Touma (on Skype from Syria) I was struck by his absolute lack of panic. He described his Art Camping project in Aleppo, where volunteers worked with refugees and members of the public to produce artworks. At the time, I found it hard to absorb some of the things he was saying. He spoke about death as something very close and real, but said it all without the slightest hint of drama. It was as if he was talking about making a cup of coffee. He described filming out of his window as war broke out in the street below in such a serene way that I doubted I was understanding him correctly.

After our conversation I saw some of the Art Camping artworks. In 2012, a group of people had walked around the city of Aleppo taking charcoal rubbings from the surfaces of buildings. Many of these buildings have since become targets of attack. From far away, we hear about the seemingly endless losses—people, objects and huge, ancient edifices—leaving us with the sense that there's almost nothing that can't be destroyed. The rubbings appear fragile, but they preserve a trace of something—in fact they have turned out to be more durable than many of the architectural features they document.

People all over the world have been sentimental about buildings in Syria, sometimes appearing to feel more for them than for living Syrians. There is real shock at the destruction of ancient historical monuments, as if it's a step beyond even the destruction of human lives. That's what makes it into the news when the relentless mortalities stop being remarkable enough to report.

In Britain, we learn about Bosra and Palmyra at school, as part of the mainstream history curriculum. We're encouraged to feel ownership of these places as part of the human story—they're not "over there", but are part of *us* and *our* history. Because of their links with the Greeks and Romans and, later, with the Crusades, Syrian cities and landmarks are something people all over the world might feel very close to. Still, that doesn't always translate into feeling close to contemporary Syrians—or at least it appears it can go either way. In Britain, we have a huge "Refugees Welcome" campaign, but then a Government who do little to help. Popular feeling can swing wildly between heart-wrenching sympathy and a paranoid fear of being invaded and losing one's identity. It seems that human beings are difficult to think about, or to know what to do with, while buildings are more straightforward.

Down with buildings

Buildings are important, too, in work of Tadeusz Borowski, a Polish writer, imprisoned at Auschwitz during World War II. For him it's the other way around—he hates them. There's a story called "World of Stone" (1959), published in his collection *This Way for the Gas, Ladies and Gentlemen*, written after the end of the war. It's a brief account of a trip to the bank. Everything seems impermanent to the narrator, except the stone buildings, which appear impervious and anti-human. Through the eyes of the narrator, architecture looks offensively solid in relation to people, who might all go up in smoke.

In another story, "Auschwitz, Our Home", Borowski speaks about how the great ancient buildings were made:

> Only now do I realize what price was paid to build the ancient civilizations. The Egyptian pyramids, the temples and Greek statues— what a hideous crime they were! How much blood must have poured onto the Roman roads, the bulwarks and the city walls. Antiquity, the tremendous concentration camp where the slave was branded on the forehead by his master, and crucified for trying to escape! (p. 131).

On one hand, ancient buildings might signify shared history, a sense of location and identity. On the other they stand as evidence of crimes against the people who actually built them. The architectural achievements that prove our high-mindedness and co-operation as a species might also just as well be considered monuments to vanity, greed, and cruelty. It's yet another reminder of the fact that whatever is great about the human race is very often (if not always) intimately linked to what's terrible.

A gentleman's disagreement

In 1932 Einstein wrote a public letter to Freud as part of his work with the League of Nations in which he asked the question, "Why War?". What is it about human beings that seems to make war inevitable? What could we change so that it could be avoided? He wrote, "I personally see a simple way of dealing with the superficial (i.e., administrative) aspect of the problem: the setting up, by international consent, of a legislative and judicial body to settle every conflict arising between nations." The problem with this, as he quickly acknowledged, was that it didn't work. The League of Nations had been up and running for twelve years by the time Einstein posed his question, and the human race was no nearer to reaching any sort of harmonious state. In fact, a second world war was looking more and more inevitable.

So why wasn't the plan working? Einstein began to answer his own question. One problem lay in the fact that the powerful people in charge of each country often didn't want to relinquish control to an external authority, preferring to retain a sense of their own absolute supremacy. This provoked the question of why the citizens of each country would give this power to a small group of people. Especially to a group who generally grant themselves privileges but don't necessarily treat their subjects particularly well. Einstein responded to his own question by saying that people in power tend to control the schools, the press, and the church, and that they use these institutions to manipulate the masses. If you tell your citizens the right things you can supposedly make them do whatever you want. But why should people go so far as to give up their lives for their countries, just because they're told to? Einstein's chilling answer is, "Because man has within him a lust for hatred and destruction", and it doesn't take all that much to call it into action. According to Einstein, people *love* to fight in spite of everything they might say to the contrary. It's easy for leaders to persuade people to kill and be killed. Most of the time this human tendency towards destruction is veiled, but situations like wars allow it to come out into the open. And that might, as Einstein explains, be strangely, disturbingly appealing. In short, he answered his own question before Freud even got a word in.

Apparently, Freud wasn't happy about the exchange. He felt that Einstein had pre-empted his response. If two such "civilised", non-violent people, involved in a discussion about the horrors of war under the banner of the U.N., can still annoy each other—by agreeing!—what hope is there for everyone else?

Freud's comeback to Einstein's pre-answered question is very concise and takes only a few pages, but it brings in ideas that he and his colleagues had been turning over for years. The questions of why, and how, human beings love and hate are central to psychoanalysis. For Freud, these two feelings are intimately linked, although he states that our capacity to hate comes before our capacity to love—it has its roots in an earlier developmental stage. We are born into a state of blurry confusion—we can't know where we end and the rest of the world begins. We gradually gain some control over the things that annoy us and make us uncomfortable, attempting to fend off the stuff we hate and to hang onto the things that make us feel better. Our capacity for love develops when separation and individuation become possible; once we have the idea of ourselves as discrete entities we can begin to long for a "lost" state of fusion.

In *Beyond the Pleasure Principle* (1920g) Freud famously put forward the idea that the phenomena of life were the result of two opposing forces, Eros and Thanatos; loosely speaking, life (or love) and death. (Of course, he was far from the first to point this out, he just has a unique way of elaborating it.) Freud argues that on the one hand life strives towards its own continuation while, simultaneously, the ultimate aim of all life is death. As well as a drive to build, create, join, and reproduce, he sees our existence as characterised by a tendency to destroy, atrophy and die. In some instances, it's easy to see how closely linked the two forces are. In the interests of self-preservation, it may become necessary to destroy something else. If resources are scarce, someone or something may have to go. If you are under attack, you may have to fight back. And, in very special circumstances, you might also sacrifice yourself in order to save someone else. As life becomes more and more sophisticated, or "civilised", the place of these destructive forces shifts. In order for people to live in large groups they need to be more careful with one another. You have to curb your in-built capacity for violence, for your own sake as well as that of the collective.

Shortly before Einstein's question, Freud had published his late, great essay, *Civilization and its Discontents*, (1930a) where he tries to explain why so much of human life involves various forms of unhappiness. He calls on his theory of the drives, and the instinctual renunciations required in order for people to live in large groups. While Freud has a very high opinion of so-called civilised life—cultures that produce music, literature, science, architecture—he also sees that these are maintained against the odds. A great deal has to be suppressed, disavowed or pushed to one side if people are to co-operate.

Psychoanalysis is traditionally very tolerant of people who fail to be "good". Socialisation is seen as a difficult, disappointing process, and it's hardly surprising that it doesn't always work. Freud talks a great deal about the things people might try to do when the renunciations required by society are too much to live up to. There's neurosis or psychosis, drugs, alcohol, yoga (he's surprisingly down on this one), religion, art, and science. All of these can work, up to a point. He also mentions Voltaire's advice at the end of *Candide*: "Cultivate your garden." In other words, keep busy with small, satisfying things. Still, in his earlier essay "Thoughts for the Times on War and Death" (1915b) Freud rather gloomily states, "In reality, there is no such thing as 'eradicating' evil." People can try, *en masse*, to ameliorate their selfish, destructive drives (by means of repression, sublimation, distraction, deflection, reaction formation) but that doesn't mean they'll be gone from the world forever.

In clinical psychoanalysis, there is always the question of whom one works with. Some people love to work with murderers, and think it's a bore to deal with the so-called "worried well". They feel that someone's only *really* interesting if they've somehow crossed the line. Other people admire those who can basically contain themselves, or who become depressed or anxious rather than directly acting out their anger or frustration on the external world. These latter types might sometimes be a bit pesky, but you could say it's honourable of them to internalise rather than to go out on the rampage.

The art of ordinariness

In Issa Touma's documentary video we meet a young Syrian woman who longs for an ordinary life and a job. She doesn't want anything extravagant, just to inhabit her homeland, and for her family to be able to work and raise children. What Freud famously termed "ordinary unhappiness" (as opposed to neurotic suffering) could be seen here as an extraordinary privilege. All the woman wants is a moderately frustrating, "normal" life, where things might go wrong, but one at least expects one's house to be still standing by the end of the week. She isn't asking for perfection, just a habitable form of dissatisfaction.

Dissatisfaction is a curious emotional state in that it may sound quite mild, but can become amplified to excruciating levels. The kind of terrifying social malaise that can lead to wars and genocides very often has its roots in dissatisfaction. Certain groups are frustrated, hungry, bored, barred access to the good life, and perceive others to be enjoying themselves more directly. Dissatisfaction can be explosive under certain circumstances, but it's also an inevitable part of being human—full satisfaction is impossible.

It can hardly be wise to "hate" the people who instigate wars. Especially if one sees war not so much as a moral problem but an economic one (in the libidinal sense as much as the monetary). People need to be rewarded for the satisfactions they give up. Social injustice is a great unleasher of violence; one socialises oneself for what? In countries with the highest murder rates, such as Honduras, as many as one third of the population are living below the poverty line, but are constantly blasted with images of consumer culture. Their dissatisfaction surely has to be expressed somehow.

According to Freud, the forces that make us "civilised", and keep us there, are complex and paradoxical—it's not a comfortable, easy process. It's dynamic and ongoing, and can be undone and redone—although social systems seem to remain more stable when there's a greater sense of fair play.

Still, the things we work on together necessarily take something away from us. Socialisation can, in itself, be cruel. In Freudian theory, war isn't something from outside that bursts in on us and ruins our natural state of peace, but is a counterpart to the hard-won co-operation that we are sometimes able to construct under fortuitous conditions.

Imagine

If civilisation is an ongoing labour, what kind of world do we *want* to make? And, then again, what's actually possible? There's the question of whether to be idealistic or realistic. In John Lennon's "Imagine" (1971) we are invited to think of a world with no countries, no possessions, no religion, nothing to live or die for, and so on. It's a very beautiful song, but maybe treats the difficulties of life as add-ons or unnecessary irritations rather than as fundamental features. (John Lennon himself spoke openly about his violence towards the women in his life—so it's clear that even he wasn't perfect.) Is it better to imagine a beautiful vision of humanity? Or to acknowledge the difficulties of life—at the risk of being fatalistic?

This is where artists are extremely important. In his *Three Essays on Sexuality* (1905d), Freud makes special mention of three types: the artist, the neurotic, and the pervert. The artist sublimates her drives through an object, the neurotic through her symptom, while the pervert tries to get direct satisfaction from socially unacceptable forms of sexuality. Freud had great admiration for artists due to the ingenious ways in which they respond to the difficulties of existence, not just making life better for themselves but also for their audiences. Artists find elegant ways to bear difficult things, and in doing so they give pleasure and hope to others. The common idea that art is an unnecessary cultural extra, only for times when things are going well, involves a radical misunderstanding of its function. Art is especially important at times when there are difficult ideas, feelings, and events that need to be addressed and processed.

The artists in the "Postcard from Syria" exhibition continue to make their work at the very limits of possibility. They have to use materials sparingly—if their paint runs out there's no art shop down the road. They may have to use paper rather than canvas and stretchers. They couldn't be further from wealthy overlords using slaves to build grand edifices. They are modestly finding ways to articulate the things that matter to them, or to document something of their subjective experience. Issa Touma's photographs and videos humanise the Syrian conflict, showing the impact on civilians caught in the crossfire of someone else's war. Yacob Ibrahim, using only the thinnest application of paint, cleverly weaves contemporary political messages into his depictions of scenes from the New Testament. Sabhan Adam creates emotionally disturbing fictional portraits, loosely based on his own physiognomy, while Thaer Hizzie reproduces, from memory, the faces of the people who matter to him (and whom he has very little chance of meeting again so long as the conflict continues). Hagop Jamgochian paints colourful visual soundscapes as a response to the noises of the war that surround him. The artists here are dealing with stories, emotions, sentimental attachments. They're certainly not making monuments. They pay attention to the things that really matter to them, sidestepping the problem of idealism versus fatalism and just doing *something*. They remind us that Syria is not a world of stone, but the homeland of breathing, dreaming, hopeful people who'd like the chance to live, work and love in the nearest thing to peace and happiness our notoriously troubled species can manage.

Wishes

Centre for Freudian Analysis and Research, 2014*

It's common to observe that putting one's most cherished fantasies into action isn't necessarily enjoyable. The transition from something imagined to something acted out is notoriously fraught. One of Aesop's fables, "The Old Man and Death", points to the difficulty. An old man, while out looking for firewood in the forest, wishes he was dead. Death appears before him as a terrifying figure and asks him to repeat his wish. The old man responds: "I was just saying that I wish there was someone around to help me get this pile of wood up onto my shoulder." The moral: "We would often be sorry if our wishes were granted."

There are at least fifteen books from the last decade, all available on Amazon, called *Be Careful What You Wish For*. Some appear to be particularly concerned with sexual fantasy, if the covers are anything to go by (bearing in mind the fact that there's also another well-known expression …). It seems safe to say that there are still plenty of people who imagine it would be nice to get what they think they want. Or at least it continues to seem pertinent to remind people that wish-fulfilment

*First published in *JCFAR*, Issue 27, 2016.

isn't necessarily a barrel of laughs. It's obviously an idea that's relevant to psychoanalysts, and to people in analysis. It's something Freud grappled with when discussing what analysis was for and how it worked. You can find very elegantly argued answers to the question of the unsatisfyingness of satisfaction scattered throughout his work. For example, in "Character Types met in Analysis: Those Wrecked by Success" (1916d) he brandishes Lady Macbeth as a prime example of the horrors of getting what you want. Then, in his introductory lecture on transference (1916–1917), he speaks about cultural constraints on sexuality and the possibility that analysis could help people by giving them the courage to overcome their inhibitions and to do the things that prudishness (their own and other people's) prevents them from doing. He then goes on to explain why this wouldn't be helpful at all; the underlying conflict between asceticism and sensuality would remain—you would simply have shifted the boot from one foot to the other.

There is a particular category of fantasy object that one often hears about in analysis, and which seems interesting in part because it frequently invokes this vexing question of translation. It's extremely common among male analysands to mention enjoying looking at images of women with penises. It isn't generally the thing that has brought them to analysis, it's just something to mention in passing as part of the general sifting through of stuff. People often say they feel awkward speaking about it, and have questions about what it means about them. Is it to do with repressed homosexual wishes? Are they actually gay? Why do they find themselves enjoying these images so much? Of course, there's a very quick, orthodox psychoanalytic answer—because it's nice to see women who aren't castrated—but would it ever do any good to present a person with this idea? Maybe to a psychotic person the idea could function as a kind of coolant, but by and large it's just a brutal way to close down a question.

An aspect of this topic that's often repeated is the fact of stumbling across the images by mistake, and being surprised at one's enjoyment of them. It seems very important that the people in the images are "feminine" in every way, apart from the presence of a penis. There may be a question of whether the people in the images exist at all, or whether the genitals are photoshopped in, because they look so incongruous.

For those who feel very attracted to these pictures there often follows the question of whether they might like to have sex with one of those people. This generally opens up a barrage of other questions. What is the nature of these images? Maybe it isn't the penis that's photoshopped in, but that other things have been photoshopped out. What if you met one of these phallic women and they had a bit of a jaw, or muscly arms, or the trace of an Adam's apple? Would the excitement still be there? Or would these visible traces of masculinity get in the way? ("Oh well, it's just a man in make up after all.") Then there are all the more practical problems. How would you find a woman with a penis? Would you go to an agency? Would you pay? Do you like the idea of sex that you've paid for? Maybe you could you go to a specialist club and meet one of these people? Or find one on a dating site? Or could you get really, *really* lucky and find one by mistake? Even then you'd have to persuade them to like you, or be interested in you, and what if they didn't? So, a fussy, anxious, bureaucratic phase of the fantasy often follows the initial, simpler phase. Nonetheless it may still be quite exciting at this point. Even very exciting. Looking into the practicalities of the real thing is a little more risky and can add a frisson once you get used to the pictures. You can start to ask questions about what you might actually do with this person if all the other stuff got dealt with. Would you want to be penetrated by them? Would you want to penetrate them? Or do something else? What if what they wanted wasn't what you wanted? What are women with penises into? The images open up a series of questions about satisfaction and how to get it, and suddenly the whole thing can start to look a bit precarious. Looking at the pictures is good but, after a while, it doesn't seem to do the whole job. But what would the whole job involve?

In 2012, BBC viewers were presented with *Ladyboys*. In style, it wasn't unlike another popular British television series about cakes. It was shown in the mid evenings, lulling its audience with a soft female voiceover, pleasant music and constant sunny weather. The series was filmed in Thailand where, we were told, one per cent of the population are ladyboys. This is a term that covers a wide range of people, from those who've had full surgery to become women, to biological men who cross dress, and people who take female hormones but haven't had any surgery. We meet the ladyboys themselves, who are all really nice people, mostly very beautiful, often unfortunately forced to work as prostitutes, and universally looking for love. They particularly want husbands, especially husbands who will support them and their families back in the countryside so that they don't have to work as prostitutes any more. They are often very frank about the idea that love and money make for a happy combination, but definitely speak about love as the most important thing.

This need in the ladyboys is, according to the documentary, very well matched by the hordes of Western male tourists who go to Thailand hoping to meet them. Especially, we're told, middle-aged, divorced, disappointed men who just want to have fun—and who have noticed that this can be problematic with women. One episode—"Men who Love Ladyboys"—focuses on two such men. The first is a British academic who is there to study ladyboys, and isn't at all shy about admitting that it's a very close study; ladyboys are his "thing". The second discovered his penchant for ladyboys after noticing too late that the prostitute he was having sex with had a penis. He was initially shocked, he explained, but realised a few days later that he had liked it. Both men, at the time of filming, are in loving relationships with ladyboys. (The academic meets his girlfriend during an episode, and then marries her in the second series.) Both argue the case for the obvious attractiveness of ladyboys, presenting them as superior types of women. Each man speaks about the very clear and definite femininity of ladyboys—they have beautiful breasts, pert bottoms, long legs, long hair, no cellulite. They wear tight clothes, high heels, and lots of make-up. They literally blare out signifiers of youthful femininity. Both men defy other men *not* to be attracted to ladyboys, because of course they are the embodiment of everything all men want. In fact, you might start to feel it's amazing that biological women bother to carry on existing when something so preferable has been discovered. The two men differ, though, on the value of the penis during sex. For the academic, it's something like an enlarged clitoris, but much better designed in that you can see very easily whether it's aroused or not, and also because you know for sure when it's had an orgasm. It's all so much simpler than sex with a woman. You might not necessarily have an orgasm at the same time, but at least you'll know what happened. For the second man, his girlfriend's penis is more of an anomaly—he looks at her and wonders how it got there, even saying he sees it as a kind of real-world photoshopping, something superimposed. He's adamant that his liking for ladyboys has nothing to do with repressed homosexuality; he's in love with a woman who just happens to have this one weird physical feature, like a sixth toe or a third nipple. He does say, however, that "it takes a guy to know a guy" and that he feels much freer and less inhibited when he's having sex with her than he used to feel with his cisgendered female partners.

So, you have two different ways of smoothing something over, all of which is very much in keeping with the soothing tone of the series.

Everybody is nice. All they want is to find true love. The ladyboys are just exercising their rights to live in their true bodies. The men are just drooling over tits and arses, like bona fide men. The academic believes he has found a solution to the problems caused by the difference between the sexes. The second man is ostensibly comfortable with the difference between men and women, and is prepared to overlook silly details, like improbable penises, in the name of true love. It's all very charming and good for eating your dinner in front of, but it's hard not to think that there's a big dose of observer effect about it. The couples really want to be seen to have good sex and find love, and are prepared to act all this out for the camera, perhaps because it would be so lovely if it could really be like that. Plus, their mums, dads, teenage children and ex-wives are almost certainly watching—they get mentioned from time to time—so it's imperative to stay on track and present the rosiest possible scenario. It starts to seem that the aim of the documentary (an aim which fits very well with the wishes of its subjects) is to make lady-boys seem *less* exciting; to keep the whole idea inside the lines of the pleasure principle and to rid it of any surrounding jouissance (which is either very kind or very cruel of the programme-makers, depending on your ideas about enjoyment).

Of course, you can search elsewhere for information about the Thai ladyboy phenomenon and it all starts to seem a bit more complex than a story about true selves and true love. The sex industry expanded massively in Thailand during the Vietnam war when American soldiers would go there while on leave. You could earn far more money as a prostitute than as a farm worker, and there was infinitely more work for female prostitutes than male ones. Thai men are small-jawed and slightly built and could apparently pass for women quite easily in the eyes of European or American foreigners. They soon learnt how to keep up the illusion, using all sorts of cunning and ingenuity in bed (faked periods, contorted sexual positions, surgical tape) and this continues to be a big part of the craft. Clients may now want to be tricked, or to know-without-knowing that the woman they are fucking has a dick.

Alongside the economic factors, there's also the fact that Thai Buddhism doesn't overtly forbid homosexuality or cross-dressing, and recommends tolerance in general. Plus, the cheapness and easy availability of female hormones, in the form of the contraceptive pill, means it isn't hard for boys to make visible changes to their bodies without medical advice or intervention. In other words, there are a number of conditions that combine in such a way as to make it possible, even desirable, for ladyboys to proliferate. It's now a huge cultural institution and part of Thailand's national identity, pulling in enormous sums of money. It seems like a "good idea" that was hit on by mistake. But now that it's come to be, there are plenty of reasons to keep it going.

The presence or absence of the penis is a question for each individual ladyboy to handle in their own way. It might come down to whether or not they can afford the operation. Removal of a penis is three times more expensive than the addition of breasts, and breasts are already out of many people's price range. It might depend on whether the person continues to enjoy having sexual sensation in their penis and can reconcile this with the rest of their being—some can, some can't. From the point of view of the individual, the question is bound to be highly charged. In interviews, subjects often speak about the difficulty of managing their transitions from one identity to another, about discrimination, and not feeling like they fit in, before, during or after. They complain about the seediness of the sex industry and not being treated as proper human beings. They talk about the difficulty of finding meaningful relationships, and of feeling like they lose their market value by the time they're thirty, that nobody wants them when they're not perfect dolls anymore, and that nobody will give them a "normal" job. In other words, they complain about all the things women have traditionally complained about, only they don't even have access to the supposed pay-offs, i.e., children, family and general domestic bliss. They can't use their looks to trap a man and then get on with enjoying the resulting child when the man gets boring. (Needless to say, there's no guarantee that cis women can actually do this either …) They feel they can't offer a man the same things a woman can, or that the things they *can* offer are even less dependable. In other words, it's true; they're more womanly than women. Whatever cis women suffer, ladyboys suffer it worse. The idea that they embody anything like a perfect solution to the problem of human sexuality would surely sound ridiculous to them. If there's a problem being solved, it isn't their problem.

So, to come back to the people who speak about the pictures they see online, and the relationship they have with those pictures; what can be said? The whole thing is generally presented by these analysands as something a bit outside the norm, something that might offer a clue, maybe give something away about their sexuality. "Why do *I* like *this*?" But mightn't that be something of a false lead? "Because you wished your mummy had a penis?" Well, that's surely no good for answering the question of your particular subjectivity. Or what about: "On the Thursday before your fourth birthday you were having a bath with your little sister, Minnie. Your father, who was having trouble with his boss, Colin, at the toothpaste factory, came home in a bad mood … and so on and so forth …" Great! That's it! That's the reason! Which is lovely if that sort of thing makes a difference to you, but what if it doesn't? (And why would it?)

Rather than taking the penis in the images too seriously—it's a penis after all, and everybody knows you mustn't do *that*—are there other ways of coming at the fantasy? What if, instead of it simply being a clue to a forbidden homosexual wish, or to a fetishistic disavowal of a lack, it could also be a way to have something to say about the impossibility of full sexual enjoyment? The most apparently complete image may also be the most excitingly unstable. For the men who have the nerve or the inclination to take their fantasy further, it can pan out any number of ways. Maybe they get frightened and can't go through with it. Maybe they like it at the time but feel weird afterwards. Maybe they like it a lot and want to get into a relationship with the other person, but the feeling isn't reciprocated. All sorts of things can happen. The one variant I haven't come across in person, only heard about on TV, is that they find a perfect form of satisfaction.

Men have a very bad reputation, in psychoanalytic circles and elsewhere, for being stupid about enjoyment. Their pathetic excitements supposedly have a beginning, a middle, and an end, whereas women are more intriguingly circuitous. But the way men in analysis speak about phallic women would suggest that they are very far from fools when it comes to finding ways to eke out thrills from the hole in the big Other, which, as everybody knows, is the only really credible way to have a good time (see p. 67–68). The penis in the picture is perhaps beside the point. The real tingle comes from indexing the perplexing division between thinking and acting, fantasy and practice, the word and the world. As Aesop's story tells us, life may be a drag, but so long as you can get wood there might continue to be something in it …

Zoolander

One of the great ongoing challenges for any working psychoanalyst is deciding when, or how, to answer direct questions. Of course, the general rule of thumb is to bounce them straight back: "Well, what do *you* think?", "Does it matter to you whether I have children?", or "What do you imagine my answer to that question might be?" This is all very well but, if practised too assiduously, it can leave you feeling like an inhuman therapy-bot.

Perhaps the commonest form of question concerns whether or not you have read a particular book, or seen a particular film. While the pretext for asking may be to check whether you already know the premise or plot before wasting five minutes of the session outlining it, the subtext may be to find out what kinds of things you enjoy. Do you get off on watching *The Human Centipede*? Do you read everything on the Booker long list? What kind of sick/super-cultured person *are* you? Still, while you might not want to get into a big discussion about the cunning politics of the latest Cohen Brothers' movie, you may sometimes choose to let slip that you know who Scarlett Johansson is. Or then again you might not.

I've worked with one person on and off for many years and almost every time I see him he makes reference to a film, invariably asking whether I've seen it. I always answer him honestly, and the answer is always "no". He continues to be shocked and amazed by my extraordinary ignorance. As it happens, I do watch plenty of films, but never the ones he does. It pains me to think of this person coming to know that I've seen *Zoolander 2* (2016). Still, if he ever finds out, he may appreciate the fact that it's a film about the mind—more specifically, about what one mind can be for another.

For those who haven't seen it—"What, you haven't seen *Zoolander 2*? I can't believe it!"—the film centres on the relationship between two ageing male models (played by Ben Stiller and Owen Wilson) who have been unwillingly coaxed out of retirement.

The big thing about the original *Zoolander* (2001) was that it had the official seal of approval of the fashion industry, who rather patronisingly applauded it in contrast to absolutely every other film about fashion—especially Robert Altman's *Prêt-à-Porter*, which just *gets it all so wrong*. "Getting it wrong" is a fashion crime, naturally. In fashion one must "know" what's right or wrong, in or out—and it's not simply a matter of being told. Buying an actual outfit as seen in *Vogue* is not in any way cool. One has both to obey and disobey if one wants to be truly fashionable as opposed to simply obedient. So, it's a properly paranoia-inducing system where the rules are not at all clear, but nonetheless one risks falling foul of them at any moment. Mob thinking is very important—you can't be fashionable on your own, fashion is a form of consensual contagion—but, as with psychoanalysis, there are different factions with different values, and being in with one lot almost necessarily means being out with another. You can't please all of the fashion people all of the time. Still, the original *Zoolander* comes as close as possible to doing just that, which might seem peculiar given the scant respect it shows for the industry. This, you could say, is what's so loveable about it. Unlike *Prêt-à-Porter*, which walks an excruciating line between trying to demonstrate a sophisticated understanding of fashion mores at the same time as maintaining a critical distance—*so wrong!*—*Zoolander* is just vicious and rude. The main character, Derek Zoolander, is a chronically vain and self-absorbed idiot who has found a perfect milieu for his fatuousness in the world of modelling. The film's chief villain, Jacobim Mugatu (Will Ferrell) is a power-crazed and unscrupulous fashion designer who wants to assassinate the new, progressive Malaysian Prime Minister so he can continue to exploit child labour. *Zoolander* portrays the world of fashion as cruel and amoral, pathetically sealed off, peopled solely by psychopathic narcissists and the weaklings in thrall to them. It does this in such a funny, relentless, semi-plausible way that perhaps the only hope for a person identified with fashion is to make a big song and dance about how much they love it.

So, when *Zoolander 2* came out—fifteen years later—fashion journalists got in a bit of a twit about whether or not they were supposed to like it. On the one hand, it was "their" film—a film about their world, originally beloved by its denizens, this time actually featuring their real gods and goddesses: Marc Jacobs, Alexander Wang, Anna Wintour, Naomi Campbell. On the other hand, maybe it had all got a bit too sucky and insidery. It wasn't actually a menace to their dignity any more. It even seemed to want them to like it. Non-fashion reviewers were also unimpressed—the film was largely written off as a cynical exercise in success-milking. The problem, perhaps, was that no-one was prepared (for this read "mad enough") to take it seriously. This shameful task had to fall to a psychoanalyst who never watches the right films, but who is at least immersed in the practice of not dismissing anything as too stupid or insignificant to merit close attention (Freud 101).

The film starts with Derek Zoolander and his former arch modelling rival, Hansel, being tracked down to their respective hideouts and persuaded to model for the House of Atoz. Both are reluctant, but ultimately can't resist the idea of being in the spotlight again. They also have strong "manifest" motives; Derek wants to regain custody of his son, and Hansel needs to get away from his demanding harem, all of whom are pregnant (including the men and animals). When they arrive in Rome for the fashion show, they are approached by a secret agent, Valentina (Penelope Cruz) who asks for their help solving a series of celebrity murders. Each of the victims has used their last seconds to take a selfie, always with the same quizzical, slightly pouty facial expression. Valentina recognises the look on their faces as the once-famous "Blue Steel", a pose invented and popularised by Derek Zoolander in his heyday. This look was so powerful it could stop a deadly blade in mid-air. But why was it reappearing in this sinister new context?

The film makes it clear early on that the storyline is, in part, a parody of *The Da Vinci Code*. Hansel is called for a secret meeting at St Peter's Basilica in Rome. He goes along with Valentina and Derek. There they meet Sting, who tells them the story of Adam and Eve, the lesser known Steve, and the Fountain of Youth. It turns out that Derek and his son are direct descendants of Steve, and therefore hold the key to the mythic fountain. This means that they are in mortal danger.

You could say that ripping off the plot of *The Da Vinci Code* is about the least cool, most cynical thing a contemporary filmmaker could do. What could signal a dearth of ideas more than pilfering one of the most financially successful, least artful narratives in the history of storytelling? Not to mention its being a story that has long since fallen below the culturally relevant radar. This "outdatedness" was certainly one of the criticisms levelled at the film, in part thanks to its crass treatment of the gender-non-binary character "All" (played by Benedict Cumberbatch), which sparked calls on social media for a boycott. Hadn't the filmmakers heard that transphobia was no longer considered a laughing matter? It was also sneered at in *The Guardian* for including a cameo by Susan Boyle "seven years after she could be considered part of the zeitgeist" (Hannah Marriott, "The Myth and the Reality: the fashion verdict on *Zoolander 2*", 11th February 2016). In short, like Derek Z himself, the film was definitely not *at all* hot right now.

In psychoanalytic practice you hear a great deal of troubling things. Anyone who wants to maintain a peachy picture of the human race should probably steer clear of this profession. (Although, to be fair, you get to see a great deal of loveliness too.) So, in the spirit of giving everyone a fair hearing I'd like to remain open to *Zoolander 2*, even if, like Tony Soprano, it eventually becomes obvious that it's irredeemably rotten. In this vein, perhaps it's helpful to start with its use of Dan Brown's storyline. If we don't write it off immediately as a pathetic admission of uninspiredness, what else could it be? It's certainly a story about encryption and deciphering, two topics close to any Freudian's heart. The embarrassing thing about it, though, is that the clues in the *Da Vinci Code* are largely so *un*encrypted that it's painful to watch the idiot detective stumble around for pages failing to see what any twelve-year-old could spot instantly. Apples + Westminster Abbey = Sir Isaac Newton. Duh! More generously, you could say it's a charming pantomime about surface and depth. It's fun to shout, "It's behind you!" while the hapless hero makes a totally implausible show of ignorance. As we so often see in psychoanalytic treatment, the "hidden" is barely hidden at all.

The other important feature of Dan Brown's story is that it concerns a famous face, and more particularly a facial expression. The Mona Lisa's smile is surely the Renaissance equivalent of Blue Steel. Still, *Zoolander 2* delicately avoids making explicit this analogy. Like Dan Brown's dumb detective, we have to work it out for ourselves. But where does it lead us? We have a story about concealment and revelation that centres on an iconic face. But there's a very important difference between the Mona Lisa and Derek Zoolander. While da Vinci's sfumato gives his portrait its enigmatic allure—"What is she thinking?"—face powder and photoshop (not to mention power-posing) have drained Zoolander's face of any sense of an interior life.

In perhaps the most overtly philosophical scene Derek, Hansel, and Valentina go to track down the evil designer, Mugatu, in fashion prison (where MC Hammer is also being held for his trouser crimes). Derek needs to quiz Mugatu about the whereabouts of his son. Mugatu is chained up in a special cell modelled on Hannibal Lecter's super high security set-up in Jonathan Demme's *Silence of the Lambs*. Hansel and Valentina are worried that Derek won't be able to withstand the psychological intensity of the meeting. Derek reassures them; his mind is closed for business—it's just a blank space where mental games have no traction.

Before entering the prison, Zoolander's friends have planted the idea that there is something he needs to watch out for. He approaches Mugatu with trepidation, on guard against potential trickiness. The problem is that Derek's mind isn't good at dealing with complexity. By his own admission, his strength lies in being "ridiculously good-looking". Still, he has evidently heard that other minds are capable of a certain kind of layering—people might say what they don't mean, for example. Or they might say what they think another person wants to hear. Unlike a person of average intelligence, who might be able to handle this sort of discrepancy without much effort, Derek finds these calculations extremely taxing. If Mugatu says, "Come over here and undo my handcuffs", Derek is faced with a terrible problem. Is this the sort of cunning double-bluff he's heard about? Desperate to show he's not a complete fool, he does everything Mugatu tells him, certain each time that he's staying one step ahead of the game. If Mugatu *really* wanted him to do this or that, surely he wouldn't just say it. Mugatu can hardly believe his luck. The sequence ends with Derek chained up and Mugatu ready to walk free. All that has to happen now is for Mugatu to disguise himself as the supermodel, and vice versa. Because he is a criminal mastermind, Mugatu has spent his years in prison making supposedly ultra-realistic masks with his feet (thanks to the fact that his hands have been cuffed). He and Derek are about to swap identities so that Mugatu can stroll out past the guards without being detected. But when the disguises are put on we see that they are only clumsy papier mâché masks—exactly the sort of thing a person might be able to make with their toes using only materials found in a prison. However, in a surreal moment of reality-suspension, the plan works.

Not only has Derek failed to read the mind of his nemesis—even though Mugatu was speaking his mind painfully clearly at all times—but now their heads have swapped places in the most implausible way. No person with functioning eyes could possibly be fooled by the switch. The entire sequence might reasonably be described as a headfuck. What goes on between heads and faces? How does anything ever get from the inside of one head to another? Can you read a face? Which are more reliable, words or gestures? And if you can't take words at face value, where else should you look?

One has to wonder whether Ben Stiller has chosen to parody this famous scene because he admires the semantic complexity of its reflections on identity and interiority. It's like he's sending a message in a bottle to psychoanalysts out there who were previously in any doubt that he was trying to reach us. (In fact it was the moment I knew for a fact that Ben Stiller was asking me, personally, to write this essay. As you can see, I am not crazy.) At this point in Demme's film, Starling and Lecter imaginatively swap roles; he is being asked to become a detective while teaching Starling how to think like a psychiatrist (who in turn has to think like a killer). As the two characters enter into each other's mindsets, their faces float and overlap in the reflected surfaces of the glass cube. As the American literature professor, Diana Fuss, explains: "Lecter's visage hovers slightly to the side and to the back of Starling's, creating the trick illusion that he is sitting directly behind her, like a psychoanalyst positioned behind a patient on a couch." (*Identification Papers*, p. 92) Starling gets inside Lecter. Mugatu doubles Derek. *Zoolander 2* parodies *Silence of the Lambs*. The psychoanalyst is an implacable mirror for her analysands. It really makes you think. Or does it?

How can one person ever hope to come to any kind of understanding with another? This, of course, is a very tricky question. As an analyst, you're definitely there to listen. But then what? Is the point to understand what the person is saying? Or what they're not saying? And does it matter whether it's *you* who understands? Isn't it more important that *they* do? It's very uncertain what gets transferred from one head to the other. The analysand might sometimes attribute great understanding to the analyst—and they might be quite wrong to do so. In Jeffrey Masson's *Final Analysis* (1990) the author describes a moment in his analytic training where one of his fellow trainees—a man he describes as "remarkably obtuse" (p. 103)—keeps troubling his far more intelligent training patient with idiotic interventions. The advice from their supervisor is to "say nothing, beyond questioning grunts" (p. 103). This plan goes extremely well; the man's analysand starts to think he's brilliant. "'Nobody ever called me profound before', he said admiringly of his patient" (p. 103). For Masson this provides yet more proof of the moral bankruptcy of the entire analytic project; the patient is paying you to understand and interpret, and if you can't do that you're ripping them off. But Masson's point of view fails to take into account the serious, structural problems at the heart of language and communication. Either you take speech at face value, and risk being an idiot, or you try to see what's behind it and find that, in trying to be clever, you understand even less.

A to Z

An acquaintance was describing the highlights of his lengthy psychoanalysis. One day he told his analyst he'd noticed that all of his girlfriends had names ending in the letter "a"—Amelia, Sophia, Frederika, and so on. What's an analyst supposed to say? What letter does your mother's name end with? What is the significance of the letter "a" in your life? Most women's names end with an "a", you twit, that's how come you know it's a girl's name. Instead his analyst simply said, "Aaaaaah …" The man was delighted by such a quick-witted joke about the sadness of all those endings.

In *Zoolander 2*, the evil organisation is named the House of Atoz. But why? Because the fashion house is the cover for a secret organisation that has traced the link from Adam to Zoolander? If so, this is yet another bit of coding not made explicit in the script. Like the secrets supposedly encrypted in Da Vinci's paintings, there's nothing to confirm whether you've got it right, or whether your interpretive zeal is just a sign of madness. Still, to keep going with the project of taking things seriously (which feels ever more ridiculous the longer you keep going) perhaps the film is slyly teasing its audience with this idea of there being something "more". We might laugh at Derek because he's incapable of reading between the lines. (He's so literal minded that he thinks an architectural model is a building that's been made too small by mistake.) But what happens when you start trying to look beyond first readings? From Atoz you get A to Z, two dumb letters. Aaaaaah! Zzzzzzzz. Who gives Atoz?

When Eugen Bleuler introduced the term "depth psychology" in 1914 he perhaps had no idea how literally people would take it. Conscious ideas were thought to splash around on the surface while unconscious thoughts were like pug-faced, whiskered deep sea creatures, too weird and ugly to venture into daylight. If you wanted to get to the deep stuff you had to go and see an expert who would teach you how to fish. Like art historians familiar with the iconographies of the Renaissance, psychoanalysts promised to unlock the secrets embedded in your dreams. Carl Jung in particular offered a ready-made map of the unconscious, its mysteries phylogenetically encoded in us, but available for exploration with the assistance of a sensitive and well-informed guide.

Further into the twentieth century, Lacan exhumed the Freudian idea that it wasn't nearly so simple. The conscious stuff wasn't on top, with the unconscious stuff bundled underneath, but perhaps sometimes the most disavowed idea could appear in full view, tampered with or reinflected to get it past the censors. Ideas like "extimacy" (*extimité*) pointed to the notion that insides, outsides, familiarity, and unfamiliarity could overlap and interweave rather than stand in opposition. Likewise, with cleverness and stupidity. As Lacan explains at the beginning of *R.S.I,* *Seminar XXII (1974–1975)*, psychoanalysis can help you become less ignorant, but it can't stop you being a pillock.

There's no measuring stick that can tell you whether a film like *Zoolander 2* is brilliant or fatuous. If you want to find it pathetic, you will. The film itself does little overtly to persuade viewers otherwise. But if you want to find it profound, you surely will too. Scattered everywhere will be elliptical signs of its thoughtfulness. But who put them there? You or Ben Stiller? And are they "there" at all, or are you just adding clues to a crime that's already been committed?

The genius of the unconscious, of *everyone's* unconscious, is something exactly like this. It's at work, stealthily, whether you like it or not. And if you don't like it, well, in that case it doesn't exist. Who's going to prove otherwise? People sometimes ask whether a patient has to be intelligent in order to do well in analysis. Do they need to be able to grasp complex ideas? To articulate difficult thoughts? And must they be well-educated in order to do this? The first part is difficult to answer because it's unclear what forms of intelligence are implied in the question. Emotional? Spatial? Mathematical? But the last part is easier. Conventional education has absolutely nothing to do with it. Very educated people might sometimes use their "knowledge" to hold unwelcome ideas at bay, while supposedly less academic types might be brilliant at expressing themselves and using other people's responses to make themselves feel better, or at least different. And vice versa. With analysts too, it isn't necessarily the ones who've read all the books who can work the most effectively with people.

All of which perhaps brings us back to the question at the very beginning of this book, concerning whether psychoanalytic concepts are necessarily helpful when it comes to understanding other people, especially when these concepts can be so hard to define and understand in themselves. Some, like "acting out", seem to fall apart the minute you subject them to scrutiny. What good can they do in the face of psychic suffering? This is the ongoing, impossible, elegant, frustrating nature of psychoanalytic work. On the one hand psychoanalysis is a system for understanding absolutely everything. On the other, it offers very little certainty. It invites us instead to put our own knowledge in question and to take the consequences of our bewilderment. If the *A to Z of London* tells you which streets to go down in order to avoid getting lost, an A to Z of psychoanalysis throws you into an indeterminate terrain and leaves you stranded. Anything less would be a betrayal of the subject.

REFERENCES

Alexenko, T., Carlson, L., Huo, Z., Miller, J., & Skubic M. (2013). *Testing an Assistive Fetch Robot with Spatial Language from Older and Younger Adults*, The 22nd IEEE International Symposium on Robot and Human Interactive Communication, Gyeongju, Korea.

Baker, N. (1991). *U and I: a true story*. London: Granta.

Barthes, R. (2010). *The Fashion System*. London: Vintage Classics.

Beauvoir, S. (1997). *The Second Sex*. London: Vintage Classics.

Benjamin, W. (1998). *Illuminations*. London: Pimlico.

Berger, B., & Newman, S. (Eds.) (2011). *Money Talks: in therapy, society and life*. London: Routledge.

Bergler, E. (1953). *Fashion and the Unconscious*. Madison: International Universities Press.

Blanck, G., & Blanck, E. (1974). *Ego Psychology: theory and practice*. New York: Columbia University Press.

Borowski, T. (1992). *This Way for the Gas, Ladies and Gentlemen*. London: Penguin.

Bourgeois, L. (1990). Freud's Toys. *Artforum, January 1990*: 11–13.

Brand, R. (2008). *My Booky Wook*. London: Hodder.

Breuer, J., & Freud, S. (1895d). *Studies on Hysteria*. London: Hogarth.

Caillois, R. (1935). Mimicry and Legendary Psychaesthenia. J. Shepley (Trans.). *October Magazine, 31st 1984*.

Camus, A. (2005). *The Myth of Sisyphus*. London: Penguin.

Dandridge, D. (with Conrad, F.). (2000). *Everything and Nothing: the Dorothy Dandridge tragedy*. London: HarperCollins.

Deutsch, H. (1963). Acting out in the transference. In: Deutsch, H. (1965). *Neuroses and Character Types*. New York: International Universities Press.

Edwards, B. (1983). *Drawing on the Right Side of the Brain*. London: Fontana.

Engels, F. (2016). *The Origin of the Family, Private Property and the State*. CreateSpace.

Evans, D. (1996). *An Introductory Dictionary of Lacanian Psychoanalysis*. London: Routledge.

Fenichel, O. (1987). *The Collected Papers of Otto Fenichel*. New York: Norton.

Flügel, J. C. (1976). *The Psychology of Clothes*. New York: AMS Press.

Freud, A. (1992). *The Ego and the Mechanisms of Defense*. London: Karnac, 1936.

Freud, S. (1900a). *The Interpretation of Dreams*. S. E., 4–5. London: Hogarth.

Freud, S. (1901b). *The Psychopathology of Everyday Life*. S. E., 6. London: Hogarth.

Freud, S. (1905c). *Jokes and their Relation to the Unconscious*. S. E., 6: 136–248. London: Hogarth.

Freud, S. (1905d). *Three Essays on the Theory of Sexuality*. S. E., 7: 136–248. London: Hogarth.

Freud, S. (1908d). "Civilized" Sexual Morality and Modern Nervous Illness. S. E., 9. London: Hogarth.

Freud, S. (1909b). Analysis of a Phobia in a Five-Year-Old Boy. S. E., 10. London: Hogarth.

Freud, S. (1912–1913). *Totem and Taboo*. S. E., 13: 1–161. London: Hogarth.

Freud, S. (1912b). The Dynamics of Transference. S. E., 12. London: Hogarth.

Freud, S. (1914g). Remembering, Repeating and Working-Through. S. E., 12. London: Hogarth.

Freud, S. (1915b). Thought for the Times on War and Death. S. E., 14. London: Hogarth.

Freud, S. (1916–1917). Introductory lectures on psycho-analysis. S. E., 16. London Hogarth.

Freud, S. (1916d). Some Character types met with in Psycho-Analytic Work. S. E., 10. London: Hogarth.

Freud, S. (1920a). The Psychogenesis of a Female Homosexuality. S. E., 18. London: Hogarth.

Freud, S. (1920g). *Beyond the Pleasure Principle*. S. E., 19: 1–64. London: Hogarth.

Freud, S. (1923b). *The Ego and the Id*. S. E., 19. London: Hogarth.

Freud, S. (1924d). The Dissolution of The Oedipus Complex. S. E., 19. London: Hogarth.

Freud, S. (1925j). Some Psychical Consequences of the Anatomical Distinction between the Sexes. *S. E., 19*. London: Hogarth.

Freud, S. (1926d). *Inhibitions, Symptoms and Anxiety. S. E., 20*. London: Hogarth.

Freud, S. (1930a). *Civilization and its Discontents. S. E., 21*: 59–146. London: Hogarth.

Freud, S. (1933a [1932]). *New Introductory Lectures on Psycho-Analysis. S. E., 22*. London: Hogarth.

Freud, S. (1937c). Analysis Terminable and Interminable. *S. E., 23*. London: Hogarth.

Fuss, D. (1995). *Identification Papers*. London: Routledge.

Gherovici, P. (2010). *Please Select Your Gender: from the invention of hysteria to the democratising of transgenderism*. London: Routledge.

Green, A. (2002). *Time in Psychoanalysis: some contradictory aspects*. London: Free Association Books.

Greenacre, P. (1950). General Problems of Acting Out. *Psychoanalytic Quarterly, Volume 19*.

Hattenstone, S. (2008). Ghosts of Childhood Past. *The Guardian, 10th May 2008*.

Heimann, P. (1950). On Counter-Transference. *International Journal of Psycho-Analysis, Volume 31*.

Hergenhahn, B. R. (2000). *An Introduction to the History of Psychology*. Belmont: Wadsworth Publishing Co. Inc.

Hoffman, M. L. (1978). Empathy: Its development and prosocial implications. In: *Nebraska Symposium on Motivation: Social Cognitive Development*. J. H. E. Howe & C. B. Keasey (Eds.). Nebraska: University of Nebraska Press.

Hoffmann, E. T. A. (1816). The Sandman. In: Hoffmann, E. T. A. (1967). *The Best Tales of Hoffman*. Dover Publications Inc.

Hornby, N. (2002). *About a Boy*. London: Penguin.

Irigaray, L. (1985). *This Sex Which is Not One*. New York: Cornell University Press.

Johnson, A., & Williams, D. (1997). *Oedipus Ubiquitous: the family complex in world folk literature*. Redwood City: Stanford University Press.

Klein, M. (1958). Klein Archive C72, frames 695–724. Wellcome Library.

Knausgaard, K. (2009). *My Struggle, Book 2: A Man in Love*. London: Vintage.

Kris, E. (1951). Ego psychology and interpretation in psychoanalytic theory. *Psychoanalytic Quarterly, Volume 20*.

Lacan, J. (1974–1975). *R. S. I. Seminar XXII (1974–1975)*. Cormac Gallagher (Trans.). Available at: www.lacaninireland.com.

Lacan, J. (1986). *The Four Fundamental Concepts of Psycho-Analysis (1963–1964)*. London: Penguin.

Lacan, J. (1988). *The Seminar of Jacques Lacan, Book I, Freud's Papers on Technique (1953–1954)*. London: Norton.

Lacan, J. (1989 [1938]). *Family Complexes*. London: Norton.

Lacan, J. (1993a). *The Seminar of Jacques Lacan, Book III, Psychosis (1955–1956)*. London: Routledge.

Lacan, J. (1993b). *The Seminar of Jacques Lacan, Book IV The Object Relation (1956–1957)*, translated with notes by L. V. A. Roche.

Lacan, J. (1993c). *The Seminar of Jacques Lacan, Book X, Anxiety (1962–1963)*. Cambridge: Polity.

Lacan, J. (1993d). *The Seminar of Jacques Lacan, Book XVII, The Other Side of Psychoanalysis (1969–1970)*. Cambridge: Polity.

Lacan, J. (1999). *The Seminar of Jacques Lacan, Book XX, Encore: on feminine sexuality, the limits of love and knowledge (1972–1973)*. London: Norton.

Lacan, J. (2006). *Écrits*. Bruce Fink (Trans.). London: Norton.

Lacan, J. (2015). *The Seminar of Jacques Lacan, Book VIII, Transference (1960–1961)*. Cambridge: Polity.

Lebovici, R. (1956). Transitory Sexual Perversion in the Course of a Psychoanalytic Treatment. *Bulletin d'activites de l'Association des Pychanalyses de Belgique 25*, D. Nobus (Trans.). (2004) *Journal Lacanian Studies 2(1)*.

Levi-Strauss, C. (1969). *The Elementary Structures of Kinship*. Boston: Beacon Press.

Lipps, T (1906). Quoted in: Hoffman, M. L. (2000). Empathy and Moral Development. Cambridge: Cambridge University Press.

Little, M. (1951). Counter-transference and the Patient's Response to it. *The International Journal of Psychoanalysis, Volume 32*.

MacDorman, K. F. (2005). Androids as an experimental apparatus: Why is there an uncanny valley and can we exploit it? CogSci-2005 Workshop: Toward Social Mechanisms of Android Science.

Malinowski, B. (1979). *Ethnography of Malinowski: Trobriand Islands, 1915–18*. London: Routledge.

Mantel, H. (2016). *Blot, Erase, Delete*. Available online at: www.indexoncensorship.org.

Masson, J. (1990). *Final Analysis: the making and unmaking of a psychoanalyst*. London: Flamingo.

Mori, M. (2012). The Uncanny Valley. K. F. MacDorman & N. Kageki (Trans.). *IEEE Robotics & Automation Magazine, Volume 19*.

Ong, W. (1982). *Orality and Literacy: the technologizing of the word*. London: Routledge.

Phillips, M. (2009). *High on Arrival*. London: Simon and Schuster.

Rabaté, J. (Ed.) (2003). *The Cambridge Companion to Lacan*. Cambridge: Cambridge University Press.

Racker, H. (1982). *Transference and Countertransference*. London: Karnac.

Rosenbaum, D., & Santamaria, J. (2011). Etiquette and Effort: Holding Doors for Others. *Psychological Science*. SAGE Publications.

Roudinesco, E. (1990). *Lacan and Co, A History of Psychoanalysis in France, 1925–1985*. Chicago: University of Chicago Press.

Skinner, F. (2009). *On the Road: Love, Stand-up Comedy and The Queen Of The Night*. London: Arrow.

Spiro, M. (1992). *Oedipus in the Trobriands*. New Jersey: Transaction Publishers.

Tallis, R. (1995). *Not Saussure: A Critique of Post-Saussurean Literary Theory: Language, Discourse, Society*. London: Palgrave Macmillan.

Turkel, S. (2013). *Alone Together: Why We Expect More from Technology and Less from Each Other*. New York: Basic Books.

Verhaeghe, P. (2009). *New Studies of Old Villains: A Radical Reconsideration of the Oedipus Complex*. New York: Other Press.

Voruz, V., & Wolf, B. (2007). *The Later Lacan: an introduction*. New York: State University of New York Press.

Wallon, H. (2015). *Les Origins du Charactère Chez l'Enfant*. Paris: Presses Universitaires de France.

Webster, R. (1994). The Cult of Lacan: Freud, Lacan and the Mirror Stage. Available online at: www.richardwebster.net.

Weisberger, L. (2003). *The Devil Wears Prada*. London: Harper Collins.

Winnicott, D. W. (1958), *Through Paediatrics to Psychoanalysis*. London: Hogarth.

Zeigarnik, B. V. (1967). On finished and unfinished tasks. In: W. D. Ellis (Ed.). *A Sourcebook of Gestalt Psychology*. New York: Humanities Press.

Žižek, S. (1995). Woman is One of the Names-of-the-Father, or How Not to Misread Lacan's Formulas of Sexuation. New York: *Lacanian Ink 10*.

INDEX